the lion's eye

the lion's eye

SEEING IN THE WILD

JOANNA GREENFIELD

LITTLE, BROWN AND COMPANY

New York   Boston   London

Little, Brown and Company
Hachette Book Group
237 Park Avenue, New York, NY 10017
www.hachettebookgroup.com

First Edition: August 2009

Little, Brown and Company is a division of Hachette Book Group, Inc. The Little, Brown name and logo are trademarks of Hachette Book Group, Inc.

Names and characteristics of some individuals portrayed in this book have been changed so that their privacy is completely protected.

Portions of this book appeared in *The New Yorker*, in a slightly different format.

Library of Congress Cataloging-in-Publication Data
Greenfield, Joanna.
  The lion's eye : seeing in the wild / Joanna Greenfield. — 1st ed.
    p. cm.
  ISBN 978-0-316-32848-7
  1. Animals — Uganda. 2. Wildlife management — Uganda. 3. Chimpanzees — Effect of human beings on — Uganda. 4. Natural history — Research — Uganda. 5. Greenfield, Joanna — Travel — Uganda. 6. Uganda — Description and travel. I. Title.
  QL337.U35G74 2009
  508.6761 — dc22   2009018357

10 9 8 7 6 5 4 3 2 1

RRD-IN

Printed in the United States of America

Contents

Contents

Contents

To my brother Matthew, who taught me to write; to my nephew Max, whose birth convinced me to stop traveling and find a home, so that I could be near him; and to Alice Quinn and Alice Truax, who made the book possible.

the lion's eye

Prologue: Nairobi, Kenya, 1986

In the dark leaves of the rain forest, we evolved from the ancestral tree shrew. Our eyes swiveled forward from the sides of the head and focused along the branches, in search of fruit or insects. Grasping hands held bark steady beneath the air, and we learned to jump from one tree to another, and then to swing hand over hand, straightening our backs. Forgotten apes lost their tails and moved the fifth finger farther from the others so we could hang unhurried from closed circles of bone.

We grew, between rain forest and highland savanna, from tree shrew to bush baby to chimpanzee, shrinking and stretching and becoming something different. For millions of years, we rested in the trees, easy in our skin, until, as tectonic plates split, the land broke and swelled and burned.

Beyond the rain shadow of the new mountains, the forest was stripped to its bone as the rain disappeared, and the ancient ocean bed lay revealed with fossils of fish and shell stranded in the white dust. Grasses washed with light rippled to the edge of the sky, and mountains hovered among the acacias. Animals fed the endless cycle of the grasslands — fertilize, eat, be eaten — each species with its own rhythm and place. Elephants crushed the thornbush as it tangled together, zebras learned to eat the old dry grass, opening the land to gazelles and giraffes and wildebeest. Insects took the dung of them all and spread it into a garden. Where forests had been, the savanna stretched from one continent to another, blades of grass flashing in the sun.

Perhaps then, separated from the trees, we lost our fur, the flat symmetry of the primate face, and the capacity for silence. Ape or human, we breathed this air back then. Our eyes evolved to this light and our skin to this wind. Neither clothes nor shelter was needed here on the highland savanna; nothing between skin and sky.

The Kenyan highlands are like no other place on earth. I think some ancestral need, some pocket of unfulfillable longing, is born with us for the home in which we evolved. When we leave the savanna, it retreats to the back of the mind and, like any childhood home, is remembered only in brief flashes that disappear if they are not written down.

Someone had given me the body of a vervet found in the road. While the others drove to the pombe to drink beer, I skinned the monkey. Skin is attached to flesh with only the lightest of bonds, and the pelt fell away from muscles with the smallest touch of the knife. In some places I needed only to pull, and the skin sucked free and rolled down.

I am no hunter and don't believe humans are born only to kill, but taking apart that body felt as gentle and right as sculpting clay. The knife knows where to go. It slides with the body, not the skin, to avoid nicks, down through silvered walls of connective tissue. At each stroke of the knife, the skin rolls away a little further, and the inner flesh, muscles purple and red, encased in more silver, shines through. The knife hisses a bit, if the skin is pulled hard enough from the monkey to create tension so the tissue stands out to its furthest length from the muscles like soap bubbles blown too thin, and the skin leaps from the body as the cords are cut. Frightening to think of our own bodies so loosely connected.

One likes to imagine skin as irrevocably bonded to flesh, and all as one unity. But it's not true, of course. We are as separate in our parts as the road-killed vervet. That is why skin moves so easily over flesh.

I didn't skin the hands and feet of my small companion because they were too much like those of a human, and I didn't want to damage the bones — though I regretted it later, when I boiled the flesh and had to peel the shrunken leather off the meat. The tail, I slit down the underside and pulled off the body by wrapping it around my left hand, gripping the front legs together with my right, and then pulling hard. Both hands slipped on the fat, and it was a while before the skin ripped away from the tail.

Then I had two separate monkeys. The fur lay in a wet pile on the left, softer and limper than it ever was before, or would be again. On the other side, the body stretched out, rigid, as if running, with its black-palmed hands and feet curled. The savanna air dried it quickly, and the silver connective tissue hardened into a second skin to replace the one taken. There was nothing of raw meat about this. Each muscle shone within its own sheath, and the whole was covered by one thin film, with little globs of fat here and there. It looked, in fact, more like the flesh of a marathon runner in the last mile of a race, with each muscle drawn like a wire under thin and shiny skin.

Before boiling the bones clean, I had to cut off the meat. This took more time; the dried skin of tissue dipped and bent under the knife but wouldn't break. I sawed through it all and threw the scraps away. Now the carcass looked like a carcass, raw and tattered, with the distinct muscles uncoupled from their strands and left halved and gaping against the bone.

With the now-familiar shock that stopped the heart, I looked up and saw, through a hole in the grove, a glimpse of the savanna. Acacia trees ran silver down into the grasses, smaller and smaller at the edges of the grove, and to the horizon, the grasses stretched in moving strands of light, dotted with the silhouettes of Masai giraffes.

Into gold distances the savanna spread, from peaks and around pillars of stone, through clouds of acacia and green heights, from one country to another. The savanna filled my chest, lungs opening and breathing without stop, one breath finished and another beginning like a sail blown taut and moving its owner on to the sea. To the curves of the earth, the horizon was lighted. The light halted the movement of time and past and future; for a few seconds, an eternity of peace.

The reassembled vervet skeleton, with its pelt stretched on a board beside it, would make a good display in the wildlife ranch's museum. While the bones boiled, I scraped the skin and thought about how I was going to find a research site so I could stay in Africa.

1

The Highland Savanna

Before I was born, my eyes lost their attachment to each other, the instinctive knowledge of how to swivel together, how to analyze data in tandem. The vision of the right eye was only slightly cloudy, but it withdrew from cooperation with the other. My eyes didn't work like two halves of a whole, and I had no perception of depth, so human faces, with their blend of emotion and social mask, were unreadable to me as a child. Only animals, with their epic passions, could pull my warring eyes together for seconds at a time. But animals ran from me.

I remember, before there were animals in the house, I used to sit on the stone ledge made by onion farmers and watch the leaves move in the trees. Sometimes, if you were watching the right place, one of the leaves would turn into a squirrel, and once even a cat. I would wait on the ledge, although Grandma said I shouldn't because stone gives you colds, looking out for toads, the only animals that let me get close. They were brown, with very golden eyes and bumpy skin that moved too easily over their backs when you picked them up.

I saw a little one crouching under a leaf and chased it with both hands out, cupped, wanting to hold it but afraid to hold too hard. It hopped twice and sat still, and I caught it in my hands, and then caught it again after it spurted out like a straw in a soda with too many bubbles. It sat still and peed once in a long, sticky stream. I turned it over to look at the stomach. It was white and soft, like the flabby skin on a baby's stomach, but smelled like toadstools, moldy and sweet. Other animals bit me or ran because I stared as hard as any predator and crept toward them as if toward an altar. But when I touched the toad, it relaxed in my hand, stretching out so I could rub it from throat to legs. Its eyes closed. I put it in my sand bucket, but my mother came out and told me to let it go.

My parents finally gave me a dog, and I followed her to the meadow in the woods. She stood at the edge, watching an invisible world, and I saw traces of the meadow's past moving through her nose and brain; here a rabbit had crisscrossed, there a deer had stopped to watch for coyotes, or a bird had swept into the grass and risen with a twisting mouse. Standing at the edge of that meadow, in grasses filled with sun and stillness, I disappeared, spread like the wind in layers of light. The incomprehensible human world of polyester clothing, smokestacks, and car exhaust vanished as if it had never existed, and I was pure, inside and out. I knew that Africa would be like this, not bounded by houses but just an infinity of lighted grasses, owned only by animals.

From the age of twelve on, I tried to build a résumé that would somehow earn me a place in Africa. I worked with hamsters in a pet store, I got kicked by horses in a local stable, I got bitten every day while working for a vet. I learned sign language in high school so that I could work with primates, and I spent my summers in college studying rhesus macaques and howler monkeys.

Someone told me that some physical anthropologists studied animal behavior in the field, so I decided to go to graduate school in physical anthropology. Then, I reasoned, I could make my life in Africa among the animals that I wanted to watch so badly. I would also be entering a community I understood, a place where I wasn't the only one who wanted to live in a tent on the savanna, or who knew that animals still have answers to questions we have forgotten how to ask.

In 1986, during my junior year at Wesleyan, my adviser told me that if I was serious about graduate school, I'd have to take off the following year to do thesis research. There were so few spaces for graduate students in my discipline that my thesis would have to be publishable to earn me a spot: I applied for a deeply coveted internship working with a signing gorilla in California. The same day that I received the letter offering me the position, a friend passed me a brochure he'd been given, because he thought I might be interested. It was a course list for the School for Field Studies, and on the cover was a giraffe floating through acacia trees, its head above the horizon. I knew I should take the internship because I'd be guaranteed data for my thesis; if I took the field course in Kenya, on the other hand, I might not even be able to find a job after the semester ended.

Without depth perception, I always had difficulty perceiving my past. If I'd been blind, my eyes would not have tried to see, and the memories would have formed intact, as sound and touch and smell. Instead, the present slid by in a blur of strained vision, of shadows half seen; there were few memories recorded for the screen of the mind. Without a firm sense of the past, I found the present impossible to read. Looming decisions often seemed undecipherable, as if my brain too were deprived of depth perception. I could think only in stark dichotomies, obvious wrongs and rights, good or bad. When choices showed themselves in more subtle shades and colorings, I was lost. I took the letter and the brochure to my career counselor, thinking that she would tell me firmly that I needed to stay on the safer path.

"Go to Africa," she said. I told her that I had to write a publishable thesis to get into graduate school. "If you want to go to Africa, go," she repeated.

"But I might not be able to do it later, if I go now," I pointed out. "What do you want to do?" she asked.

Want to do? Didn't everyone want to go to Africa? "I want Africa," I said.

"So go."

The plane landed in a September dawn, just as the sun rose. I leaned backward, to look through the one open window. At first there was nothing but an arc of darker sky in a multitude of small lights as the sun below blanked out the stars on the horizon. For a long time, the darkness hovered there, then slowly became a lighter arc within the star-studded sky. The gray haze expanded, widened, and stretched. In a line at its base, a sliver of crimson spread.

The beginning was undramatic. Rays of light fingered from below the curve of the earth and moved like soft piano music, touching in brief dances across the grasses. Stars above the half circle paled and winked out. Then, with a crash of light, the crimson spread to fill the arc of gray, and the grasses below it glowed beneath a dark sky. Like colored light from a prism, the rays spread higher, rising and falling but blanking the stars they touched. Halfway out, the sun no longer arced: it soared across the curve of the earth, then rose in its entirety. The light of the savanna is like nothing else. The sun dwarfed the earth and filled the grasses with a burn of gold.

The passenger beside the window stirred and pulled down the shade, but I was glad to sit and catch my breath for a while. I had wanted Africa all my life. I had been wrong about everything in the human world, but I had been right about the savanna. This was my home.

The other students and I drove through zebras and waking lions to a tent camp an hour east of Nairobi, and almost immediately mounted a truck bed to jolt out onto the grasses. As if my eyes could breathe, I filled with light and spread my atoms across the horizons like white laundry lighted by the sun. Time halted and never began again. Part of me would always be there, on the savanna, breathing its lighted dusts and exhaling my own.

The field-study site sat in the center of a wildlife ranch, one of the few in Kenya. The owner let the researchers and students stay on his land because he wanted to prove that hunting wildlife was better for the land than raising cattle on it. For the next few months, we were going to be doing research on giraffe ecology and studying wildlife biology with the teachers there.

The following day we returned to the savanna with our binoculars and telescopes and notebooks, jouncing through the blue shadows of the kopjes and acacia shrubs into the blaze of sun. Everyone wanted to be up front, out of the dust that roiled up under the truck. On tiptoe there, we rode it like a bucking bronco with the wind in our faces, and hands locked tight on the rear window's roof. The sun beat down on us even through the wind, and the savanna spread out to the African horizon, as old as it had ever been. All in all, it was the cleanest I have ever felt.

We set up our telescopes on windy hills and sat down with binoculars on knees to scan the horizon. I was always the last to see the animals. My father had taken me bird-watching since I was two, but I had never seen the birds with more than one eye at a time, and they looked blurred and flat. I couldn't believe that, even here, it was no different.

The giraffes we had come to study wandered everywhere. There was no need to drive right up to them, but we did it anyway. The closer, the better. Every now and then we could hear the *scuff, scuff* of their feet or feel the sudden gust that twitched their ears.

That first day, as we rattled and creaked across the savanna, we saw a giraffe we'd been watching from a distance finally rear back and stilt away from a faint green tree. This, our teacher explained, was an acacia. Silver leaves sprouted so small between its huge thorns that the bush looked like a man whose height was all in his feet, turned upside down. The thorns jutted in all directions, casting shadows that on another tree would have belonged to the leaves. This type of acacia was called a Whistling Thorn, named by natural history.

The bush didn't just whistle, though; it shook and rattled the thorns together like bones clicking. The thorns were as long and dry as shards of sheared-off branches, and it took only a small wind to set them squeaking and rubbing up against one another, with little taps and clatters. As the wind passed, the bush sat still, so faintly tinted it looked like nothing more than a small cloud drifting over the grasses. The scent of a wild animal hung over it in a secondary cloud of musk and freedom.

Leaning forward to see what the backlit giraffe had done to the acacia, I touched the branch. There were no gaps in leaf or thorn. The foot-long tongue must have stripped the leaves erratically; the giraffe had stood there for an age, curling its tongue in yanks at the branches and shaking the ants off in slow motion. The only real signs of the giraffe's assault were the ants, still swarming, with antennae flailing, up and down the east side of the bush. It was the ants' homes, the teacher told us, that whistled. Acacias grow hollow balls amid the thorns for the ants to live in, and the ants pay rent by swarming over the antelope and giraffes as they graze on the leaves. Giraffes have tough tongues and long eyelashes, but they don't stay long once the full force of ants has been roused from its whistling homes.

The bubbles clinked and clattered with dry silver sounds like the thorns, but they also whistled. A breeze picked up the thorns and tossed them into a tangle, and I heard the wind faintly blowing over all those hollowed holes. Through the tinkle and clicks and squeaks, and the rattles and rubs, wove a little high-pitched scream, or maybe a moan — the movement of the thorns like all the wind captured in miniature and magnified for our eyes.

Sometimes in the night the teachers let a few of us joyride with them in the Land Rover across the starlit savanna. Moths came from nowhere and swarmed around the headlights, swirling into the windshield like gusts of dusted wind. Holding out flashlights to search the road ahead, we stretched our arms over the sides of the jeep to keep the hordes far away from our eyes and mouths. They landed and crawled on clothing with tight fingers, searching for the light. We learned not to touch our bodies, to avoid leaving a smear of corpses behind.

Once, passing under a tree, we shone our lights up and saw a snake draped there, looking down, bemused by the car, its noise, and the lighted hurricane of insects drawn after it. Bush babies' eyes, we learned, are the largest — bigger than lions' — and it was a treat to shine our beams into another tree and see the vague gray huddle of a body with two headlight eyes turned on us. Another time, the wildebeest herd, with its gold-flared eyes, raced around us so fast the moths were whisked away, and we were surrounded by the clatter of hooves instead.

By day, I recorded the behavior and feeding patterns of giraffes. In my free time, on the nights we weren't out looking for animals in the dark, I'd tear myself from the moonlit horizons to work on the future. I would sit at a table looking out over the savanna, my face tingling with sunburn and powdered with sweet dust, writing to scientists to ask for a job. The moths would circle around my head as if it were a secondary light, while an unsnubbable mantis stalked its prey from my shoulder. I felt like the earth itself, surrounded by the eating and the eaten.

Again and again I wrote the same letters and sent them off to the oblivion of the post office, like prayer cards tucked into crevices of rock or, released, fluttering up into the wind, to a god alone. "I have worked for a pet store, a nature center, three veterinarians, and a riding stable. I have studied Hanuman langur affiliative behaviors in a zoo, rhesus macaque sibling interactions on an island in South Carolina, following order in Panamanian tamarins at a field site in Panama, and daily patterns of feeding in howler monkeys on Maje Island in Panama. I am studying a semester of wildlife management at a giraffe research station in Kenya." I feared that there would be no response. This was going to be hard and bitter labor, finding a research site; I had no right to one by virtue of degree or character.

"I'll bring a tent," I would plead, "and my own food."

When it came time for spring break, the other students went on safari, and the teachers dropped me at the Nairobi International Youth Hostel. I was determined to talk to the scientists to whom I'd written, to try to find a way to stay in Africa. Backpackers looked up from their cooking stoves and said hello in a few different languages.

Nairobi Town was dusty and hot, as if even the low mud buildings at its edge blocked the wind, ending its continent-long search. I left my backpack in a locker at the hostel and trudged to the main road.

Hanging my wallet inside my shirt, I buttoned my pockets and climbed onto a matatu so crowded the conductor braced his back against me, clung with hands and toes to the door frame, and pushed until the crowd inside groaned. Forced closer to humans than I'd ever been, resting against their weight with feet raised off the ground, rib cage so crushed I wondered if I'd be able to breathe, I felt fingers grope around my hip and slide along the edges of a buttoned pocket. "Hey," I said, and "Tchah!" a woman shouted. Shaking her arm so the whole crowd swayed with her, she burst into KiSwahili so loud I couldn't follow. The hand withdrew. "You are a bad man," she added. "Do not rob the Mzungu." The matatu screeched to a stop, and horns blared past. Someone groaned. The conductor grinned, opened the door, and stepped out. A man in a business suit paused on the step and looked at us, but it was too late. The conductor had planted himself in the door and blocked his getaway; the crowd swelled and absorbed him.

I stepped off the bus onto broken pavement. Pickpockets lined the boulevard. With a rush of bead necklaces and orange-dyed giraffe carvings, they dived at me. "Mzungu. You buy, you buy!" they screamed. Hands stroked along my pockets, pushed me gently from one vendor to another, and shook me by the shoulder. "You buy, you buy," not caring whether I bought or was robbed, one or the other. "Tell them 'sitaki,'" a teacher had said. "They'll go away." But they didn't.

I wavered for a long time, blocked by hands and giraffes made in China. The shouting came closer and closer to my ears; it seemed to pierce right through them, from one to the other. No longer gentle, the hands grabbed and pushed. "Sitaki," I said, "sitaki," and they paused for a second, then flung themselves back into battle afresh. Some of them wore the fanciest new clothing — 1980s-style disco shirts in plum and puce — and others the gray rags so common in Kenya. They must have felt the guilt pouring from me. I had always given money to beggars on the streets, lovingly saved every piece of clothing for local charities, and played Peter, Paul, and Mary on the recorder with my mother when I was little. One traveler's check in my pocket would have fed any of these men's families for a month.

Hierarchy is the curse of wealth written clear in Africa. I had too much, no one else had enough, but mine wouldn't go around, and if I gave it away, I'd have to leave. I was trapped more by a lifetime's beliefs than by their arms. But I was also burning for that office door. When I finally breathed in deeply and, shouting like a maniac, pushed and pulled my way through them, slapping fingers from my pockets, I left behind more than machine-dyed giraffes.

Every day of that week, I rode the matatu filled with pickpockets into town and walked past mud huts to cement buildings with hordes of men bashing and pulling and swearing and yanking me around to look at their giraffe statues while their other hand tugged at my pockets.

When I had left the United States four months earlier, I had been so shy I wouldn't ask waiters for a glass of water. That strange burning determination that had made me reject a guaranteed research site to come to Africa changed my character overnight. In Kenya I hammered on doors and waited with oxlike patience to be thrown out; remade appointments that had been broken; and waited six hours for a man who said he would see me at eight and never did, and came back the next day to try again. And the next.

In a wildlife services office, two secretaries sat talking. I held out my résumé with a cover letter. "Can I leave this for the director, please?"

"What do you want?"

"I want to volunteer at the research site of one of your projects."

"We do not accept volunteers."

"But all of the sites are staffed by volunteers."

"That is not my job."

The secretary put it in a pile of résumés two feet high, all for a permanent job application in administration.

Another secretary in another office put it carefully on the floor, with a stack of papers, three scrunched-up paper balls, and two lunch bags.

A third secretary told me about her family, and I gave her a recipe for ginger tea, good for colds. She buzzed me through to the director, then said, "I'm sorry, sir," when he yelled at her and showed me out.

I ran out of résumés and had to hike out to the white people's suburb to make more copies.

The archaeologist turned to me and said gently, "No, I am sorry. There really is nothing we can do for you. Even PhDs have problems getting clearance in Kenya." He opened his filing cabinet and pointed to a thick folder, bent and shedding under the weight of paper. "Everyone wants to work in Kenya." Why wouldn't they? From his back window, a giraffe passed through an acacia stand, treading with immense thought. The sun trickled down through the leaves, and three Thomson's gazelles froze in a patch of light. They looked at me until I turned away. I had two names left to try, out of thirty-seven.

Tears had stung my eyes at the sudden kindness. But I knew that what he said wasn't so. The backpackers I'd met at the hostel who had been working at research sites had had no qualifications.

One had been a farmhand, one a cook, and the third had been unemployed.

I rode the riotous matatu home every night and in the evenings would sit on the bench under the acacia tree by the hostel office, learning KiSwahili and telling the managers about my day. My life on the savanna hinged on the little black address book filled with names.

Turning from their cooking stoves, the backpackers had asked first, "Where are you from?" Meaning, *What are you leaving behind?*

Then, "Where have you been?" *What are you looking for?*

Last, they asked, "Where are you going?"

What are you going to become?

2

The Lion's Eye

The teachers picked me up from the semester break, and we left again in the bus for a safari, to compare the different ecosystems of the different reserves. There was light without shadow. Giraffes passed like dinosaurs in the distance across a sun that arced from one horizon to the next. Under the reflected glow of mountains set on plains, we looked for a rhino but found the lion first. He sprawled on a bump in grass that was eaten so short it looked like a lawn. Because he was higher, we saw him long before the others. Wind rippled the ends of his mane and one ear ticked back toward us while his eyes looked away at the mountains, though only one eye could see even the near hills. The other was swollen shut over a cascade of fluid and flies, and ticks attracted to the softness of wet skin. The tail flicked as we came nearer, and he pawed once at the black cloud on the left. With noise, the insects rose, then settled again into his silence. We drove toward him on an angle to look but not chase, and he swung the other ear back at us. The sun was straight above, burning on the gold and the black, the healthy and the crawling.

Cresting a twin hill, we saw the others in the incline, the largest pride I'd seen since coming to Kenya. We were too excited to count then, but there must have been thirty-five lions there. Young of different ages turned fat bellies in the grass and suckled from the nearest female, and two old ones stroked each other's heads with so long a rasp that the very grass seemed to rumble in a purr. They lay stomach to back, paws folded together, eyes shut in a melt of peace and hot fur, and the smallest of the babies played with their tails, making a forest of them. A young female strolled toward them, head and eyes heavy in a purr, and one broke away to bump foreheads with her and knock her over with a washing. More infants poured between the three, so round they rolled under the tongues that licked them in no particular order, just as they came within reach.

With binoculars, I twisted the angles of light, and suddenly each eye had a separate, perfect vision. Each still saw the world in different colors, but I could see the lions with both eyes. For the first time, the animals popped into focus, and with this new depth perception, I saw crags and hollows and wrinkles in the lions' faces, and could smell the wind as they lifted their noses into it.

The lions lay on the savanna in a hollow, with nothing but a few mountains in other countries between them and the edges of the earth. The savanna highlands of Kenya rested just beneath the sun, and the light filled the grasses as if they were clouds, seen from above. A whisper of wind eased through the grasses, and a faint whistle sounded over the baboon rocks. A giraffe stepped out of the acacia stand and looked down its nose at the lions and our truck. Then it flew away. One leg creaked down, then out, then another, and another, and the last, and the giraffe that had been a tree was running across the savanna with a grace so slow that she tilted and skimmed like a rigger dipping into waves under still sails.

A weaverbird clattered away in a flash of yellow and wing, disappearing like all the yellow-and-gold flights of all the animals I had ever seen.

The lions were all related, the older females as grandmothers and mothers, the younger ones as mothers now too. Only the male was unconnected; he had fought another male to stay with this group, and if a new male sent him away, he could die. Males are too heavy to easily run for prey; the females do that. And he couldn't see from that eye. He lay with paws ahead and his back in that curl of thought that only lions have, looking at the hills. Like the pods of an amoeba, tendrils of young moved apart from the group, pacing shoulder by shoulder away, then romping back when the others stayed. They bumped heads with the purring old ones and pushed at their faces with too-large paws or bit vampirelike into sleeping necks, and the females lapped them with love and humor.

One old female got up and stretched, curled and uncurled her tongue, and yawned her back straight, then followed a mass of young, who moved with new speed and certainty toward the tree. We drove into the shade to watch them straggle in. The old female lay on the roots, and the others danced in after, then her sister wrapped around her, and they moved only to greet the others, each time with a thunder of satisfaction. Pieces of hair spiraled off as young slid and grabbed and walked on top of them. And at last, the male followed too, head down and one eye sharp with gold, that incredible gold of a lion's eye. We could see only that one eye from this side, and his belly, a paler fawn, tight with good life and wildebeest legs.

There, as he raised his head from the mane and smelled the wind in nods and sucks with tail twisting round, he was alive. A lion is as nothing else on earth: fire and flames, a flickering silence that is peace complete, a strength that moves without sound and dies all at once. He turned and lay down away from us, and we were sorry that we could not take pictures of him as he had been; all we could see was the eye squeezed shut and the flies crawling over one another to get at it. So we took shots of him blackened but far from dying while the cubs pounced by the tree and the mothers licked them clean. I keep those pictures in a fireproof box, but they are shadows when compared to that shining lion I still carry with me.

The teachers drove us back through zebras' and lions' eyes to the research center, where there were only a few stands of acacia woodland but acres of scattered acacia shrubs. One thicket of shrubs circled the center of the camp. The other students had gone to drink pombe, and I sat alone on the ground, scraping the vervet bones for a display. I loved bones, the curves and twists, like dancers' poses, the whiteness, the clean, dead smell, and it was a while before I looked up and saw a giraffe standing nearby. She knew I was there but had forgotten me. I had been moving constantly over my gems but with absorption, like a giraffe feeding on a favorite food. As soon as I lifted my head, she stopped browsing and looked at me.

I tried to fake an interest in the bones again, but she could tell the difference, and I couldn't help looking up at her. Though she was only fifteen feet away, the acacia branches hid her almost completely, the spots and mottles merging with patches of shade up her neck. Standing still and watching me, she was invisible. I stared through the silver branches, repainting her face in the shadows, but any direct look is a threat; only predators stare. Soon she had had enough. With long backward-hinged legs, she stilted out of the trees and disappeared behind them. Feeling as if I'd been cut in half, I returned to polishing my bones.

In the last week, with our projects finished and the monkey bones mounted on the wall of the museum, we drove all over the ranch. In the lighted grasses, standing against the sky, impalas and zebras and wildebeest and giraffes mingled in symbiotic relations, each watching for different predators or finding new foods for the other.

One night after dinner, I walked alone through powder to the watering hole. Other students had gone to the watering hole casually, with beer; I wondered if I'd see the unevenness in the ground before I fell, or would miss a snake that others would spot. But the animals ran from the truck in the daytime. Maybe if I sat quietly in the night, they wouldn't notice me, and I would have another of those moments, so rare in America and so constant here, of entrance into the wild. It might be possible to stay in one of those moments forever, everything in life filtered through a lion grooming in the sun, or a giraffe feeding. Under the moon, the grasses had shrunk, as if the wind had stretched them with light during the day. The trees, as uncolored and unusually silent as skeletons in grass, hovered over my hair. Whispering in puffs to the ankles as I trod in an unseen depression, clean and cold dust shifted over my sandals. It was my first time alone on the savanna, and near the end of the semester. No one had answered my letters. I listened for lions.

The path wound away from the road to the east. Grass shrank from my knees, and through my shoes I felt a track hardened into the dirt, a separate pool of light. A mirror of a giraffe's foot, an echo of its absence painted in water with a reflection of the sky, clouded at one edge where my foot had been. Shifting away, I wiped my shoe on grass. One of the teachers had told us never to touch water in Africa. In the thickest mud, the liver flukes could survive. "You never recover," he said, "even after they're dead." He wiped mud from his sneaker with a handful of grass.

There was the watering hole, lighted and glistening, so clear that clouds formed and reformed across its surface, dark and moon-glowing. Predators might be waiting at the edge for gazelles to drink, so I squatted on the path, which always made me want to go to the bathroom, and watched for a while. Nothing came, though I heard rustles inside the grasses. I sat looking at the bright water and the flattened landscape, and then put one hand in the hardened ridges of an impala track, barely touching it.

The pond was dead. There was no sign that anything still living had made these tracks, or would ever come back. A white feather fluttered in one step, lifeless as a wing of pine needles.

I had been in the hostel for a month since the semester ended. It was the last week of December, and I was lying dizzy with a passing bout of dysentery when I paged through my appointment book and found that I had visited every single person in Nairobi who could have helped me. My deadline for leaving Africa to find a research site at home fell the next day. Without hesitation, hand still weak, I wrote in my notebook only, "Call embassy — get visa for Tanzania," and laid the book on the blanket to drink water when Tom Butynski appeared at the hostel office and offered me a research site with chimpanzees in Uganda.

Chimpanzees in the rain forest. I did not deserve chimpanzees, but in one second, I had leaped in and taken the research site — taken the dream that was more than I expected, and beyond my qualifications.

"Yes," I said. "I would like to study the chimpanzees at the bottom of the mountain." Where is Uganda? I wondered to myself, thinking of dark hills like Vietnam, and piles of bones.

3

Ugandan Mountains of the Moon

I n The Varieties of Religious Experience, *William James defines a mystical experience as having four characteristics. First, ineffability. It defies expression: "no adequate report of its contents can be given in words." Second, noetic quality. Mystical experiences are "states of insight into depths of truth unplumbed by the discursive intellect. They are illuminations, revelations, full of significance and importance, all inarticulate though they remain; and as a rule they carry with them a curious sense of authority for after-time." Third, transiency. "Half an hour, or at most an hour or two, seems to be the limit beyond which they fade into the light of common day. Often, when faded, their quality can but imperfectly be reproduced in memory; but when they recur it is recognized; and from one recurrence to another it is susceptible of continuous development in what is felt as inner richness and importance."*

Last, mystical experiences are passive. One can prepare by "fixing the attention, or going through certain bodily performances," but when the mystical state sets in, the mystic feels as if "he were grasped and held by a superior power."

Through the mud of the main street, a white bull wandered. Slow and ponderous, like an elephant musing in front of a mountain, he thought and ate and drifted forward. Even with the clouded sun straight above his horns, he stood in shadow under a sky as dark as a lid on a bowl.

It rained a little, mountain cold, washing tracks into the red mud on his legs. He was a Brahman bull, with all the excesses of the breed: the straight wide hams, the great hump, and the dangling added muscles of chest and throat. A mist rose around him because he was hotter than the rain, and behind him the mountains steamed too. Head up, he smelled the air, and turned his horns about to look up the road. As far as one could see, from this edge of Uganda toward Zaire, the mud was red. He lowered his head and, on the side of the road, walked on, among women strolling to market with baskets on their heads and men carrying chickens.

"You will never find these chimpanzees," the hotel guard in Kabale had said outside the ruined white walls, while crowned cranes tiptoed past. "Eh," someone said in obligatory agreement, then added, "These chimpanzees, they will find you and come and kill you. They are very bad animals." "Eh." Someone else sidled forward, hands cupped to hold his words. "And when the rains, they come, the chimpanzees go so far away, even past the mountains." "Eh," they all agreed.

I sat in the back of the truck, afraid of the men, except the old one, but I looked forward, up the mountain, around my shoulder. It was all fields of scrubby dirt at the bottom, with small, dirty children screaming after us, shouting, "Mzungu, Mzungu," their rags flapping against legs of bone. Two churches, a Catholic one and a Protestant one, leaned together in the valley below the road, shrouded by sticks of smoke from the huts.

Kayonza lay a week's journey by bus from Kenya and its savannas. I had taken a bus to the Kenyan border and then another, through angry border guards, to Kampala. Another bus to Njerere.

This morning, after a week's wait in Kabale, in the ruined hotel of the aristocrats, I'd finally gotten a ride from the lumber poacher up the mountain to Tom's gorilla center. From warmth to cold, sun to rain, an infinity of horizons to mountains like walls.

We passed madly driven pickup trucks full of shouting, laughing men and thumping with loud music. Ours was silent. The men sat, looking away from me, except the youngest, who leaned his leg on mine and tried to catch my eyes with his flat pupils. An old man scolded him and he moved away a bit but grinned at me like a vampire. They have a special look, children raised as soldiers. I'd seen city people in Kampala ducking into stores as these dead-eyed boys walked down the bullet-riddled street. They are separated from the rigid hierarchies of people raised in times of peace. Too much power and too many deaths. Now they live in peacetime as if they still hold a gun in their hands and can take prisoners at will. The old man grew up in a quieter world; the young one was lucky to survive a war in which twelve-year-olds were shooting at one another. Who could blame him for hating white people, in a land that ticked gently at the foot of the mountain for hundreds of thousands of years before the British gave them factories and new hierarchies?

Through the wreckage of the richest land in Africa we bounced, past potholes as big as cars, telephone poles rotting in the mud, a country ravaged by its own leader for no known reason. Idi Amin had ordered his soldiers to destroy phones, electricity, plumbing, and factories, and burn any village at random.

Even with the young on my left and the old on my right, I could do nothing but look up ahead to where the forest began with a brutal chop, one second too exposed, the next second a dark carpet over the hills. But we had miles to go, through mud huts and fires, chickens and children, red dirt and banana trees. Sometimes a cement house popped past us, standing alone, as if wealth had made its owners lonely. A red-haired child flashed past, pale curls among the dark ones of his siblings, then another. The dust roiled behind the truck, bouncing up and down in clouds, as we revved over boulders. The men sitting over the rear wheels covered their noses with shirttails and waited patiently.

I had been pressed among them in the wall of dust, picked up last from the white hotel at the end of Kabale. As we jolted away, a young man on the road had grabbed my shirt and pulled me backward off the truck. I hung on with my legs to the side while the others watched expressionless and moved away from me. The old man in the front of the truck shouted at the young one running beside it. I felt my shirt shake up and down, then relax, and I pulled back up into the truck. The old man made someone else clear away from the second-best seat, on the spare tire in front next to him. The young man ran alongside the truck for a while, jeering, but I didn't watch him. I could barely see, with the flaws in my eye, and the world had burst into color. Up front, in the truck bed, we could breathe the clean air coming from the mountain, and smell dust, the smoke from a thousand old fires, and wet leaves.

We were closer. High enough now on the road, we could see that the wisps of mist — that on the bottom were just pockets of heavy, wet air — were in fact clouds gathering themselves out of morning dew heated to steam. Heavy and thick as they rose, the clouds-to-be broke off and spiraled into columns, rising faster and faster and whiter and still lighter, spreading gravity-free in all directions with tendrils and shoots smoking off from the edges, whirling off as they got lighter and higher, so the whole valley was sleepy and wet under a lake of mist, but the far mountains were ringed by separate clouds.

We bumped along on the rocks, in the dust, with our own plumes twisting behind us so we felt a tremendous sense of going somewhere fast. What was gray below was white above, like some early zealot's idea that humans are dirty and only heaven pure. They were better than angels, those clouds. We passed above one, and a man leaned his tattered sleeve down to let his fingers ride in the cloud, as a canoeist might drift a hand in the water.

A ribbon of road stretched out above us, winding back and forth in switchbacks so steep that they dribbled rocks. What might have taken an hour straight up took five to loop and loop around the gash cut into the last of the Mountains of the Moon. An old man and two children came out of a mud hut to shout — "Mzungu, Mzungu" — and women shrieked with laughter. They lived on the right-hand side of the road, on a steep, dusty hill. Impossible, one would have thought, to keep their babies and chicks from rolling off the edge of the hill onto the road, and from there off the crumbling side of the mountain, down two thousand feet into the clouds.

As one sits in a car, the crunches and creaks of the tires usually echo back from all sides, but with the straight fall to the left, we could hear only the rattles bouncing off the in-cut stone, and nothing on the other side, as if we were drifting along on half a car. The other half's sound fell deep into the valley, where someone might hear it at the bottom as they moved around in the gray mist.

The path dipped down again, and we passed through a cloud following the road up the mountain. One second the rock was clear and sharp around us, tinted with light, and the next it was shadowed, wet and smoky, our cheeks cold and damp. I smiled at the old man, grateful that he had protected me. On the other side of the clouds, with tendrils of vapor clinging to our tires, we saw a cluster of liana vines pouring over rock, swaying its leaves and flowers like a bead curtain. Two birds hid in there and flew out as we passed. Moss as green as ferns sparkled with rain left behind by the last cloud that passed by, and water trickled from its roots in great lichen-stained falls. Butterflies hovered around and drank from pools in the moss, resting beaten wings to lower their heads and lap the water. A crystalline fly buzzed in and out of the curtain, and something scuttled quickly under a swaying leaf. The air was suddenly full of possibility.

The vines twisted on the right thicker and thicker, white flowers cupping butterflies as the truck spread its dust. The air smelled of leaves and moss, and water running over rock, and still, faintly, of clouds. To the left, the last of Uganda twisted up and down, far into the distance below us, and beyond that, Rwanda and Zaire. The mountain where Dian Fossey lived loomed up ahead—the tallest and the only white cap in that rolling carpet of green. I thought that I was very happy to be here, after all, in the bouncing truck, on the crumbling road over the clouds, with orchids on the stone, and monkeys and maybe even gorillas ahead. I had always known I would have to work harder than anyone else to earn a life on the savanna, and here in the rain forest, on a mountain in a war-torn country, I would find sacrifices to set on the altar.

I smiled at the men, and some smiled back, and they all shifted uncomfortably, still half afraid, except for the younger one. "Me, I want to see chimpanzees," I said in Rukiga, very proud of myself, but they didn't burst out laughing, though the villagers in Kabale had rolled on the ground, slapping their knees. Murmuring, they repeated it: "The Mzungu wants to see chimpanzees." Bats swooped over our heads, catching bugs, and we passed some that were nestled upside down, hanging inside the lianas.

A sign struggled out of the bushes on long arms. THE IMPENETRABLE FOREST OF UGANDA. The trees shut around it, and we passed from light to dark, warm to cold, dust to mold, in one second. Ahead, I heard monkeys calling, and a turaco.

4

Guest of the Gorillas

I *n Kenya, when we drove out onto the savanna at night, wildebeest*
stood gray and shapeless against the separate shadows of a cloud
and the dark, bent grasses. Their eyes, a second constellation, stared
as our headlights passed over them, and winked from the moving
shapes. Something snorted and ran, and the eyes blinked out and
reappeared in profile, flowing away from the headlights in separate,
hovering globes of light. The movement was, like everything on the
savanna, myth and clarity. Stars had been swept away, as if a cloud
meandered by, present only as an absence.

"I am not always regretting my palm trees and my panther. I should
have to be very melancholy for that. In the desert, you see, there is
everything and nothing."

"Yes, but explain —"

"Well," he said, with an impatient gesture, "it is God without
mankind."

— *Balzac*

It was hard to breathe up there on the mountain in Uganda.
Human noise faded first to a humming of accumulated echoes,
then to an emptiness. It was a while before my lungs filled with
air. I turned to the edge, away from the white cabin.

At the end of the mountain, under the pines, a chicken clucked by as if drawn on invisible threads through a strange land. The pine trees held their breath, and the chasm sank so deep, the silence hummed in the ears. A thousand drums thumping in my pulse, I had ridden past savannas and mountains and red mud roads, in blue-and-yellow matatus, with dust sucking through the windows and curling like feathers about my neck, and the bone-jarring bumps and all the drums and pickpockets and screaming beggars and throbbing engines and shrieks of laughter and questions and complaints and spiced tea and green tangerines and sticks of samosas, hot and yellow triangles of pastry on branches, and arguments over price and border guards with their ferocious scowls—one human more or less—and the poachers whom I begged for a ride, and that last silent truck traveling the mountain, always on its edge; they were all thumping and jangling and drumming on still in my blood. I had breathed too deep of this world. And here there was silence, the emptiness of a home half lived-in.

It was not the light and space of the savanna, neither a home nor an opening of the eye. It was the entrance, in the absence of humans, to the human world. And, though the hut perched on a cliff, and was surrounded at every other border by smugglers and thieves, it was the kind of house I had always wanted, without knowing it. No electricity or plumbing, no traffic or human noise, no aerosol spray cans or blue window cleansers. It was just a hut, in clean air, above a wilderness.

Into the gap left by so many human presences, two children appeared silently around the corner and stood, looking at me. A new restlessness surged through me, and I almost wanted to lift my backpack and hike into the forest, thinning away huts and human controversy until I was in land unmarked and unstamped, clean of human alteration.

But it was just a cloud, one of the last of the day, rising from the bottomlands. It rose in a solid wall, a few feet from the cabin, and blocked out the sun, first in part and then with a wet draft of eclipse. My backpack rippled as if it had flashed over on its side and back again, and then the cloud soared overhead and dwindled on the ground into a small, dark spot, and the children and the trees were lighted again along their sides.

The children hovered in a solemn line, diagonally against the trees. The girl stood closer than her brother, one dusty finger in her mouth, belly jutted forward and her flat bare feet planted firm in the dirt of the yard. Her older brother leaned sideways under the weight of a baby and watched me.

All three were smooth-limbed and relaxed, with slow-blinking black eyes, but the boy arched slender and tired behind the baby. The infant perched on one dusty hip, a plumply gleaming Buddha, arms creased with fat and belly bulging above short legs. He shone like satin, naked except for a round good-luck charm tied on a thong underneath the widest part of his belly.

"Hello," the girl said firmly. "Hello, Mzungu."

She asked my name, then crowed, "Eeeh, eeh, Mzungu." She pointed to each child in turn, snapping out names: herself first, "Jean-Marie," then "Henry," then "Eh eh Mzee," jutting her lip at the firm little baby. She walked past me as I unlocked the door. Eyes glimmering and shoulders hunched around the baby, her brother Henry sidled in after her, gazing around the corners of the room, then glancing back at me once beneath lowered eyelids.

As I hovered on the dusty doorsill, not sure where to go or what to do, Jean-Marie turned to watch me and murmured, "Eeeeh, Mzungu," with the mixture of laughter, cheek, self-mockery, and warmth that only Africans can put into the vowel. I swung my pack over the stone step, into the little alcove filled with rough shelves of pots and red lanterns for the researchers who camped near the gorillas. I didn't look at the children, careful to neither welcome nor repel these explorers of their own backyard.

The walls were thick and dark, but mountain light fell through window and door in a column that sparkled in reflection on the covers of books and the blades of machetes.

Just inside the door, I stopped, not sure where to sleep. Tom had told me to use one of the bedrooms, but I didn't want to get in the way of the gorilla volunteers when they came back.

Henry put Mzee, whose name meant *honored elder,* down on the peach-colored couch, and the two older children flanked him like acolytes, legs swinging as they stared at me, waiting. Cement and stone walls loomed over the small, shining bodies, but the children fit in the sooty cavern in a way I did not, and I wondered why they found it so strange. Leaning the dusty backpack against the cement wall, I unstrapped the sleeping bag.

A shadow suddenly stretched into the light on the doorsill, cutting across the room. Jean-Marie and Henry stood up with their legs leaning against the peach cushion.

"Eeeeh, memsahib, it is good to see you. Dr. Tom told me you were to come. I am Luke, the campkeeper."

Luke turned his back to the children but took my hand between both of his and clasped it while he talked. Dark eyes, the whites brown with age, fixed warmly on mine as he bowed up and down over my hand with the rhythm of his welcome. Finally releasing me, he asked if Tom had given me the keys to open the bedrooms, since he had none. When I nodded, though I wouldn't use them, he turned to go, glaring at the children.

Mzee, with an expression of removed concentration, sent a tiny golden arc of urine into the air. A patch of peach fabric quickly darkened into a circle before him, and he bobbed his head down to look at that too with dreamy interest. Jean-Marie, eyes sparkling, snatched him to her belly and ran for the door, calling, "Eeeeh, Mzee, ee, ee, eeeeeh." Henry slipped silently away as the campkeeper shook his fist and yelled after them.

"Eeeh, memsahib, these children, they are bad. They know they should not come in the research station." He picked up the couch cushion.

"I'm sorry I let them in, Luke. I didn't know."

"Their father, he does not teach them respect. Olin, his tribe, it is very bad."

"I'm sorry, Luke. I'll wash the cushion if you show me where the water is."

He recoiled. "Eh, memsahib. It is my job."

I watched him lift the cushion. Leaving my backpack next to the naked couch, I walked toward the doorway and halted in the room with the lanterns to look at the edge of the mountain. Dark clouds crept over the forest thousands of feet below, too far for a watcher to see the movement of trees beneath the wall of rain; just the quick slashes of silver as a new line of trees, surprised and conquered by the assault, shook their leaves upside down and swirled about in circles.

Air currents played with the dust, and with a depressed chicken in the yard. I stepped over the gray stones of the doorway and into the gathering storm to look at the waves of the forest. Grit and chicken feathers stung my face. Luke carried the cushion out into the yard and held it on his knees while he scrubbed beneath a pump.

The couch smelled of urine and rain that night. I knew the next

35

few months would be the most difficult of my life. I stretched out my sleeping bag and fell asleep with human complaints ringing in my ears, and the rustle of wind in mountain pines.

"And then this moth-essence, this spectacular skeleton, began to act as a wick. She kept burning. The wax rose in the moth's body from her soaking abdomen to her thorax to the jagged hole where her head should be, and widened into flame, a saffron-yellow flame that robed her to the ground like any immolating monk. That candle had two wicks, two flames of identical height, side by side. The moth's head was fire. She burned for two hours, until I blew her out.

"She burned for two hours without changing, without bending or leaning—only glowing within, like a building fire glimpsed through silhouetted walls, like a hollow saint, like a flame-faced virgin gone to God, while I read by her light, kindled, while Rimbaud in Paris burnt out his brains in a thousand poems, while night pooled wetly at my feet."

—*Annie Dillard*, Holy the Firm

5

Batuko's Bed

The tectonic plates that met in East Africa split apart and bulged up into mountain height. They left a rift between them that ran from Lebanon down to Mozambique in the south, filled with river and some of the world's deepest lakes. The rift split Kenya diagonally, decreasing its height as it tapered down. To the north lay the deserts of Somalia and Ethiopia; to the west, the untouched rain forests of Uganda, and its original volcanic hills. The highland savannas, at the highest edge of the rift, spread in a giant flat mountain, so wide one can stand in the center and see the horizon in any direction, and the curve of the earth a continent away. Sun and moon cover the sky, and at night one can see stars beneath one's feet.

The river waters the rift, but twice yearly rains fall on the highland savanna. The animals in the sky, like the separate parts of a machine, tend their garden of grass with urine and feces and flesh.

A shadow passed over my face as if a cloud had covered the moon. Without the heat of the fire, the couch plummeted into chill. The fire still crackled with flames, but the stronger smell of mud and sweat wafted toward me in another shadow of cold air. I woke slowly without opening my eyes. "Buga waka," someone said. I held my eyes shut another second, hoping he'd go away. He said something again. I opened my eyes. A shadow in shredded clothes leaned over and peered into my face. The movement wafted a breath of rain to me again, with a strange smell of mud and the wax of clothes worn into a second skin.

"Bulagawala!" he shouted, chopping his arms down. I kicked up in the sleeping bag and sat against the wall. He spat out another round of words. Firelight flickered down a muddy uniform and the rusted machete resting against the wall.

Crusted feet stamped the cement floor. With a crescendo of shouts, the man hopped into the air. I hoped Luke wouldn't be angry about the mud.

The ranger leaned forward again, eyebrows beetled and mouth firmly closed.

"I'm sorry, I don't understand," I said.

"Eeeh?"

I repeated in French, then KiSwahili, Rukiga, and English.

"Eeeeeeeh." Slowly the hands opened. One gnarled mitt slapped his leg. "Batuko." He chuckled, eyes sparkling.

I told him my name, and the huge hands cradled mine. "Eeeh, eeh, eeh."

Stepping back, he flapped a hand at the couch.

"Batuko," he said, and folded his arms.

I crossed my legs inside the sleeping bag, trying to identify languages. Was he saying that he was supposed to sleep on the couch? Tom, the director of the research site, had told me I would be alone, but Batuko was wearing a uniform. He pointed, flapped, and shouted.

I told him I still didn't understand.

"Me!" he shouted.

One middle finger was missing, and part of another.

"I see, yes, ndiyo." I nodded. The muddy silhouette swam in the dying firelight, and my eyes drifted shut, then opened.

Batuko peered forward, muttered, and pointed at the couch again with his mouth, jerking his head. I waited. With a groan, he turned, stamped, and hobbled from the room. I slowly released the edge of the crumpled sleeping bag. He stomped back in, mumbling, and spread a blanket on the floor. Straightening, he glared briefly at the couch, then lowered himself piece by piece onto the rug and subsided in front of the fire.

A log fell in the fireplace with a crash, sending tendrils of sweet wood smoke into the room. A stab of light shot up the barrel of the rifle clasped in one wide hand. I lay down slowly on the couch and slid back down into the zipped sleeping bag.

Dreams are different in Africa, perhaps because sun and moon are both so large that the circadian rhythm is stamped into one's blood with alterations of light. One sleeps both deeply and lightly, as if one's body has lost weight and floats above the bed. The events of the day also weave into a lullaby of wind and sun and monkey screams.

A bellow rang through the small room, shaking the couch. I sat in the sleeping bag, rubbing one eye, then the other. The fire glowed dully beneath ashes, and the room was cold with a damp that struck ice to the bone, but sheets of gray morning light fell from the cracks around the shutters. Unzipping the bag, I slid my feet reluctantly into wet hiking boots and squatted in front of the embers. Somewhere outside, Luke's high scolding slid in volume around Batuko's roar, gradually muting him to a shout.

I opened the door and stepped off the cement floor and onto the dirt of the yard. It was my first morning in the Impenetrable Forest. Cold and damp though it was, the air was pure, and smelled of clouds and pine and wood smoke. The edge of the lawn fell steeply down to the dark rolling sea of the forest a thousand feet

Joanna Greenfield

under me, where clouds filled the ravines like rivers. The forest, so far below, echoed with silence, as wisps of cloud began to rise toward our noisy plateau. Chimpanzees, gorillas, and elephants were wandering about somewhere in the endless green carpet.

A thin chicken clucked around the yard, scratching a wide circle around Luke and Batuko. Clutching the rifle in one hand and the half-eaten machete in the other, Batuko stamped puffs of dust and shouted. Luke must have been able to understand Batuko. He snapped a few sharp words, and turned to me.

"Good morning, memsahib. I hope you sleep well. This man, Batuko, he bother you last night?"

I explained that I couldn't understand Batuko, but I thought that I had taken his bed.

"Eeeeh, eeeh, memsahib, this man, he was supposed to sleep in the house to guard it while it was empty. He was supposed to go home when you came, but he did not like this. He is buying a new wife, and his youngest wife is very angry."

BaKiga men are obliged to sleep with their wives a certain number of times a month, or the women are allowed to divorce them. Luke said Batuko already had more wives than he could handle.

Batuko stepped down a path into the cloud. Legs invisible, he turned his head back to shout. The cloud muffled his voice as he sank down the trail into a distant mumble that disappeared in the wind.

Luke cooked beans for me and told me stories of the BaKiga tribe. Tom had written of forest officers who took farmers from their villages and told them to poach or smuggle or cut trees for sale. If the men refused, they were thrown in jail as poachers. One officer had made his fortune sending mahogany down the mountain for sale in the west. Food wasn't given to prisoners in Ugandan jails; their family was told to bring it. Without transportation, family couldn't come, and the prisoners died slowly for the crime they'd refused to commit. Though few men did refuse.

"Can I help you cook, Luke?"

"No, memsahib. No. Please. That is my job."

6

The Missing Monkeys

In Uganda, it was hard to see birds through the canopy, but on the savanna, birds were everywhere. One day we were standing in the truck bed and a bird of purple and blue flew by in a stream of light. We were standing, with dust pouring in jolted rivers over our toes, the giraffes ahead on the horizon—and suddenly a lilac-breasted roller, shining as if dipped in water, so blue it dropped sparks of mirage as it twisted in its flight, streaked a shimmer of light beside our arms. It seemed to pick up the universe and put it down in a fresher place.

The roller didn't fly for long. It jumped from the acacia in a flutter of different blues, then tilted and dipped and swooped along in one tearing glide, with each indigo glitter streaking from beak to tail in one long stroke after another. Then it settled and landed on another acacia, indistinguishable from the first, and watched us go by. We strained back to see the catches of light in the bush, and suddenly it streaked by us again, in triangles and spears of color.

I sat on a cold rock, watching the rippled mountains below, and the morning clouds still rising in wisps and spirals, and wondered what I was supposed to do.

A game guard had appeared in the room with lanterns, and told me that I had met his children, and that he hoped they hadn't bothered me. He said that he worked with Dr. Tom. Then, instead of taking me to the rain forest, Olin led me to a rock above the cabin and left me on the road, facing a tree planted below my feet in the clouds.

The sun baked the cold out of my skin, but my stomach filled with ice as I looked across that sea of dark trees. Where would I find the few chimpanzees in all that? How could I follow animals that walked in the trees faster than I could run? No one knew how large their territories were.

I didn't want to be here, on a road between two villages, when I could be in a tent in the rain forest, or back on the savanna looking for a research site. I couldn't start without him, but each extra day that Dr. Tom took to come back from his conference in Kenya made research seem farther away from possibility. I needed at least three months of research to write a publishable thesis.

But still, against all odds, I was here, a part of Africa like any ancestral hominoid, about to descend to an ocean of life and death and something that modern humans have lost. All my life had led up to this point, and all my future was held hostage to it. If Tom realized how unfit I was for tracking chimpanzees, I would talk my way into his gorilla research. And if he turned me down there too, I'd hitchhike to Dian Fossey's old site in Rwanda.

Creaking and clopping on the rocks, an old donkey rose from below the curve of the cliff. It stood in the shadow of the overhang and watched me for a second. The saddlebags on its sides almost dragged on the road. It looked like a hobbyhorse stuck in a garbage bin.

A man trudged up and stood in the dust beside the donkey. He balanced a cloth sack of potatoes, as long as his torso, on his head. "Hello," I said in KiSwahili, not knowing what tribe he was from. He said hello back with a jerk of a nod, then he and the donkey turned their heads and looked at the tree and back at me.

In an upper branch, just below my feet, a big monkey poked its wrinkled face through the leaves, chuckled a threat, and without haste leaped out of the tree with an arching, glorious, open-armed swoop that looked as if it would end in trees that were smaller than pinheads at the bottom of the mountain. But it landed with an unnecessarily loud crash in a tree below the edge of the cliff, and screamed a brief defiance from its cover there.

It was a blue monkey, *Cercopithecus mitis*. Wrapped in a gray cloak with a tinge of yellow at the tips, like a mink coat fading in the sun, the male bobbed a threat at me, raising and lowering its scowling brows. Stunned, I stared back, and it screamed and shook the branches. Hastily, I lowered my eyes, but it had had enough and soared again to another tree, which shook and absorbed it instantly.

"Monkey," I said weakly to the man. The donkey cocked its ears and tilted its head to get a better view of me. One of the bags sagged in the dust, and I saw the outline of plantains at its bottom. "Many monkeys," he agreed politely in KiSwahili, and watched me write the time, date, list of vocalizations, and an ad libitum account of the sighting. I closed the notebook and looked back, wondering whether I should say something more, and what he had meant by "many monkeys." The donkey snorted, swayed back and forth for a second, and then propelled itself forward, clopping its feet heavily through the rocks. "Good-bye," I said as the man followed it. "Good-bye," he said.

Suddenly a multitude of monkeys poured to the ends of the branches at my feet to scream a threat at him. Bobbing, bowing, shaking the tree, they barked and screamed and chirred. I flipped open the notebook and wrote frantically and uselessly. What sex were they, what age and rank? Gray faces with white fringe popped out and withdrew again. The donkey kicked a white rock as it disappeared around the bend. The rock soared out over the edge and hovered without moving for a while, then slowly shrank into thin air and silence. Sinking back into the tree, the monkeys disappeared again. From the leaves spread a chuckle of irritation.

Olin came to bring me back for lunch. He looked at the empty tree, and the monkeys poured out to the ends of the branches again and screamed at us as we left.

A few days later, Tom's volunteers screeched to a stop in a cloud of dust; poured, athletic and shining, into the hut; and threw open the locked doors of the bedrooms. Mountain light from the windows of the largest bedroom met the rays from the open doors, slid across the dark floor, and settled into a silver radiance, a haze of wood smoke and pine trees and mist. They strewed backpacks and notebooks on the cement floor, stepping around a splintered wooden box that sat in the center.

7

The Real Volunteers

The eye has many parts: electrical pulses, fluids moving in and out, muscles small and large, shifting panes of glass reflecting light back and upside down—it has an inside, containing drops of the sea from which animals came, and an outside, which evaporates its moisture out into the air, to maintain the electrical, moving whole. In every human, each eye has its own rhythm of movement and its own slant to the windows that reflect light. The wrong bend to a pane, and the eye compresses its light into a blur; the wrong slant, and it sees the world backward.

The movement of waters and electrons and small red muscles, all pulsing at their own rhythm, re-creates the world, true or false, for the brain behind it, like standing not before or reflected in a mirror, but within it, on the thin edge of reflection, a third reality created by the movement of light waves on a shimmering surface.

What we see of the world is illusion, a cropped and tinted still, filtered through eye and nerve and brain and flashed back again onto some screen in the mind for viewing.

Suzan stood smiling before me, as strong and wiry as Jane Goodall. "Watch out for him. He likes to create drama. He had the whole Dartmouth football team fighting before we graduated." Charles grinned and pumped my hand. "No, watch out for Ted.

He's from Harvard. You know how you can tell someone's been to Harvard?"

I shook my head, feeling short and out of shape beside these slender aristocrats, as if I'd stepped into a glittering cocktail party instead of a mountain hut without showers. These were the sorts of people who I imagined populated the animal-behavior world, people who could hike all day, make honored friendships with local tribes, and walk through a *National Geographic* special with grace.

Growing up, I didn't know that my eye was flawed. I thought I lived in a whirling world that moved past without coming toward or going away from me, and that other people had a courage that I couldn't find to navigate the ground that rose in stairs or disappeared beneath their feet in holes that looked like shadows.

"They'll tell you before they tell you their name."

A tall blond man with glasses strode through the doorway, hand outstretched. "Hello," he said in a Boston blue-blood drawl. "I'm from Harvard. Where did you go? My name's Ted." With Charles blazing with laughter behind me, I admitted to a secondary Ivy League. There was a long silence. Ted nodded like an adding machine, clicking me into place, then said kindly that he knew some people who'd gone there and told me their names.

"Actually," I said reluctantly, "I'm still there. I'm taking off between junior and senior years to do my thesis research."

The fire snapped and crackled on the wall. "You do understand you probably won't even see the gorillas?"

I looked at the floor. Tom hadn't told them he'd given me the site that a professor had turned down. "Um," I said, and told them about the chimpanzee offer. Luke must have begun to think long silences were natural in this group, because he didn't look up for this one as he bustled about, settling new equipment in its place.

I waited, heart in mouth, for them to erupt with rage. Mountain light moved on the dark floor in ripples of wind.

"What will you do about your thesis if you don't get enough data?"

Chimpanzees are far harder to track than gorillas. It can take years to learn their routes well enough to see more than glimpses of them.

"I don't know," I said.

"You won't get into graduate school without it."

"I know."

We ate bread from Kenya, toasted in the fire, and I wondered why Tom had gone to Kenya to find someone to set up the chimpanzee site, with so many more experienced people here. Most of them had already finished college, with honors. Maybe he had really wanted me to help the volunteers all along. It only occurred to me years later that Tom might have already offered the research site to his volunteers and that they had turned him down.

"Tom said you could read those," someone said, and nodded at the box. Papers poked through the slats, old and stained, and new and fresh.

8

The Box of Ecology

Two volunteers stepped off the edge of the cliff and climbed down into the clouds to track gorillas. Charles worked on the new gorilla research center. I sat on the floor by the fire and read through dozens of papers from scientific journals to the dusty bottom of the box. Feeding competition, mixed-species interaction, ecological niche separation, vocalizations, and foods found in the Impenetrable Forest. Even by the fire, the hut was as cold as a refrigerator. I shivered and leaned over the papers. I had learned more about primates from one page of Jane Goodall's book than I had about monkeys from all these papers.

A small pit of fear settled in my stomach. I'd come to this continent because I was convinced human beings had lost something essential that primates still had. If I could read a hundred scientific papers from the best journals without learning even a question to ask that would help me find what I was looking for, where in the world could I look?

Early animal behaviorists wrote anecdotally about their subjects, telling stories of what they had seen much as a journalist would record a game, or a war. Until the Greeks with Aristotle began the science of classification, these stories could have been complex portraits of a species, or mirrors of the world the researcher wanted to see—husbands and wives and dutiful children. Often, high-ranking females in female-bonded groups were assumed to be male, despite breasts and a lack of external genitalia.

Science has always warred with religion; it classifies the unseen world into categories from which predictions can be made. A thunderstorm is no god's triumph if the wind has made thermal masses collide, nor is scarlet fever the swift response of an evil spirit to sin. As far back as the human record can reach, we have studied stars and planets and migration patterns. And humans have always looked to animals to recover some understanding that we have lost.

Aristotle sorted animals into groups. Pliny expanded his work with stories of the animals as beautifully written as haiku. Linnaeus discovered techniques to classify them based upon physiology, and Darwin explained their overlapping evolutions. Fabre wrote that his lack of education was an advantage; he had never learned not to see. He described the social patterns of insects as if he lived in a garden of bright images.

E. O. Wilson's sociobiology later explained most of their actions as the desires of their genes to survive. Other scientists misinterpreted this to mean that all behaviors have an evolutionary purpose, just as they had earlier misinterpreted the work of the early ethologists Lorenz and Tinbergen. But we animals are more than capable of producing fertile offspring in parallel with other unrelated creative and destructive behaviors. Because the ethologists (ethnologists study humans and ethologists study all animals) focused on the most basic ineradicable instincts in a species, some scientists today still speak of other animals as mindless bundles of fight, flight, and parental instinct.

When Jane Goodall wrote *In the Shadow of Man*, the scientific world was therefore ill-prepared to receive stories of chimpanzees not made in our image — with the largest of a group being the husband, the second largest the wife, and all others their children — but as political beings with friendships, antagonisms, love of their offspring, and desires for power, with the ability to make tools in one place and carry them to another. Goodall was called an anecdotalist for her ethnography of a nonhuman species. Thousands of students who had read the book with pounding hearts — here was the tip of the explanation of what humans were meant to be — found themselves in graduate schools where Goodall was never mentioned, studying the different rates of slash- and pick-grooming techniques. There is no science of ethnography for animals as there is for humans, because we are not allowed to suggest that other animals have emotions until we have proved that they do. And personalities cannot be quantified.

Science became further dehumanized in 1974 when Jeanne Altmann, a mathematician, replaced other forms of behavioral research with statistical analyses. The limitations of this approach were further compounded by the fact that most ethologists studied males of the species, since there were fewer in a primate group and they were more distinct in appearance than the females, who tended to be closely related. Still mired in an incorrectly understood sociobiology, scientists set out to prove that the most aggressive animals reproduced most often. Because dominance hierarchy in females wasn't studied, many assumed that the females didn't have one. The baboon researcher Shirley Strum changed that and set the balance back in order. Females of most primate species are the social core of a group — an interrelated hierarchy for life.

Long before I began my research on howler monkeys in college, the standard of research had been set. Take ad libitum data — write about everything that happens, stories and all, until you have found the question you want to answer. Choose six or so animals of the age, sex, and/or dominance level you want to study. Arrange a rotating schedule every day of fifteen-minute focal samples of certain behaviors on one individual, followed by a one-minute scan of the group as a whole. The latter can have its own list of categories to mark, or be a simple ad libitum cover of all behaviors, so that you can understand the motivations for the focal sample animal's actions. At the end of the scan, move on to the next animal on the list for another focal sample. A simple t-test or chi-test at the end, and you can reproduce behavior in a formula as clear as algebra. If you have asked the right question.

During the fifteen-minute focal sample, most behaviorists recorded in columns behaviors such as hitting, biting, chasing, and threat lunges. Then, in the scan, they might write down any of these behaviors in the group as a whole, or they might choose a separate set to watch in that minute. At the end, they could in theory construct a pyramid calculating dominance levels of individuals by how many times those individuals were the biters rather than the bitten.

The rules of research are simple; most sites use the same basic structure. But the categories of data taken can be chosen at random for the preliminary study. Finding the question that needs to be answered is the difficult part, and I wouldn't be able to watch the chimps long enough to choose focal samples. I'd have to sample, as a group, any animals I saw and take whatever data that I could. Most researchers work for three to six months on a research project, but chimps can take years to habituate.

I spread a paper on my lap and pulled an orange notebook, already soft and tattered, from the belly of my pants. "Foods eaten by primates...," I wrote.

When Dr. Tom arrived, he found me sitting on a heap of bricks, copying illustrations of chimpanzee foods from a botanical book.

"Very nice. Concentrate on L'Hoest's monkeys too. They're almost completely unstudied, they're so shy." I was so afraid he was going to tell me I couldn't go to work with the chimpanzees that I couldn't look up, as if eye contact would change his mind.

Charles trotted by with a huge pile of bricks in his basket, shouting abuse at the workers. "You are so weak. Even the WaZungu children can carry more than you." The workers ran behind him from the road to the new gorilla research building site, roaring with laughter, and telling him they needed his watch; he should give it to them.

"I can't find a Mutwa Pygmy yet to track chimps for you. Do you want to go to the gorilla camp with the volunteers for a while to map nests?" Tom asked.

"Yes," I said.

"You can't watch them," he said. "I'm going to habituate them slowly, to only a few people, so they'll still run from poachers."

"Yes," I said.

"Batuko can take you."

9
Batuko's Walk

*W*e spread across all continents, adapting nose and hair and the color of skin to each sun and moon. As societies grew more complex, from nomadic herders or subsistence farmers to multilevel societies with specialized tasks (and with many humans named for the tasks they performed), language expanded to cover more needs of past and future tense. Dependence on the language of the body almost disappeared, unrecognized because it cannot be named. But deep within sinus and brain, all the connections of the original primate within us can still read scent and pheromone, constructing a world we cannot see.

We stepped off the side of the cliff, into the air. A small path wound down, so steep it was invisible again after the first few rocks. A few hundred feet below the overhanging peaks, the air was warm. In the sun basked antique ferns, dinosaur-size, vibrating with thick clouds of calm insects. Streams ran zigzag through backlit fronds, and would someday cut canyons between these foothills, if the trees were left there to hold the soil. I hiked, gasping, down the wall of the valley through the tangled roots of the slope and then up again into one hill after another. Vines and early trees mingled into a dense shrub. My boots slid left and right into its cracks. Lifting my feet from each trap with two hands, I swore and struggled on, and Batuko skimmed ahead in his bare feet, straight up without pausing for breath.

Tom had sent Suzan and me down to camp in the forest with Batuko and another tracker. Both of them were ex-poachers.

"Look for the gorillas, but don't get within sight of them. Just record the nests." At the last second, he picked one of the oldest workers from the building site and sent him down with us to cook.

Simon, he said his name was, but Suzan and I both wrote it down as Silver in our research notebooks. It was hard to hear him, he was so quiet.

I stopped, wheezing, leaning hands on knees, with the whole of the day left to finish. Studying chimpanzees on my own had never seemed possible, but what would I do if I couldn't keep up with gorilla volunteers either?

"Stop, Batuko!" Suzan shouted, but he floated on. Still heaving for air, I trailed her on shaking legs. Six hours left, at least. I had always sat still, in a whirling world, and I was poorly prepared for these slopes. Suzan waited halfway between us and shouted again. She had been a track star, and was hardly sweating. I had barely been able to finish a mile after a year on the track team. Batuko cackled and explained with waves of the hand and incomprehensible shouts of French, English, and KiSwahili that the gorilla nests for her study were set on the slopes of the hills.

The forest could have been empty or full, lighted eyes behind every shadow, or abandoned to insect and bird; the canopy here released neither scent nor sound. I bent and breathed knife blades of air. Suzan waited, but Batuko shrank into the distance again. I straightened, shifted my backpack, and, dizzy with breathlessness, slid along the slope. We climbed through deeper trees, lined with lianas and reaching roots. Here the light closed itself into a still, unstirring bowl, a dark and fungal scent of air too wet to breathe. The soil had always been soaked; one could tell. The leaves dripped water for days after a rain, passing drops from branch to branch to ground. There was no evaporation here, where the air was as wet as a river and clothes clung with icy grip to any bend of skin. We walked on the sides of our feet, up a wet slope, ankles shaking with the strain. Batuko passed out of sight, and Suzan called again until he stopped and waited for me. Like an evil guardian of the forest, he stood laughing in the shadow.

I didn't know we were on the peak of the hill until the soil leveled, then dried, and leaves crackled underfoot.

"Tchah," Suzan's tracker spat without explanation. "Batuko, he is a bad man," another tracker added. A hush fell. The beans boiled and turned in a sludge that smelled of dirt. "This man Batuko, it is that he is a poacher." Suzan and I sat with arms on knees. I was too tired to wash or drink water. Small insects crawled among prickles of sweat, and my ankles throbbed with an ominous dullness, merging with a pounding headache so that my whole body vibrated without rest.

Simon turned away. Bald spot gleaming like toffee in the firelight, and lips pressed shut to show he hadn't said anything, he finished stirring the beans and ladled them into two bowls. They scorched my knees dry and warmed a chill I hadn't felt, of drying sweat and dust. The beans tasted like buttered popcorn and steak. "This is great, Simon," Suzan said, and he turned and waved his arms. "Eh, eh, memsahib." A frill of wrinkles across the balding forehead eased. He smiled and turned back to the fire.

My legs felt hammered, whipped, and ironed. I shifted them sideways, and they shook with the effort. I was afraid to go out tomorrow but couldn't say anything. Tom, and then later his wife, had spent weeks in the forest trailing the gorillas. "We carried tarps and wrapped ourselves in them at night," he had said. He would never let me go out to the chimpanzees if I couldn't follow the gorillas for two days.

"You know," Suzan said, "the men can travel faster without us. We can send them all out to find nests, and then go from one to another for the next few days." I nearly groaned with relief.

Batuko stomped back into the clearing from some mysterious excursion. One of the men translated Batuko's English for Suzan. "Batuko, he is very angry and wants very much more money and he wants that you must to take his nephew too, for much money, or he will leave."

Suzan thought for a while. "Perhaps, Batuko, you should go and speak with Dr. Tom about this. It is Dr. Tom who pays your salary, not me." A hush fell in the clearing. Simon stirred the beans without looking up.

Batuko suddenly waved a panga and a rifle over his head. "Blaaagh, blaaa, blaaagh." I don't think anyone understood him, but the game guards shuffled their feet in the leaves and looked away. Sputtering to a halt, he stood over Suzan and glared.

"But there's nothing I can do," Suzan said. Then she told him we'd decided to let the men find the nests and bring us to them.

"Back to the new wife," someone muttered, as Batuko stomped on those flat feet up the path, his back rigid with fury.

"Batuko, it is that he is a poacher. It is that he does not like to have the WaZungu in this forest."

"Tchah," said Simon, in another direction. A boy bobbed his head.

"It is that Batuko, he take these people who want to see gorillas, and Batuko, he make it so they cannot walk in the forest, it is that it is very hard, and it is that they do not want to come back, and it is that they give him much money, and Batuko, he does not have to take them to the forest again." Suzan pieced together that several groups of researchers had come to the edge of the forest and hired Batuko to take them in. He had dragged them through the most impenetrable patches of the rain forest. Most of them never went out again but gave him the full fee. And he could poach without interference.

In a clearing the men led us to the next day, huge nests lay close together, of ferns drying in the sun. The gorillas had taken handfuls of stems and broken them down into mattress and pillow. The imprints, one of a huge head, another of buttocks, showed in shadows of crushed fern. These vast beds clustered together so closely that the gorilla scent hovered, a solid wall, clean and musty, perhaps a little salty, like that of a sleepy dog. Here had lain an adult, one child beside it; in the center, cavernous, the silverback male had rested, larger by a third than any of the others, and beside him too, a small gorilla had curled.

As we climbed up from the cavern, an unearthly scream rose with the rising clouds to our narrow path. Like Dante passing out of the lowest levels of hell, I stopped and turned to watch. From the dark forest hills, flashes of light shone in waves. Far below, a tree, no larger than a fingernail, caught the sun on the white underside of its leaves: an invisible chimpanzee rocking, perhaps disturbed by our progress.

10

Journey Down the Mountain

O*n the Masai Mara, birds yellow and lilac and cerulean blue sang in the thornbushes. Some chirped as sharp as insects, creeeaak, creak, and a small brown bird warbled like water. We had to stop under the tree and feel the dryness crackling the skin of our cheeks to believe that this was a bird and not a fountain or waterfall. It gurgled and glugged and rushed through descending notes so quickly that one smelled water, and yet there was also some-thing of a bird's liquor in it. The lions were not fooled, though the cubs would stand, outlined against the horizons, under the tree and look up with ears pricked and one paw resting gently on the bark.*

Across the reserve, wind rolled out from the sun and changed with every movement of the grasses. Hush, hush, hushshsh, it soothed. Hush. It crawled a little faster. Hushshssss. The animals rested their heads in it. Hushushush.

I sat again on the pile of dusty bricks. It was larger now. The BaKiga carriers, with Charles among them, must have worked hard while I was gone. Uninterested in the gorillas, Charles had become the full-time supervisor of the building site: now my boots barely touched the ground. Tucking them under me, I bal-anced the yellow notebook on one knee and a botanical book on the other. Carefully, I copied the drawing of a leaf that one of the papers had listed as edible to primates. Tom hadn't said anything more about my research site, except to say that Batuko had told him we had sent the men out to look for the gorillas without us. I had read down to the bottom of the splintered box again and made notes and hovered over all the books that might have pictures of foods eaten by chimpanzees. While the BaKiga carriers ambled slowly by, half as many bricks on their heads as they'd carried when Charles worked with them, and the ever-present ravens croaked their amusement, I worked on, drawing every pore and follicle.

Hour after hour, I waited for Tom to come and tell me to go home. I wondered if I should beg to go out again with Batuko. But what would I see, with him running us to exhaustion away from the animals?

One day in late morning, a shadow slid across the trail of spilled bricks. I looked up, startled. All the other volunteers were gone, and even Charles had left for a supply trip.

"I found you a tracker," Tom said. The notebook slid from my hands into the dirt.

Olin and Luke came out to watch me leave and, separated by tribal hatreds, stood far apart on the stones of the road. The volunteers had gone down to the gorilla camp, and this was a small, silent group, though the wind below the mountain's edge murmured with a faint clang, like the distant banging of cymbals, or beating of wooden drums.

Olin looked at the food and said the basket was too heavy for Simon. I took jars of kidney beans out and shoved them deep in my backpack and then, when he didn't move, pulled out some more. Hurry, hurry. My legs were shifting in place. I had no right to this site; it should have gone to a professor or to one of the gorilla volunteers. Hurry, hurry. The wind rose from the chasm, rushing like trumpets in the pines. Dust tilted and settled in small clouds. I took more jars out and looked down the path. Between pillar and fall, it curved out of sight. I felt as if some stranger at any moment would open the door of the research center and call Simon back, saying that they needed him to cook for the gorilla camp, and that someone with a graduate degree wanted the chimpanzee site.

Olin shrugged and helped lift the basket onto a tall man's head. "This is Gabriel, Simon's cousin. He has come to help you too."

I wondered what had happened to Akit, the game guard Olin had brought to meet me, and his brother Patrick, who spoke almost perfect English and grinned with a crocodile smile almost as wide as Gabriel's.

As soon as the basket was on — even though Gabriel smiled at me, as sinister as a Cheshire cat — I was sorry I hadn't taken out more food. But Gabriel and Simon strode away, already laughing and telling stories. Olin called something after us, and around the next bend we were on a narrow road set into the cliff, with the rain forest below us, clouds rising to our feet, and a silence that rang in the ears.

"When the sun appears in the eastern horizon it at once permeates the whole of our hemisphere and fills it with its luminous semblance. All the surfaces of solid bodies turned towards the sun or towards the atmosphere illumined by the sun, become clothed and dyed by the light of the sun or of the atmosphere. Every solid body is surrounded and clothed with light and darkness," wrote Leonardo da Vinci in his journal. On the savanna, with nothing to cast shadow but the branches of the acacia, the sun had lit the world.

*　　*　　*

I breathed in a deep, trembling breath of white dust and pine. Whether I found chimpanzees or not, I was walking in hiking boots, wearing army pants, with a heavy pack on my shoulders, into an unrecorded rain forest. I hadn't believed that this would happen, and I woke suddenly, a different person from the one still sitting at home in a blurred world. This road led to more than a research site; it led away from a life within walls and into the past that so many humans have lost.

The road from the hut stretched down the mountain, past two huge women in swirls of scarlet, yellow, and green cloth, and their slender husbands, carrying woven baskets of potatoes and banana stalks on their narrow heads. The men were so long and thin that they walked beside their wives like spousal shadows stretched against a wall. In the beginning, we walked fast, and the land peeled away like layers of an onion, each with a different color and deeper smell. At first, the air was cool and the path lined with pine trees along a road strewn with dust and white rocks.

A foot trail disappeared down to a meadow, through the switchbacks. We slithered to the bottom — I, overbalanced and stumbling, the other two calmly pacing down. From there we could see the whole of the Impenetrable Forest, mountain after mountain marching down into a blue mist and endless hills, slashed with black-shadowed valleys. From these green waves, at the edge of Uganda, the mountains of Rwanda rose into the horizon. Dian Fossey, Jane Goodall's second in primatology, had lived and died there with its gorillas.

In emerald waves, the foothills curled below. On top of the mountain the people had slashed and burned the forest and planted beans and potatoes down the bare sides of the reserve. With each rain, the stump-filled slopes would slowly slide into the valleys, along with their gardens. War removes rules. People had moved away from it into foothills too steep for crops. We walked past rumpled fields, into tilted valleys. Around a bend, the men stopped, and I panted down to them and stood with the weight of the pack hanging on my hips.

A spicy bush spilled onto the road. Gabriel leaned over its branches and whistled. Through the leaves, straight down beneath our feet, under rolls and mountains of mud, perched a little hut on a ledge. A soft colorless hat lifted from under the hill, like a mushroom growing in dark soil. Underneath, a tattered pants leg straightened and followed it. I thought a child had unfolded from the invisible slope, but a wrinkled face tilted a few inches up from under the hat. The man dropped a sack of potatoes in the dust.

"This is Kamumbo, memsahib," Simon said. "He is the Pygmy you meet with Gabriel. We ask many places for a Pygmy, but he is the only one who will come."

I said hello in KiSwahili and held out my hand. He took off the mushroom hat. The tips of his fingers touched mine reluctantly. Then with a blank face, he waited, looking away. Except for his height, he looked less like a child than a hobbit; his legs were so slender that his feet, gnarled and flat, spread beneath him like the base of a statue. He had a grace different from that of the BaKiga, shifting as if the strength of his feet and hands weighed down his narrow limbs. But even with feet so out of proportion to a child's body, Kamumbo looked unaware of his skin and settled into silence. He was deliberately looking at nothing, and thus invisible.

Simon snapped an order in Rukiga. Meekly, Kamumbo crammed his hat on his head, and tore some branches off the bush and twined them into a ring, winding them on the crown.

With an exhalation, Gabriel lifted his basket onto Kamumbo's head. The child-size legs sagged, and I closed my eyes. Simon took Kamumbo's sack of potatoes and passed his load to Gabriel.

Gabriel grinned at me. "Simon, he has a bad chest," he said in fluent KiSwahili.

"Tchah," said Simon.

The BuGanda and the BaKiga, like most of the tribes left behind by the great wash of kingdoms from north to south in the Bantu migrations, had formed roving herds of cattle, and settled into plots of land. The men slashed and burned the land and then, with the women, sowed the fields in rotation. Each garden needed to be cleaned of the wild again and again; trees grew as fast as weeds in the exposed soil of the rain forest. They lived in small clusters, a man and his wives' huts, and then there was the next compound, spreading in a far-flung village of people who knew one another as well as they did their own children.

On the edge of the mountain, around a bend, perched a hut with a grass roof and terrace. Men stood talking, chickens clucking around their feet. Quietly but without looking at us, three of them disappeared down a path, like Kamumbo in reverse, gone with a step downward.

Simon put the sack in the dust. I sat with a thump, falling backward onto the pack and kicking like an upturned beetle.

"We get beer, memsahib." They came back with pitchers of a sour brew, thick with millet, banana fibers, seeds, and insects. I strained a mouthful through my teeth and gave it back. They drank fast, looking at the crowd watching us, then walked away while I curled and uncurled on the ground, rocking forward to stand.

"These men at the bottom of the mountain, they are bad men."

"Eeeh, very bad."

* * *

The road curled and flattened on the side, away from the mountain. It was Switzerland's hills we walked through now, green velvet dotted with white flowers. The sun pulsed on the back of my head.

Simon, laughing with Gabriel, turned back. "Memsahib, you must to walk fast. If you walk slow you will be tired." I tried but felt like I was dragging boots of lead, hips stiffening under the belt of the pack; after years of fighting for Africa, I had now only my own body left to struggle against. Simon told me stories and asked about America. I said there were many houses and not much room to walk and that I liked Africa very much.

"In this village they are bad men, eeeeh so bad," Simon said, as we cut down a switchback past a cluster of huts. "In the forest they like so much to poach and to take gold and to smuggle these things to Zaire." Simon gave Gabriel the bag with Kamumbo's potatoes, took my backpack, and walked fast with it on his head.

When the Tanzanians invaded in 1979, they had cut power lines, destroyed plumbing, and burned factories. Because inflation was so high, no other country traded for Ugandan shillings. The ancient trade route, which had carried ivory and slaves and gold and weapons so long ago that the names of the first kingdoms have been forgotten, was closed. The road was too damaged, the border guards and soldiers at the roadblocks too hungry. And Uganda had nothing to trade but bananas and beans that could be bought in any country. In the Kabale market, the women sold only red-and-blue plastic plates, iron pots, and unsharpened pangas. Refusing to retreat to the barter system, the BaKiga, in the triangle of Rwanda, Zaire, and Uganda, had turned to smuggling: cattle, gold, stolen goods, humans, and timber.

As we descended, the dust turned red and the farms tilted on their slopes and children clung with curled feet to the grass and ran slanted after us, shouting, "Mzungu." Simon told one story after another of poachers and smugglers and gold miners.

In the dark hills at the bottom of the mountain, the road widened and stretched into a village. Simon and Gabriel stopped.

Silent and unmoving, a crowd of men blocked our path. The air felt heavy here, as if the dust had sunk down into the valleys.

The men wore the same clothes as the top-of-the-mountain people, a jumble of male and female missionary box clothes sold on the black market. Only the spears planted in the red road looked African. Hand-hammered metal glinted through the dust.

A few men stood on one leg and leaned on their spears like the Masai lion hunters on the savanna.

A thin layer of fixation cells covers the visual cortex. This single-celled film takes all the million details of a single scene, cuts out the unnecessary, and fits the images from each eye into a single photograph with depth, color, and shade. Let anything interrupt one fragment of the electrical journey to this point, and the eye sees a flat world, or one bereft of color.

11

Poachers' Village

The spears etched trails of shadow in the dust, one black line after another like the bars of a cage. My feet ached with the throb of broken blisters. When I was walking, they had been an itch and a feeling of something wrong. Standing still, I found that each was outlined as a lack of skin. I was afraid that once I stopped moving, I'd never start again. Facing an ocean of faces, I wondered what to do. I wanted to pass them so badly that I felt as if part of my body had left game guards, blisters, and the crowd behind and gone striding ahead into the rain forest alone.

"You." Straddling the dust in front of them, an old man pointed the palm of his hand at me. In the village beyond him, a tree twisted its roots into dirt packed like cement. One chair perched lopsided in its narrow shadow. A few square huts, and then off into the distance, running along the red-dust road, gardens of banana trees and beans. Another small path wound up the hill and out of sight. The crowd stood so thick that the main road itself had disappeared and spread out from behind them like a peacock's tail of dust.

A murmur of threat rippled across the crowd. I looked at Simon and Gabriel for help. Leaning forward, the old man shouted a stream of some language that might have been English, if slower.

The men looked away. He grabbed my hand and held it hard, pulling me toward him.

I was so startled that he was shaking my hand, it was a while before I realized that he hadn't stabbed me. He smelled like oilcloth and dust.

Murmuring, the crowd moved closer. Arms knocked my shoulders, and a hand pushed through them. Not sure what to do, I kept shaking the old man's hand, smiling. He shouted and leaned on my hand and glared. My hips ached with pain. Scowling, he faded to a murmur. I kept shaking, and he loosened his grasp and faltered to a stop. Still smiling, helpless, I let my hand lie in his. He snapped out an order and fell silent, waiting.

The flawed-of-eye are never sure where a blow has come from. It is always safer to stand still or sit. But I had known someone would give me a research site, just as I had known I'd live in Africa someday. A village of men with spears standing between me and the chimpanzees was as ephemeral as dust.

There was a long pause. Someone was standing on my foot, and another BaKiga was leaning his full weight on my side, tilting me toward the old man. "It is that this man, he say that you must to give him a job and very much money, memsahib," someone said.

I waited for them to tell me what to do, but they looked away. Stumbling in KiSwahili, I told the old man that I had many workers, but that if I needed someone, I would tell him. He dropped my hand and stepped back, smiling. Dredging up Rukiga, I added, because he was old and worthy of respect, "Sebo."

The crowd melted into a gust of laughter.

"Eeeeh, eeeeeh, eeeeeh."

Arms slapping knees, the men and their spears milled in circles, and patches of red clay appeared between their feet.

Women and children popped up from nowhere and shouted with the men like a crowd on market day with a good story to tell.

An old woman, almost bald, pushed a gnarled, dusty hand through the crowd and past my face. A pain stabbed the side of my head. I clapped a hand to my scalp, not sure what had happened. She scuttled to the edge of the crowd, then stopped, leaning over her hands. Part of the crowd broke away and followed her, and I could breathe again, and move my foot.

Arms thrust a baby toward me. "She speaks Rukiga," they said to one another. The baby melted into my arms, then leaned back to look at me. Holding my shoulder with gentle fingers, she leaned back as if to nod to the refrain. "Aaaaagh," she screamed instead, calm and horrified, looking at my face. "Aaaaagh," and the villagers laughed and told one another about that as a man took the baby back, so the two stories wove together—that I spoke Rukiga and that the little one was afraid of the Mzungu.

The crowd parted for a man taller by a head than any of the others. He pushed through the last group around me and took my hand. "Mr. Olin said that you would come," he murmured in perfect Oxford English. "He is a good friend, from my tribe in the north." The smaller group murmuring around the old woman parted without his asking.

"She is pulling the hair she took from you to see if it springs back into a curl when stretched. They have never seen a white person. I am Brother Odel."

He led me to a white plaster building on a hill over the mud huts. With his own hands and the help of the village, he had built the monastery. Simon, Gabriel, and Kamumbo disappeared without telling me where they were going or when they were coming back.

Books lined Brother Odel's study, the first I had seen since Kampala besides the ones at the gorilla research site. A middle-aged man limped in after us and scowled as he squared himself into a chair. I sank down on another, expecting him to throw me out of the forest. Brother Odel sat too, with a more than priestly grace, and introduced me with a smile and a nod, then smiled at the man as well. I'd learned in Kampala that after Museveni had chased Idi Amin to Saudi Arabia, and installed his army of orphans as guardians of the peace, he'd selected a government midway between the principles of socialism and communism. Each village elected a representative. These delegates in turn chose regional leaders.

The representative planted his cane and leaned over it. "So, why is it that you are here?" His speech too hadn't the faintest trace of Africa. He asked me about the research, its value to the villagers, and its dangers. Questions that took scientists years to ask. If I was going to be forced to leave, I'd at least argue my case well.

As if singing for the forest, I took a deep breath and told him the story of his own country, how the war had forced people up into the inhospitable hills, and there they had used their flat-land tools to slash and burn the forests that held the earth to the ground, and how the rivers that ran through Uganda and beyond were filling with that loosened dirt and killing their babies with a stew of bacteria.

"And why should we save the gorillas when we are starving? Because Westerners like to look at them?"

I told him about how the gorilla groups had been separated by the clear-cutting all around them so that they couldn't cross the mountains to breed and of how other countries had come to live off their gorillas and the tourists who came to look at them. "And buy," I said, at a loss to think what tourists could buy in these markets of plastic plates and multicolored beans, "buy art that people make . . ."

He propped the cane and stood, said, "Well," and shook my hand without conclusion.

I woke in a cinder-block room with one wall missing, like a stage set, on a real mattress. A dusty hand pushed a pitcher of water across the floor. Peering around like a criminal, I stripped with moans of pain and poured the water over my head in a rush. I pulled on my shirt without drying, just as Brother Odel strode around the corner.

He led me quickly, then slower as he realized how stiff I was, from the monastery to the packed dirt square. The crowd parted around us, now laughing and pulling at my hair, until we climbed to the peace of another three-sided hut. I looked at the edges of the crowd. Simon and Gabriel hadn't come back.

With the leaders of the district, I ate eggs and ugali, unripe plantains that had been boiled to a mush and tasted like paper. The villagers held glossy babies and watched without envy, though eggs were precious. "Mzungu." "Eeeeeeh, Mzungu."

"Wa," a man said, in a suit that could have come from a boardroom, if it had had a shirt with a collar underneath, and slapped his hand on the table. "Wa," said someone else. Chairs grated, and I braced to push mine back, glad I wouldn't have to eat any more of the ugali. It was already clinging to my teeth in a sour paste that would stick for hours.

"So," said the first man. They turned and looked at me.

The representative limped from the crowd as the politicians led me to the dust beneath the village tree.

"Eh," the villagers said. I had explained how soil erodes when trees are cut. The representative had translated in ringing tones. They sounded pleased. And again, as I told them the forest was dying, and its soil washing into their river, they laughed. "Waahaha." I stumbled and scolded, and tried to stop myself, wondering why they weren't angry.

Square fields stretched behind and to the sides of each hut. Every fourth or fifth lay fallow, marked by the fast-growing grasses of the lowlands. Long swaying trees, like eucalyptus but not, shaded the edges of the land, and held the dried humus with their roots. In one row of them along the road, white tails hung down—colobus monkeys, waiting for us to leave so they could raid the crops. "Bleah, bleah, bleah," one of them said, in a rush of breath as faint as wind. The representative waved his cane and talked for a long time, far longer than I had spoken.

Once again I tried to think of something stunning to say that would save the gorillas and the land, but found that I was going around in circles. Here was my chance to save the forest and these people's lives and I had blown it already. I paused, thinking of Jane Goodall's firelit speeches to her neighbors, which had formed bonds of loyalty that saved her research site over and over again.

Shining faces gathered round before I'd tapered to a halt, and long fingers shoved through the pack of bodies to grasp my hand. "Eh!" the crowd shouted.

"What did you say?" I asked the representative as he leaned stolidly on his cane.

"I told them what you told me last night. It was very good." Suddenly Akit and Patrick magically appeared and pushed through the villagers, shouting, "Wewe, let the Mzungu move." Ten steps behind them, in the shadow of the trees where the colobus monkeys had been, Simon, Gabriel, and Kamumbo hovered, almost invisible.

We left the representative behind in a shouting village. Some of the villagers split off and followed us, prodding my shoulder, tugging on my backpack, and offering their milk and bananas.

The trail from the village ran along a wall of forest. Simon and Gabriel stood past the last hut, separate from Patrick and Akit, as if campkeepers and game guards were two separate species.

The trees shook and thrashed as we passed. "Bleah, bleah, bleahh," the colobus roared in a whisper, and poked shriveled faces below the leaves to duck a threat. The trees, far above the dust, were outlined in gold, a separate world.

The old man and the villagers stopped and watched us go, still talking. "Eeeh, Mzungu."

"Eeeeh."

"Eeeeh."

The trail wound through red dust and neat square fields. A flock of chickens followed us into the sudden silence as the last few villagers watched us walk away. Most of the chickens too fell behind, until we reached a small circle of dust that ended in a footpath no wider than a shoe, stretching up the hill. The last chicken circled, kicked, clucked in triumph, and then jerked herself away as Simon shifted my backpack to his head and stepped into the bushes. The foothills, still in the morning shadow of the mountains, stretched above, one on top of the other at random, like peaks of crumpled tissue.

12
Entrance to the Forest

With a grasp and slither, wet bushes parted like the train of a dress against my legs. A few flowers shook themselves off their leaves onto the path. Brushing through the orchids, hips stiff and bruised, head back, I looked up at the arch of trees that closed off the light.

It was a damp and cool cathedral that we walked to that morning, with rain still fermenting on the leaves and trickling through to the ground. Small streamers of light fell through the canopy at its edge, so I saw dark bushes, black trees looming over, and those rays of light with flares of gold at the bottom, lighting a few sharply defined leaves.

My chest thumped with jarred beats that shook deep into the stomach, catching each breath in its center with a pause and stillness. The men shifted, impatient, but I stayed on the threshold.

They stopped and stood inside the shadow of the forest, thinking I was tired again, but my feet had stopped hurting. I looked up, to the top, and across the valley to the foothills of the mountain, the last horizons.

Like thread woven through a pattern, or ships standing immobile on a changing sea, the desire for Africa had passed through every incarnation of my childhood. In every loss there is a compensation. Without depth perception, one cannot ride a bike or read a human face, but in those seconds that one does see, the human world slams shut and one disappears into light and wind, one animal like any other.

Roots twisted and climbed so high above the ground they had woven themselves into branch and leaf in the darkness. Vines as thick as trees twined about their hosts, and down through the castles and towers of the ground. Mud, flung twenty feet high in the rainy season, clung in pale stains to tree and bush before turning to dust and sifting slowly downward through the columns of light in the entrance as sparkle and fog.

The savanna had been the purest of light, a sea of it in every direction to each end of the world, lighted gold set within the sky. It should have hurt to leave it for a world without light. Instead my lungs filled with the dust of gazelles and wildebeest and lions, as if in leaving the savanna for the rain forest, I was entering it forever.

Along the trail, human or chimpanzee feet had worn the roots into gloss. I stepped across the threshold into cold air. The shadow of the canopy slid with the wind, lighting silver into gold, and darkening the path into invisibility. Root and bush and fern twisted one above the other into a floor with an infinity of layers, stretching across the path. Looking down to step around a root, I walked with a thump into a branch and fell into the tangle, hands sliding past an infinity of wet, dusted bark. "Eeeh, sorry, sorry, sorry, sorry," the men said, hovering at a distance. I laughed.

"Eh, WaZungu." They laughed in relief. "Eeeeh, the WaZungu, they are very weak." I wouldn't have gone that far. They crowded around again — "Sorry, memsahib, sorry, sorry" — and pulled me through the roots to my feet.

In the foothills of the Impenetrable Forest, one can look down and place one's feet among the floor of the roots, or look up to duck the branches. Ten minutes later, I stumbled over another root cluster. A polite echo of *sorry, sorry, sorry* rang up the line. My boots caught in the roots, and I had to reach with both hands to twist each one out. I would have taken them off, if I could see under the roots to the forest floor. But if the vegetation itself was so dangerous, what lay underneath?

Patrick walked alongside me, telling stories about his future. "Me, I will to get work and buy a new wife. She will work very hard and I will buy eeh so many clothes, you have not seen. Me, all I need is a hundred thousand shillings to buy a goat and some beer to buy a wife." He looked at me sideways.

"Eh," I said.

"Then I will have so many children and they will work very hard. Then me, I will build a house with cement and I will have a generator and a lightbulb and will be very rich. If I had fifty thousand Uganda shillings, I could buy this goat and some chickens and tell them I will give them beer later."

Moss hung down like weeds and swayed gently with the weight of the water inside it, as drops collected, ran down, and hung trembling from the strands. Dust and water splashed from each held branch, or arched from sprung roots.

"Eh."

"Wewe, you will not give them beer later," said his brother, Akit, walking straight and strong, so much darker and taller than Patrick that they looked more like Simon and Gabriel than each other.

"Me, I know. But them, they will listen to me."

"They are very stupid," said Akit.

"Even twenty-five thousand shillings would be good. I could buy a goat and tell them I have chickens and beer. Then they will give me a wife, and if she is no good I can give her back and will lose only one goat. This I can do for twenty-five thousand."

"Eh," I said.

He glanced back at me. "For ten thousand even, I can buy the goat and promise to pay more. Then I can give the goat to the father, and if the wife is no good, I do not pay for the goat."

"Eh."

"Or perhaps memsahib can buy me this plane ticket for America, and I will get a wife there." I slid along a root and scrambled face-first into a bush. Three arms pulled me out. "Sorry, sorry, sorry, sorry memsahib."

"For five thousand even..."

13

Building Camp

*T*here was only one other thing my eyes took in with ease as a child. As the school bus crossed the marshes on a small cement bridge, I could see down the river to the horizon, and up the river toward a bend of trees. In the swamp that ran alongside it grew cattails and rushes, as naturally gold as they were tall. They burned semi-translucent; each blade glowed separately in the morning sun as if lit from within. Together in their bending, high-feathered swamp, they bowed under the weightlessness of light. Sometimes there was mist rising from the water, and altogether it was the only masterpiece I ever saw in my suburban town. I don't know why I needed to see those rushes so badly, or how I knew Africa would be the same, but it was.

The trail curved down a river of roots, to the bald branches of a giant fig tree. Roots flowing from its bole had left no room for other trees; its branches spread into emptiness, silhouetted against the sky. Past this royalty, we broke from darkness again into green light, a clearing empty of tree and sapling alike, but still roofed with intertangled canopy. Perhaps a fig had grown there too, and fallen and died, its trunk washed away by softening mildews and rain, before its seeds had time to grow. I stepped over a root and skied down the mud into a split, wondering where we were going.

"Eh."

"Sorry, sorry, sorry. Sorry, memsahib."

This was a different forest from Batuko's. It was cold and wet down here; where the clouds began, the trees stretched high above, out of sight, fighting one another for sunshine. I walked, head down, hands out, sliding on wet roots.

Through the fig's clearing, only thirty feet above, shimmered a drier forest on the peak of the hill. I was afraid the men would pick that piece of land for our camp, which was too close to the village. I wanted to go deeper and farther into the forest to a place where no human would have been. We struggled on for a few minutes. Suddenly, the men dropped their bags. Straightening, I panted and watched them to see why we'd stopped. This clearing was as dark and roofed as a house without windows, tilted on a hill. Green light swam at the edges, and a few stray rays fell in the center on a sea of tightly woven ferns.

Bending over machetes, Simon and Akit slashed clear an oval on the hill. From branches woven with vines, Simon built two tables, and Akit bullied the others into helping him cut saplings. "Memsahib," someone said. I wondered what they were doing. After less than an hour's hike, we couldn't be far enough into the rain forest to see chimpanzees.

"Call me Jo."

"Yes, memsahib," Simon said firmly, glaring at the other men. "Yes, memsahib," they echoed, except for Gabriel, who said, "Yes, Jo," grinning like a kid. "Eeh, eh." He laughed. The others turned and scowled, and he hung his head and scuffed one bare foot in the dust. "Eeeh." He shifted the saplings in his arms. "Memsahib, where is it that you want the house?"

In the twice yearly rainy season of Uganda, the clouds that rose from the valleys opened and dropped eight to twelve inches of rain sometimes in less than an hour. Remove the trees, and the soil slid down the slopes, swelling with dead leaves and fragments of tree and all the thousand bacteria that broke it down to dust. The soil washed down into the ravines, which became streams, and from there to the river, the beginning of the Nile, where, exposed to sun, it bloomed into dysentery. But while the trees were there, the roots held the hills together. I wondered how I'd see chimpanzees in that tight-woven wall, even if I found them.

The rainy season hadn't begun, but the trees dripped with runnels of water as the morning rain filtered hours later through a canopy so thick that neither light nor wind nor sound moved through. Now cut smooth with machetes, the sloped clearing glistened in the seawater light. Neither insect nor rodent nor bird scattered from the slashed bushes, as if the forest had been wiped clean long before we came.

I waved a vague hand at the hilltop, invisible through the canopy, but probably as flat and dry as my parents' backyard. "Maybe up there, where it's flat?"

Gabriel and Patrick argued with sharp jerks of the hand. "Wewe, you are not a temporary game guard even. You must to get the wood for the fire."

"Wewe"—with a twist of the head—"you are this temporary game guard. Me, I am to help the Mzungu with the camp," Gabriel said.

"Is there anything I can do?"

"No, memsahib," they chorused together and, planting their feet in the mud of the clearing, leaned their weight upon the saplings. The tarp tied between them lifted into a roof.

Aelian, in anecdotal imitation of Aristotle, recorded stories about animals he'd heard from conquering troops. With equal weight, he told of the birds that clean crocodilian teeth, and of the phoenix that rises, newly feathered, from its own ashes.

Some trees need flames to release their seeds from the hardened cones. Whole forests must burn to let the seedlings grow from their parent ashes. The savanna maintains its grasslands against the world's desire to make trees by cropping grass and seedlings alike with its great herds of elephants, giraffes, and antelope. The big animals also prune the surviving trees into inedibility, and a multitude of smaller species are grateful for this narrow remaining shelter. The savanna has held itself still for millions of years with this machine of perpetual motion. The zebras pass through first, cropping the coarse, dried grass that holds the light like lanterns. New shoots, released, grow and are eaten by the gazelles and rhinos. The grass, in any stage of life, feeds the largest biomass of mammals in the world.

They carried back one tree trunk to hold a fire in place on the slope, and another for us to sit on.

At a loss, I finally opened the tent bag and read the instructions in the green light. Again and again, I pushed the poles through their fabric tunnels and watched the tent jerk itself from my hands, flatten, and fall. On the sixth try, I reread, and pushed the poles through the same tunnels, and with a hiss, the tent rose, expanded, and became a home. The men took it from my hands as I wondered what to do with it. Without interest, they dropped it in a terrace they'd dug in the steepest part of the hillside. I looked at the grooves water had cut into the slope and wondered again why they hadn't set up camp on the hilltop. Someone said something, and Akit dug a trench around the tent with his machete. Something crashed into a tree near the clearing. The men didn't turn away from their tasks. A cat-sized face poked out of the branches and said, "Chirr." It bobbed a threat. White nose and puffs of cheeks gleaming in the shadows, it chirred again, and I laughed. Insulted, the redtail monkey withdrew, like a clown sliding back into his overpacked car.

They set a woven mat, their only piece of furniture, in front of the fire beyond the edge of the tarpaulin roof.

Akit disappeared long and quiet into the forest and came back, walking with the BaKiga measured gait, carrying an entire tree on his shoulder, air bubbling and whistling through the goiter on his straight throat. Gabriel clicked his tongue, and Patrick turned. Twisting his shoulder, Akit dropped the tree with a crash that shook the hill. As he jumped away from the rebound, Patrick and Gabriel, in synchrony, ran down the slope and caught the ends of the tree, wedging stones beneath it with their feet. I was surprised already, to see top-of-the-mountain men working with those from the bottom-of-the-mountain tribes.

While they worked, Kamumbo stood in the shadow at the edge of the clearing. As the men set logs beneath the tree, he bent and folded ferns at the edge of the mud into a bed that lifted him off the ground. Turning his head away from the others, he closed his eyes and slept. I had thought the men would order Kamumbo to do all the work, but somehow he had known that they wouldn't let him touch the camp they were building into a home.

Gathered around the fire made from a whole tree, with the men on one side of the log seat and me on the other, the rest of us listened to the flames. I had never seen a fire made with only one log. But this tree, after its base logs had been consumed, burned at its end like a torch, alone. Sitting apart, hunched with a lantern, I wrote data on the monkeys I had seen that day, while the men talked in low voices by the fire and Simon stirred the beans and Kamumbo slept. I hadn't found a question in the gorilla station's box of papers. They were about small things, not something burning that needed to be answered. I'd begun to wonder if I would ever see the question or just fumble blindly, collecting any data I could, and then find at the end of the trip that I'd missed something huge. But like a clock ticking slower and slower, I stared motionless at a page, with one ear cocked to the singing of wet wood. As the light of an invisible sun drained out of the leaves, complaints and accusations faded, and the men drew in to the fire in their separate groups.

Simon scolded at first, then laughed and said, "Wewe," as the stories rolled from Gabriel. Gabriel laughed too. No, he didn't have a wife who needed to go to the doctor. But there was a bike he was supposed to buy for the research station. He looked at me and cocked an eyebrow. You'd have to be insane to ride a bike up or down that mountain road. But at the bottom, a bike could save hours of time. We laughed and said, "Eeeeh," while Kamumbo slept with the gray hat pulled over his eyes.

With a slither and thump, my sleeping mattress slid down the length of the tent and bulged through the fabric behind us.

I pushed the mattress back up its slope and crawled into the tent. Between plastic bags of clothes in a row, I found an animal book. Backing out, I sat on the log. "This is what we saw today." I pointed at the monkeys. "Eeeh." They nodded. Patrick murmured some of the names in Rukiga, and I wrote them in the research notebook. Hunched shoulder to shoulder, their faces a foot from the pages, they watched the pictures go by.

"And this is what I want to see."

"Eeeh. Empundu."

"Chimpanzee," said Patrick. They nodded. There was a silence, then Patrick said, "They want to kill you."

"What?"

"These animals, they must to kill you. They are very bad."

"I want to see these animals very much. I came from America to see these animals."

After another long pause, Gabriel said, "The WaZungu, they are very strange."

"Tchah," said Simon, and pushed him. "Wewe, you are a bad man."

"No, these are good animals. I will show you how to talk to them so they won't hurt you."

"Eeeh," they said, and Gabriel took the book and flipped the pages. They laughed and murmured at the lion. Simon reached forward and touched it with his finger. "Me, I to not see this." Gabriel scowled and nudged him away. "It is that there are no more. This animals, it is dead." Patrick took the book and said, "Yes, it is so. This animal, it is dead."

I paused. "In America, we want to save these animals, so they do not all die."

"Eeeh!" The mattress once again slid down the tent like a snake in sand, *thump*. It strained at the door of the tent, tilting it forward.

The tree raised flames from below our toes to our shoulders, burning without smoke, though it was so wet that water danced on its bark. I sat on the log above, the book on my knees with notebook beside it, pants clinging with cold. Chimpanzees walk miles a day, sometimes in ancestral paths through the tops of the trees, sometimes on trails shared with a dozen species, road maps in the mud from one fruit tree to another. They travel within the bounds of a territory, separated from other chimp groups by consent, but some males cross over and sometimes females too disappear from their rounds, leaving their whole infrastructure of family behind, to pass across invisible lines.

No one knew how large the chimpanzee range was in the Impenetrable Forest. Every species' pattern is dependent on the spread of the food it eats. No one knew what trees grow in the Impenetrable Forest, or what the chimps eat there. Knowledge of edible foods is passed from one generation to the next by example, so chimps in different areas tend to eat different foods.

The BaKiga sat on the far side of the fire, talking in low murmurs. Bent into the light of the red lantern, with the notebook tilted to its side, as I used to read books under the sheets with a flashlight after bedtime, I wrote: history that the men told me, of gorillas killed in the area, six taken to Zaire to sell for food, two more killed in defense of hunter or dog, and five killed because the BaKiga were afraid the government would take away their land for the gorillas.

Lifting the lantern, Simon squatted beside the log. "Now you can write," he said, holding the lantern aloft so it threw light on his face and back down upon the paper.

I sent him back to his dinner, and then I wrote instead about him, remembering what he looked like, with the lamp hissing and curling its flame around his face and him glowing at me like Father Time, ready to squat there all night while I wrote.

The fire roared up loud and dry, and all the trees crackled and leaned in toward the tunnel of smoke. Through a small hole in the canopy, stars showed bright. Lying with feet braced on the tent mesh, I breathed wet air. It was enough to be here, like standing on the edge of an ocean that no one had known was there, or watching from the shadows as Greek gods played out their myths. I was home for the first time, where humans began, living next to a trail built by the primates we were meant to be. The sleeping bag was cold and already dank with my sweat from the hike.

Zipping the tent door shut and lying back in fire-tinted light, I listened to my heart pound.

And then the chimpanzees began calling, whether from near or far I couldn't tell. Their calls echoed over the hills, down the foothills, and through the mountains.

The forest hushed as if those reverberations had struck everything living into silence. Chimpanzees will eat almost anything; even lions are afraid of them, and walk quietly when they hear those epic wails. My chest hurt with a stab of pain so sharp that I thought I'd stopped breathing. I'd taken in a great swelling breath of air when I heard them again. Later, feeling my face in the darkness that their echoes had left behind, I realized it ached because I was smiling so wide the corners of my lips had cracked.

14

The Chimpanzee Nest

With a murmur, someone kicked the log and it crackled into flame. With effort, I lifted my face from the firelit tent door. The sleeping bag coiled around me like a boa constrictor. With one numb hand, I pushed myself off the door flap.

The trees hung their feathers and, through the zipper of the tent, I saw the top edge of a cloud forming on the stream below, wisps of green-tinted gray rising along the hill to a window in the clearing's wall. I must have fallen asleep after the chimp calls because the sun was now rising behind the canopy. One of my hands held the tent from my nose. Outlined in condensation against the nylon, the fingers shone green. My knees and elbows had slid down the air mattress into the groove between zipper and floor. Struggling, I pushed against walls that moved away, trying to heave myself off the fabric and wondering again why the men had chosen the steepest of slopes.

The chimpanzees were long gone, so far away that even the echoes of stillness had disappeared.

Simon stood below the tent with his hands folded.

"Memsahib. It is that Gabriel, he find a chimpanzee nest so close."

The path was wet with morning dew, and dark beneath the

rising mists. Stiff and still sweaty from the hike into the rain forest, I clambered over vines and roots from darkness into light and then into a black cave again, with only patches of sun filtering through. The path sharpened into a narrow vein over the valley. Trees thinned, and suddenly, where a tree must have rested on its feet and disappeared upon falling, there was a small widening, lighted like a milk box with a candle set inside.

I knew how to measure and map nests, but I sank down on my knees to learn what a wild chimpanzee smelled like, and took data as an excuse to stay there. I bent over the tangle of ferns and branches and put one hand in to stir musk and salt and wild fig smell from wet leaves. Something leaned with a click into the present the way it had on the savanna when I watched the light on the animals. But this present snapped me into my body, not into nothingness, so I was very suddenly myself with more flavor and spine than I'd ever had before. I held out the ruler on my jackknife and knelt there for a while, pointing it in different directions while Gabriel watched intently. Without breathing deeply, I was bent over with air, flooded.

For a few seconds of halted time, I wandered with the chimpanzee, sleepy and filled with the juice of ripe figs, pausing to bend ferns into a bed of sunshine. It was probably a young male; females usually travel with their children. He would have strolled the path until he was tired, then bent the ferns into a luxurious bed, slept for an hour or so, possibly missing his mother, who used to hold him in her bed, and then an hour or so later, stretching, rising, and ambling away. The bed would slowly separate into its leaves and disappear over time. Chimps and gorillas don't go back to their temporary homes.

Damp leaves hold scent a long time, but at last, I'd had the best of it, or gotten used to it, so I measured again and wrote numbers in my notebook, and explained what I was doing to Gabriel so he would know how to do it himself after I was gone.

"With the ruler, you measure how deep, how wide, how long, and how thick the nest is, then you write down the direction it faces, and the leaves it is made from."

"Eh." He looked startled at first, then watched my face and saw I was serious. Squatting down with me, he took the ruler from my hand with both palms as I offered it, a sign of ultimate respect in the BaKiga.

Colobus monkeys had called the night before, an hour of creaking echoes — "Bleah, bleah, bleah" — one waiting politely for the first to finish, then replying, "Bleah, bleah, bleaaaaah," until they were so excited that the hills rang with their scolds. "Bleah, bleah, bleah, bleaaaaaaaah."

The notebook was cold as I slid it back into my waistband, as if it had soaked in the rain forest like a sponge. Looking back as we left, I watched the nest, perched in its pillar of light.

Gabriel crashed ahead of me on long, flat feet. "Eh!" he shouted, already telling the tale of the nest, before we could see the clearing. Through lunch, the men told one another what he'd said, and still murmured as Gabriel and I left on an opposite trail to look for more nests. The chimpanzee scent was gone.

The clearing seemed to tilt steeper when I came back. In the slope of the hill, someone had carved a square and set the tent back in place without the book of instructions. I unzipped it and looked inside. In yellow-tinted light, the air mattress lay almost flat, a welcome bed.

From my arms, in the sudden movement of air from the tent, I smelled a waft of chimpanzee fur.

*   *   *

From the natural wellspring of classification rose the naturalists of behavior. Actions too can be recorded, and used to settle species into categories. Territoriality, for example, nocturnal or diurnal, arboreal or terrestrial—patterns and certain characteristics hold true throughout the species, and can be used to define it.

In a leather-bound book, Darwin's grandfather had written an epic poem on evolution. Perhaps, though the family had paid little attention to their elder's heresy, ancestral lines and ideas resounded in Darwin's ears as he stepped off the Beagle *onto island rocks, and saw the infinite variation of species, and the adaptation of animals to their environment; long beaks for one food, short for another.*

In mirror image of St. Augustine, Darwin took the question of his time and rewrote it as a statement that was its own answer. The man who ended the rule of religion in favor of science didn't ask who built the world. He wrote that the world had built itself.

15

Empundu

Movement toward light is one of the earliest instincts. The first one-celled organisms lifted themselves to the surface of the sea, not by a resistance to gravity but by an attraction to the sun. Each evolutionary order orients itself to light. Plants lean toward the sun by emptying pockets of cells on one side, and filling others. Reptiles, who cannot regulate their temperatures, lie on lighted rocks to heat their blood until it speeds fast enough to carry nutrients to muscles for movement. And mammals absorb the sun's nutrients through their skin.

"Empundu," Gabriel said, so casually I thought he was beginning a story.

He looked at the forest and back at me, eyebrows raised. "Eh," he said in approval. Flat-topped and green, the hill across from our camp spread through its wrinkles upward to a small fig tree. The forest waited, as silent and absent as any land before a storm.

"It is there, memsahib." In the sudden hush of the forest, the valley lighted itself without shadow. Leaning forward on the wet log, I held my breath. The glow of the motionless valley spread to our clearing like a torch. It was a clear evening somewhere above the canopy. Still no leaves moved. Jerking his head, Gabriel pointed with his lower lip. "It is there, memsahib."

*   *   *

As children, we see emotions more clearly in animals than in humans. They are lit from within, glowing and sparking with thought. A deer wreathed in mist, sniffing the air, a rabbit in perilous flight across a meadow, a cat lying limp on its back in the sunshine, puppies clamping on to ears with sharp teeth and squeaking in mutual pain. They live with a pure delight. Humans are raised to think of the future, postponing pleasure and sedating our longings, locking ourselves in a cage of wood and wallpaper.

As if the trees had hushed, listening to an invisible step, the silence deepened. Long after I should have seen them, I realized that Gabriel was looking at shadows between the leaves, darker than the rest. Without breath or sound, without stirring the leaves, the shadows crossed the ridge. Fragments of a dark shape slipped behind the branches from one tree to another, then another followed and another, coming faster and faster. We sat in a theater built like the Colosseum, in seats so high they seemed part of the drama, with all the world in microcosm across from us on the stage, hidden so close we could see individual leaves.

The sun was still out, and the trees across the valley low, so we watched the chimps' passage like sailors seeing whales come nearer, more by displacement of water than by any flash of skin or fluke. Naturalists look not for animals but for disturbances in the movement of air and light and leaves; animals make a habit of invisibility.

We watched those shakings of branch and leaf, those sudden leapings of trees, shift and pause on the other side of the valley, first far away toward the curve of the last foothill, then closer and closer, silent. Of the primates in the forest, only chimps bend trees as they walk in them. Gabriel made excited conversation in whispers louder than speech. Simon told him to be quiet, then forgot and shouted in his excitement for me when a chimp looked out. It silently disappeared.

As the sun rose and slanted the hill into silhouette, color drained out of the leaves. Decrease in light or distance brought the crashes to us, so each toss and wave of a tree was accompanied moments later, it seemed, by a crash, and sometimes a grunt. We sat quietly on our log, and the whole forest across from us shook and wavered in a spreading of movement. The hill was smaller than ours, so we looked down at an angle and thus saw flashes of fur that would have been invisible from beneath.

Most primate species live in female-bonded groups. Daughters stay in the ancestral group and form small villages of defense, grooming, and mutual child-rearing with their relatives within the sometimes vast expanses of animals, clustered by the hundreds. Chimpanzees have perhaps the most fluid of all arrangements, because they travel such great distances. Only a female's youngest offspring are certain to be with her, and both males and females might any day disappear over the unwritten borders into another group's land. When an older female goes into heat, rules dissolve and a rioting group of males and females follows her wherever she goes, fighting and screaming and embracing.

I wrapped my arms tight about my knees, as if holding in my breath with a wall of bone. I'd been trying to watch animals all my life. We don't know when our eyesight is flawed, any more than we can see what others see in us. The world is the way we see it, even though our vision grows and changes.

A cluck rose like mist from the valley to the northwest. Three shadows of chimpanzees, and fragments of more, climbed slowly into the fig tree from a vine touching the ground. In dots and flashes of shadow, a small shape rose slowly behind a larger one. The larger swiveled its head and looked over its shoulder, straight at my binoculars, then drew back in the leaves. A primeval hoot wafted down, slow and uncertain. Thunder rolled across the valley. Hums rose as the thunder sank in and died, and low hoots murmured into the leaves. A bundle of shapes moved. Within the leaves, an infant dangled by one hand, holding a pulp of figs in the other. Time slowed, and my vision sharpened, as if the gloom of the forest had given clarity to sight. The tornado world slowed to a stop so that time neither moved nor changed, and one breathless moment continued without end. An infant, glossy in dark leaves, shimmering like a peacock.

Simon laughed with delight and flapped his hands. The infant and its mother screamed and disappeared. The valley hung silent. A pulse pounded in my eye, flashing light through the forest. Chimpanzees had walked across the valley. Though they were gone, their images returned in echoes filmed on the leaves they had stood among as if my eye held mirages from the past. I told Simon it was perhaps better to be still and not stare. Eyes sparkling, Simon wrapped his arms around himself. I wondered if I should have spared Simon the criticism. Surely the chimpanzees had left when they saw humans.

Two branches spread open, and in that sea of slight movements, another chimpanzee suddenly appeared. For a second I thought he was an arboreal gorilla. His back was turned to us, as grizzled as that of any silverback, and his shoulders spread wide from branch to branch as he held them apart. Simon rocked back and forth, laughing silently. The male turned his balding forehead toward us and bowed in the homage of a chimpanzee threat. The branches shook beneath his hands. Retiring into the still-moving leaves, he sat again with his back to us, draped on hip and elbow like a Greek statue, each visible muscle clear and overlarge.

Hoots rolled out and around, probably from him, closer together and louder, building. A different old female, lower lip sagging, peered out over her infant's head. Without moving, she puffed her face into a ball and watched us. Leaning back in the crotch of a tree fifteen meters high, almost visible, the male stared with her. Pieces of fig trickled through the canopy and fell thudding onto dusty leaves. A monkey clucked nearby. The chimps climbed higher. The pink rump of a female in heat flashed through the leaves and disappeared. "Eeeeh!" someone shouted, and I choked out a whisper: "We must be very quiet." Akit and Patrick had left to collect more food; otherwise the noise would have been painful.

The male broke branches and threw them down, leaning back against the trunk of the tree while they crashed and cracked below. Pointing, the men screamed with laughter. In a swoop, another chimp popped out near the big male. It was an infant. A branch fell. Hoots—quieter and farther apart. One of them urinated, and I smelled diarrhea. Oblivious to the rage of titans, the infant played near the male.

"Eeeh, eeh, eeeh!" shouted the men.

The chimpanzees screamed and shifted backward into the canopy.

"Hush, you must be very quiet," I said for the third time, hissing.

Hoots, very quiet. Something fell, possibly feces.

When a minute passed without calls, I climbed slowly to my feet to look. An arm poked through the leaves in a "go away" flap upward, and I heard the male shift against the tree, scratching, nervous. The next time I looked, he turned his head away, hooted, and peed.

"Eeeeh, eeh, eeh!" the men shouted.

"Shh," I said this time instead, so slowly that I spat, and it must have been an international signal for silence, because the men sat still. Wishing them gone, and overwhelmed with guilt, I sat hunched over my knees, trying not to stare at the chimps.

Something crashed nearby and then moved in the tree across from me. The female still in the fig tree climbed down, and the infant sat in her lap. No hoots, even when I looked down to write. Clouds slid across the valley into a lighted haze, very quiet. The female stirred in the tree, and a monkey clucked in the north.

The chimps left silently. I heard one quick thud and a rustle near the fig and felt rather than saw a movement in distant forest. One of them grunted fifteen minutes later, already an echo of distance. The brief green light of dusk fell on the trees. It would be too dark to see them soon anyway.

In the forest, sounds I hadn't realized were silenced began again. The cicadas buzzed in after-echoes louder than their song.

"I stood on the grass with the lights in it, grass that was wholly fire, utterly focused and utterly dreamed. It was less like seeing than like being for the first time seen, knocked breathless by a powerful glance. The flood of fire abated, but I'm still spending the power. Gradually the lights went out in the cedar, the colors died, the cells unflamed and disappeared. I was still ringing. I had been my whole life a bell, and never knew it until at that moment I was lifted and struck."
    —*Annie Dillard,* Pilgrim at Tinker Creek

16

Chimpanzee Soldiers

Rain rustled closer in the canopy, stirring the trees. Small night sounds hushed into a silence so deep that the chimps' cries seemed to thrum on long after they had stopped calling. They beat in my blood like movements of the heart, as if the ancestral human in the primitive core of my brain was calling; passion without deception. A small group of colobus monkeys said, "Bleah, bleah, bleah." The fire crackled and snapped in the rain, and the men talked in low voices. Across the rain forest, a last hoot rippled and swayed.

The forest hummed and shook. Perhaps an earthquake had passed—the mountains still rising. The beans lifted from the pot and spilled into the fire, first a cascade of froth, then swirling beans, then an explosion of infuriated ash. Simon leaped toward the pot and lifted it with the palms of his hands into the edge of the red embers. "Eh, eh, eh." The men talked and shouted and explained the chimpanzees to one another. "We must be quiet," I said, though I was sure that the chimpanzees had already gone forever, now that they knew we were here, square in the middle of one of their feeding grounds. "That is why we are here, to watch the chimpanzees. They will go away if they hear us."

"Eeeeeeh," they agreed, and moved closer to one another and shouted and waved their hands from there.

I turned my head away from the smoke and closed my note-book with shaking hands. At the age of eight, I had read about chimpanzees in Goodall's book and had thought simply, not that I would earn the chance to watch chimpanzees, but that Africa had always been my home and that I would be a guest in any other. And, though I had failed to earn it, here I was. A lifetime on the savanna hovered near, growing in a notebook that was suddenly rich with its opposition, the rain forest.

As if the fig tree had sprouted a fruit as large as a sun, at the top of our own hill squatted a black bundle. Without movement of the trees, a chimp had climbed to our side of the valley and been feeding there, invisible until now. It was minutes before I realized that other branches too were snapping nearby, and that the crack and thump wasn't the beating of my heart. "Eeeeeh." "Eeeeeeh." "Eeeeeeh." Backs turned to the fig, the men shouted and slapped their legs. Kamumbo glanced at the chimp, then away.

Pushing both hands on the wet log, I slowly shifted to face the fig tree. The lump didn't move. Simon and Gabriel bent, laughing, and held on to each other's shoulders. "Eeeeh, eeeeh, the chim-panzees, they come." "The chimpanzees, they come."

The chimpanzee lifted its head into silhouette and looked down at us. Silently leaning back in the crotch at the top of the tree, it turned its face away and pushed figs one by one between teeth and lower lip. I pulled my head down and breathed out to relax, but I couldn't. My body stiffened with excitement so tight it hurt.

A branch cracked across the valley. Turning carefully away from the old chimp above us, I watched the male on the far hill appear and recede again, scowling.

The men shouted and pointed at him. The lump above the

tent snorted and disappeared behind the tree. I saw one flapping breast as she swung away. Holding the notebook against my knees, I wondered what to write. "Chimpanzee, adult female, time, height in tree, type of tree, vocalizations."

Near the fig beside the path, trees rustled and bent. The chimps had climbed in silence around the valley, after the old female. Perhaps because they had always slept there, one by one they made nests in the trees above our heads.

Invisible branches pulled aside from others. More like the rush of water than a military snapping of rifles, the chimps wove giant nests of leaves. As they worked, I heard, over the men's loud conversation, a gusty sigh as one of the chimps settled into bed. Across the clearing, an infant peeped in fear and then silenced itself.

With that strange perception that one feels only in an absolute silence, with a single stimulus, for a moment my feet left the ground. I settled carefully into the bowl of branches with a mother that smelled of salt and fur. In the windless canopy, wrapped in wet leaves, I stared at the ceiling trees and swayed with the beating of a larger heart.

Simon, still talking, leaned toward me with a plate of beans, but I could barely hear what he said, listening through his talk to the movement of leaves and a small, almost invisible murmur. I didn't want to eat. If I were to stay in the rain forest, I would melt away, thinner and thinner, and at last, disappear completely.

A chimpanzee turned in its nest, a crackle of leaves and a small sigh and then a choked scream as if it dreamed of anger.

With a crash and slither, Akit and Patrick walked into the clearing, sacks of beans on their shoulders, through a gauntlet of hoots and screams.

"Eh," the men in camp said quietly. Calm, without eating or warming themselves at the fire, Akit and Patrick lay on their mat with Simon and Gabriel and pulled the blanket over their heads. Kamumbo sank into his bed of ferns, head turned away from the chimpanzees, as if listening.

A chimpanzee cooed, a small wisp of sound, like a child seeing something unbearably beautiful: gingerbread houses with gumdrop windows, or rocking horses with spun-gold hair. Leaves rustled in a river of ripples along the valley. Then the unseen chimp screamed, and the others sat in their nests and shook the branches in a small hurricane.

A scream ebbed and faded from the tilted foothills into the mountains, a pulse of the chimpanzee call and a ghost of its own return. On and on it vibrated in the ears long after the physical disturbance had passed. Perhaps sound, like vision, is captured and returned in the cells that have memory, thrown back and caught and thrown again in its own echoes.

The men turned and murmured on their mat, and from the silence of my still slightly tilted tent, I listened to the chimps listening to them.

"Memsahib," someone said from the dark. "Hoot," something said, and rustled uneasily.

"Call me Joanna, or Jo, whichever you like."

"Yes, memsahib. Memsahib?"

"Waaaaaaaaagh." The hills rang with primeval rage.

"Yes?"

"These chimpanzees, they must to come and kill us this night when it is dark. These animals, they want to eat us." The men were lying very still. The mat didn't rustle, so the speaker hadn't moved his hands as he talked.

"You must be very quiet and move slowly. If you don't look at them, they will not come to hurt you," I said, thinking, guiltily, that the chimps might throw branches in territorial display, but not really trying to hit anyone, more to see what we would do.

"Eh." Silence fell.

"These animals, they to chase us back to camp. We come from Ruhizhia and eeeh they come so fast and we run, run, and then we are here."

The child-size Batwa Pygmies, driven back into the forest by the BaKiga migration and their spears and axes, moved with the animals into the depths, coming out only to trade. They brought meat and honey, strange fruits, and leaves that cured disease, and the BaKiga gave them trade goods in exchange, from the lands they had taken over. The BaKiga made small excursions into the forest, cutting firewood and snaring small animals, but no farther than the outer trails because the Batwa wrapped their forest tight within walls of stories, of man-eating chimps and gorillas that hunted people and snakes that rolled like hoops. For centuries, they had held it intact, until the British declared the forest a reserve and threw the Batwa out. They gave to each adult male Mutwa a piece of land, a shovel, and some seeds, but the Batwa didn't know how to farm. The BaKiga found them sitting at the edge of the forest on their bags of seed and took the land and turned the Batwa into their slaves.

Chimpanzees tie men to trees and beat them to death, the men had told me. Their soldiers will follow BaKiga for miles in the forest and then throw branches like spears, killing them. Chimpanzees meet in groups for dances of war, and then raid BaKiga farms.

"Why did Kamumbo come," I asked in a whisper to change the subject, "when all the other Batwa would not?" It was wrong to talk while the chimpanzees slept, like shouting in church or speaking as a movie unfurled — one of humans standing upright against gravity and leaving these dark woods.

No one answered. Silence buzzed in that forest where even the leaves were so heavy with water that insects crawled in their multitudes without a sound.

"They must to kill us, memsahib," a voice spoke out of the dark.

But by the next day, the chimpanzees had disappeared, except for flashes that might have been shadows of wind-turned leaves, and hoots that echoed from mountain heights.

17
Kamumbo's Beating

The estimated age of human evolution has been shifted back again and again with each new discovery. We are always older than we think. More than five million years ago, an ape walked erect on its feet. It had exchanged, for some mysterious value, all the protections of the mammal—speed, fangs, and strength. They must have had tools, those apes with foreheads and all their retained infantile characteristics. But a modern human alone and naked on the savanna would starve, or be eaten. Tools and a close cooperative society saved our fledgling skins. That half-human ape—had it already lost the bliss of the wild?

As if a bowl had been placed over its valleys, the rain forest emptied into a dense silence. A bird flew straight up from its tree, and an insect gasped somewhere. I sat on the log as Simon stirred the pot, watching the light fade in the valley.

We are built of these flashes of light; these towers of photographs and the physiological responses to them live on as long as neurons fire. Eyes that had been bordered by tree and building now flashed with lighted oceans and giraffe outlines in gold, and eagles glowing with white and black over the curve of the earth. And now, in darkness, chimpanzee eyes.

*   *   *

"Eeeeh, he is so bad, this Mutwa. What is he doing that he is so late?" Simon scowled at Gabriel, who chewed a twig, grinned, and shrugged. The forest loomed dark and impassable, as if some sort of end was near. If someone was late, he disappeared forever; if the food was gone, it was gone forever. We had eaten the cabbage and tomatoes, and Simon had fed me the bread and pineapples, fending Gabriel and Patrick away, until the bread grew green, then yellow, whiskers, then softened into a puddle. It was maharagwe for breakfast, lunch, and dinner, the kidney beans boiled into a rich stew.

I looked down at the notebook. It was filling with flashes of monkey fur and flickers of green, guesses of height and species and age and sex, none of it good enough for a college thesis, and not even feces falling through that thick-woven canopy of leaves for study.

Kamumbo fit in nowhere, neither top-of-the-mountain nor bottom, neither Ugandan nor Mzungu. The Batwa could live anywhere in the forest, passing from one country to another. Arguments against Kamumbo could go on for hours if I listened.

Long spirals of steam spun from the beans. The men murmured and looked at the blank forest. "Memsahib, it is that this bad man, this Pygmy, he take this food and he go away and he does not want to come back." "These Batwa, it is that they are not men, they are animals." "It is so." "Eeeeh." "Yes, memsahib. It is so. It is that they are animals."

"Eeeeeh." A gray shape tapped like a quiet drum down the hill across the valley, feet skimming over the roots as if barely touching them.

With a rush, I closed the notebook and thrust it in my

waistband, dropping the pen in the thigh pocket beside its ink stain. The humidity was so high that the ink had liquefied in the pen and always ran, fresh and black to the touch. We stood, and Simon lit a lamp, though Kamumbo had walked through the forest in the dark for hours. We all needed light. Even with the fire and the lamp held over Simon's head, the clearing was dark in a way that made us all twitch and want to run.

The hill across the valley flickered silver through leaf shadows, moonlight filtered at an angle. Without wind or rain, the trees tangled into a carpet as dark and still as a lawn. No monkeys moved, and no birds called a warning. The forest rested, hushed. From the tree over the fire, a leaf dropped and spiraled on wind currents of smoke up and down, fell to the side, and rolled, heavy with water.

Across the valley, we saw his gray rags glinting in the sharper flares of the lamplight, the same shade as the dirty burlap sack on his head. Kamumbo ran as if on clear ground. Knees rising past his midsection, those flat feet cleared roots and branches with a soft, syncopated punch—*tack, tack, tack.* Simon rustled and clicked. "Eeeeh." The sack was only one-quarter as full as it should have been. Kamumbo floated down the hill and across the stream, head bent, and silently *tap-tapped* his trot up the hill to us. Akit and I took a step backward, and Gabriel receded into the shadows behind the clearing. Only Simon waited for Kamumbo, with the lamp held steady over his head, and the light pouring and hissing down over his face.

Kamumbo's feet stepped into the clearing, and he put the sack on the matting by the fire. Clasping hands before his groin, he looked at the ground. Simon opened the sack, and everyone stepped nearer. Ten or twelve sweet potatoes lay curled in the dirt at the bottom.

"Eeeeeh. What is this? Wewe. You are a bad man. A very bad man. Where is the food of my wife? Me, I tell you go to my wife and she will to give you food. What is it you do?" Simon flapped his arms. "Eeeeeh, you are a bad man."

Akit murmured and moved nearer. Kamumbo stood with head bowed, like any Batwa before any BaKiga. Akit said something sharply to him in Rukiga, but Kamumbo didn't answer, and Akit turned away with a breathy "tchah."

I didn't know what to do. Some siphoning of food was expected; it was just the BaKiga way, like tips in America, but with so little food, we couldn't stay in the forest. Kamumbo ate little, slept outside the tarp even in the rain, and treasured only his hat. Next to Simon, he seemed the least likely one to steal.

Simon rapped out a KiSwahili question so fast I couldn't understand, but Kamumbo shrugged. It was Gabriel, at last, who asked Kamumbo what had happened. Kamumbo said very little, but Gabriel told us a lot. "Eeeeeh. Memsahib. He say he go to the house of this man Simon, and he go to the research center of Dr. Tom and take so much food and he walk down the path, and these three men they come and ask him where he is going and he say to the house of the Mzungu and they say he is lying and they take his food and his machete and they beat him with their sticks until he fall down fast, fast and they go away and Kamumbo, he does not know what to do, so Kamumbo, he go to my home and ask for food and they say he is a bad man and a Pygmy, but they give him these potatoes for him to cook and he come but it is many hours and it is night so he come slow, slow and that is why he is here."

We stood silent for a while. Simon said, "Eeeeeh," disturbed, and Akit shook his head and clicked. I said, "I'm sorry, Kamumbo," in English, then in Swahili, and wished I had the courage to take his hand, but I could tell that, like the BaKiga, he didn't want to be touched by a Mzungu. He dipped his head once without looking up, and Simon pushed the potatoes into the ashes of the hottest coals. "Are you hurt?" I asked in KiSwahili, but he didn't answer.

The smugglers and poachers had threatened the men before when they'd gone to collect their food but never hurt them. I sat with hands in my lap. If I wrote to the park officials, they might throw me out of the forest. At last, I pulled the notebook from my stomach in a rush of cold air, turned a page, and asked Gabriel to ask Kamumbo for details. He didn't answer. I looked up from the flickering page. They were standing there, awkward and miserable, afraid of me.

I saw, in snapshots of memory, a man in a suit, slapping aside a peddler in Kenya, another spitting, "Wewe," within a store, a fat man on the road to Kampala riding a motorcycle through a silent town of gray and frightened faces. No quarter given. Even after all this time, after all I had done to get them to trust me, they thought I was writing to the police to report Kamumbo as a thief. I cried, "No! Me, I am writing to this district man to tell the police of these bad men. They should not beat Kamumbo and steal his food."

The men didn't answer. They still watched me with blank faces, as if I were about to hurt them. In their separate corners, they looked no more like one another than like their tribal enemies. The brothers were as different as the cousins. In a tribe so small, they must all have been related, but height, shape, nose, and mouth were unique. Akit stood a head above his brother, tall and as dark as a Nubian, with the Arabian nose of those northern tribes. Ennobled by the goiter, he looked down over that warrior's nose, blank and impassive. Beside him, his brother looked like a businessman gone astray, neat and formal somehow, despite the mud on his clothes. One would think he had come to sell computers to a king without electricity, and was being listened to with polite scorn. Patrick was the only man with an expression, but it was so masked I couldn't read it.

So the lamp hissed and flickered, the potatoes burned themselves soft in the ashes, and the fire twisted itself around all of us while they shuffled and coughed, and at last Gabriel said, "Eeeeh, memsahib, these bad men, they are the police."

Into the clearing, the potatoes spread their scent of burned earth and baked bread and ashes, and the tree above released, in response, moisture in a slowly settled cloud, wet leaves and potatoes swirling in a spiral lifting through the canopy. I felt alone, and far away from home. As I closed the notebook, it slipped back to the last page used, line after line of question marks. "1030 hours, adult blue, sex?, height about thirty feet, eating unknown food, 1035 hours, leaves tree."

In the distance, a colobus called *bleaah, bleaah, bleaaaaah,* as if it murmured, "I vant to drink your blaaaahd . . . ," and a blue monkey answered as quietly and far away as a nightingale.

18
Leopard

*F*our months earlier, by a river in an acacia forest on the savanna, the trees stretched separate yellow barks to the sun. The great uplifted branches, with their sticks of leaves, mingled with the silver of the dead ones. In one tree, so old the bark on the trunk had died and silvered while the top had grown on, a leopard lay stretched on a branch.

I looked after someone had told me it was there, and felt unworthy of Africa because I could see each branch, silver or yellow, or black where it was sketched against the sun, but couldn't see the leopard. Then someone else pointed and said she had two cubs with her on the branches above. I strained to see, sick with dismay. If I missed three leopards on a bare branch, what else was I missing in Africa?

I had thought that on the savanna, where the eye was open all the time and vision had become a series of layered photographs, I would see clearly, but I was still the last to find an animal.

Don't look for a leopard, look for movement, *they told me.* Wilderness is seen in the corners of the eye. When the wind moves the branches of an acacia, look for the leaf that doesn't move, or one that rises against the tide of the rest and twitches again with the others. The tail will stand out, a branch bare and curved, susceptible to irritation.

Binoculars twisted the angles of light until each eye had a separate, perfect vision. And still I couldn't see it. My right eye hurt, as if

I had crossed it to look at my nose, and the weight of my entire body rested there.

The savanna spread beyond the tree, moving with light. Long grasses bent and swayed with reflections of the sun, and the animals that swam slowly through its sheaths glittered too, an ocean of lighted fur. The only human presence was the truck rocking and tilting in those waves of light, dust rising behind its shell.

John Muir, hiking the Sierras with morose shepherds, climbed down a ravine to study geological layers. Like Darwin, he formed his scientific theories by looking at the earth and thinking about what he saw. On the way back up, through the sharp stones of a waterfall, he stopped and looked at the lighted water over the mountain.

"No pain here, no dull empty hours, no fear of the past, no fear of the future. These blessed mountains are so compactly filled with God's beauty, no petty personal hope or experience has room to be. Drinking this champagne water is pure pleasure, so is breathing the living air, and every movement of limbs is pleasure, while the whole body seems to feel beauty when exposed to it as it feels the camp-fire or sunshine, entering not by the eyes alone, but equally through all one's flesh like radiant heat, making a passionate ecstatic pleasure-glow not explainable. One's body then seems homogeneous throughout, sound as a crystal," he wrote in My First Summer in the Sierra.

Like many transcendentalists, John Muir had learned to live with flawed vision. One eye had been damaged in the factory where he worked as a young man. It was a tubercular lesion of the eye that sparked Emerson's key trip to Europe; Emily Dickinson was learning to live in the darkness of possible Bright's disease; and Thoreau watched his birds through half his early eagle vision.

*   *   *

A small lump on one branch moved, and, by staring through the binoculars so hard my ears buzzed, I saw, more in negative than with certainty, slowly coming into focus, a leopard lying not on her stomach but on her side along the branch, as flat as a layer of bark. She looked at us and lay back for a minute, then heaved up and stood still. Even with the leopard silhouetted above the branch, it was hard to tell her apart from the tree. Slowly and deliberately, she turned and walked to the trunk, and then, in fifteen separate molasses-slow movements, she fell down its bark to the ground, where she paused and moved her ears around. The young ones leaned their faces and paws over the crotch to watch her. She lifted up her head and sniffed with two nods, looked at us with indifference, and, putting her head down, disappeared.

I thought she had stalked off under the grasses away from us, but a minute later, her head appeared again, swimming through the grass toward us, ears back, then forward. Of all the animals, the lions and elephants and eagles, she cared the least about human noise. Slowly, she walked in front of us and into the grass on the other side of the road. The tail waved a black tip that looked like a milkweed seed and then was gone, grass among grass.

19

The Forest Ranger's Threat

Remove an animal from its cage, and if it has been there long enough, it will mark, in worn patterns of earth, the dimensions of its old home in the new. In the largest meadow, a single line or a circle.

Kamumbo paused at the edge of the clearing. He didn't look back at me, but I hauled on the backpack and followed. A mist of bean-heated breath plumed behind me as I climbed the hill past the wet roots of the fig. Hidden past a bush, a narrow trail led to the side of the hill. The night before, I had shared my food with the men, and now the others had left to collect more from their families and from Dr. Tom's camp. As soon as I had put aside the letter to the police, their faces had returned to life, and, like a paused movie, they had bustled on with their separate tasks. Kamumbo had ducked away from me and disappeared, but the next morning he stood at the edge of the clearing and waited.

Leaning over a tangle of ferns beneath a tree, Kamumbo, still without looking at me, bent the stalks into a mattress. Standing next to the nest like a butler, he waited. I lowered myself with care, clutching the stems, feet slithering on long roots.

He disappeared like the Cheshire cat, unsmiling but only half visible, and then faintly still there after he had trotted into the bushes. So quietly it was almost inaudible, something squeaked and then rustled in the branches, as if turning away to stop itself from screaming. I lay rigid and braced myself, afraid to move, not sure what animals he had found.

The ferns bent beneath me. Just as I thought I'd land in the mud, thrashing, the fronds caught together. Lying still, I rose, then lifted into the air.

The hills fell so evenly down that the valley was too narrow to hold a tree. Below my feet, the slope glowed, lighted ferns stretching as high as walls. The stalks of the ferns poured a stream of ants over my boots. Lying there in the lighted air, my mind floating too, I saw myself as if watched by a chimpanzee perched above. A pale thing, tense and rigid, like any predator.

Breathing in the heavy air, I relaxed my toes, then my knees and hips, and looked randomly at the sky. The bed of air was the most comfortable I'd ever lain in. But one can't think of something else when one might be lying below a family of chimpanzees. They had disappeared two weeks ago, as if they had come to see us and then gone over the mountains to a quieter valley. With the next breath, my body had frozen into one rigid log again. Butterflies rose and twisted in the light, blues and golds and reds. The valley hummed and twitched with a multitude of insects.

Suddenly a shadow cursed as it crashed into a tree. I burrowed in the tangle of ferns and parasitic vines and thought of hiding behind a bush. The last time we'd had a human visitor, I'd had to sit for hours, stumbling through three languages, aware that something was expected of me but not sure what. I hadn't realized until he left that he'd been trying to ask for a bribe. But right now I stayed on in my living nest, because I had never liked to move, even in Africa.

A uniform passed through the smoke of bushes in the clearing below. With a yell, he flipped backward, then crashed down the hill. It was the muddy patch below the fig. He'd stepped over the root and landed in a split, one foot skiing downhill and the other trapped behind. We had all learned to walk sideways past that spot, clinging to the tree like a lover. Simon and Gabriel rushed up the hill to apologize. "Sorry, sorry, sorry, sir." "Eeeeh, eeeeh, sorry, sorry, sorry, sir." I lay chilled and hunched in my nest. He had come to throw us out of the forest. If I waited long enough, perhaps he'd go away until I had sent someone to Dr. Tom.

Kamumbo must have answered a question, because Gabriel climbed to the blind. "Memsahib, it is that the forester, this man, he must to see you."

Lying frozen in my hammock of ferns, I wondered if I should tell Gabriel to say he couldn't find me, but he had turned and hurried down the path, across the root and out of sight. I lowered my hands to the mud, struggled up, and slid down the hill after him.

Broad and balding, the forest officer sat with a mug of tea in his hand, scowling. Simon hovered by the fire and wrung his hands. Holding the bag of gray sugar on his palms, he reverently poured three teaspoonfuls into the mug as he saw me walk into the clearing. The officer looked up and pinned me to the trees with a glare.

"What are you doing in the forest?"

I told him Tom had taken me to the president's office to get clearance under his permit. A silence fell. The forest officer cleared his throat and told me the laws I had broken.

Simon moved from foot to foot and looked at me in agony. The ranger was going to order me to leave the forest. I breathed deep in preparation for an apology. This was my home, and my gateway to a life on the savanna. I would rather die than leave. A few hours of groveling was no price to pay.

I thought, *I will say, "I'm very sorry. I didn't know that I was supposed to speak to you."*

Then, stomach freezing with horror, I heard a stranger's voice come from deep in my chest. "I am here with permission of the president's office to do research on chimpanzees."

The fire crackled and snapped. Simon stood hunched over the sugar bag, staring at the ground. The forest officer — I almost took a step backward — swelled without movement, waiting for me to finish.

I didn't know what to do once I had made that clarion stand. For a second, I stood paralyzed. The men were locked in position, looking away from me. The only thing I could think to do was talk about the path I'd taken for research clearance, to turn assault into the polite giving of information. On and on I talked. Tom had brought me to Uganda on his research visa, but we'd trudged for days through the red mud and smoke of Kampala, past buildings with broken windows and bullet holes, visiting offices for permission to set up a research site in the rain forest. My voice cracked.

The officer rose suddenly, like a dragon unfurling its wings. My lungs stopped working. He handed the cup back to Simon, thanked me, and left, saying he'd be back. The men stood silent. I hiked back up to the bed of ferns, legs weak, and lay down. Chimpanzees had come and gone in my absence; the valley smelled of musk and salt and something wild.

20

Earthquake

Fabre rebelled, saying that beetles were more than a carcass. But the age of observation had passed. Literature separated itself from science, except for a few naturalists here and there, like Gilbert White. The American transcendentalists combined the passion for nature of the European Romantics with the elegant logics of Hegel and Carlyle. Like Fabre, they wrote about nature as a glorious science, recording fact with poetry.

Jane Goodall, untrained, went to Africa and wrote what she saw, in simple detail, without walls or separation, and engraved her stories in history. The chimps made tools and used them. Political alliances, friendship, betrayal, war, maternal love unto death: they had stories, just like us, and a literature of melodrama. But how does one write Shakespeare from whispers in the wind and half-seen shadows?

Feet braced against the ferns that were still standing, I lay again the next morning along fronds so strong they held me still and almost dry above the chill ground. Ants and gnats crawled without stopping now, probing the end of my pants, but, breathing carefully, I stared at the sky. The valley lay quiet and empty. One branch whispered and stopped; another cracked and then silenced itself.

Coos as gentle as those of murmured pain echoed behind the trees. With a rustle, a chimpanzee leaned forward out of the leaves and peered down at the top of my ferns, then closed itself into the canopy as if shutting a thick velvet curtain on an unwelcome dusk.

I turned my head and slid one hand to the side. Coos rose to hoots, then shrieks, as I pulled a leaf from the vine. Holding the leaf with one shaking hand, as Goodall and Fossey had done, I pretended to eat, and picked another. The screams hushed. A young chimp pulled aside the leaves and threatened me and disappeared. The tree shook, bounced, and screamed defiance. Slow, like a gorilla, I pulled and "ate" and broke off another fragment of vine.

I tried not to look at the chimps, but eyes evolved first to find predator and prey. It is almost impossible to prevent the eyes from turning toward motion. I held my head down and away, staring at the darkness between the stalks of the ferns. The trees muttered and dispersed invisible chimpanzees into a semicircle behind the fig tree. Without a branch stirring, or the smallest breath to tremble a leaf, the canopy above my nest hovered.

A boom cracked into the silence, just one, as if a chimpanzee had broken a branch or a policeman had fired a rifle. I clutched the ferns, wondering if the officer had sent in the army. A faint tremor shook the ground and thunder rolled into the distance. The hill sat on a slant above the others, and the whole forest was laid out below me, hill after hill shaking and cracking, one after the other. The wave hit each hill so neatly, like dominoes falling, that I couldn't believe it could happen to this solid ground.

With a roar, the hill across the valley shivered and shook itself. A few trees fell over like loosened hairs, but so slowly I still wasn't afraid. While I was still thinking, *Those goddamn soldiers aren't going to get me,* the other hill waved. I couldn't feel any change, but the rumble deepened, more of an order now than a threat. It seemed displeased that I sat while it displayed aggression before me, but I knew better, at least, than to stand on wet ferns to meet an earthquake or civil war.

Still, I couldn't help wondering about my sanity as I watched a mountain dance, and was almost relieved when my hill picked up the rumble and vibrated under me. The tremors had passed slowly on the other hills, but this one rushed below and through. Holding the stems of the ferns, I turned and watched the other hills bow and turn away from the noise like a tidal wave collapsing. It rushed into the distance, faster and faster. Soon it was out of sight, and I lay back in the ferns and listened to the thunder of the tectonic plates in a clean sky.

The earth, like skin, is not as solid as we think: it can move and be moved; there are flames underneath, hidden from view.

Simon hurried into the clearing where I sat and, turning his hat in his hand, told me not to be afraid. Invisible in the trees, chimpanzees cooed, then screamed, and gradually faded into the distance. Washing in on their wake, hidden monkeys emerged, screeched a late defiance, and crashed into the trees near the fig.

21

Rain Dance

With constant glitter, as if the earthquake still shook it loose, dust fell from the branches, settled into fabric, and disappeared. Beans released a clean scent of earth into the clearing; garlic, greens, tomatoes, and chili peppers roiled in turn to the surface of the pot. As I slid down the hill toward the campsite, Simon added a pinch of gray salt from a plastic bag that had once held used batteries sold as new.

The tree swayed over the fire, bent toward its warmth as if to an invisible sun.

"Empundu?" Simon asked. Lifting the machete, he sliced a branch from the tree over the fire. With four strokes of the blade, he peeled the bark, then with another two shaped the thick end into a spoon, and dipped it into the beans to fish out the other spoon he'd made.

"Empundu zabura." I sat on the mat in front of the fire, with elbows on my knees, breathing in the scent. If I had clung to a tree and watched the earth move, with a pale predator staring at me, I would have thought this valley cursed too.

My stomach hurt so badly that for a second I couldn't breathe, and I wondered if it was grief or some new illness. What I had seen during the earthquake had been a different group of chimps passing through, then leaving in haste. The groups weren't coming back. I had gambled a life in Africa and lost.

A shadow moved at the corner of the clearing: Kamumbo was squatting silently there. I hadn't seen him slide out of his crouch below the trees. Branches crashed in the distance, and we jumped to our feet. Kamumbo was three feet away from me, but I had to look hard to see him, he stood so still.

"Empundu?" I whispered. He nodded.

I crept down the path after him, stepping over the clear stream. He had never taken me up this neighboring hill into the theater where we had watched chimpanzees screaming. A trail zigzagged through its ferns to a small fruiting tree. The air was thick, so close to the bottom of the valley. I paused in a burst of sunshine and breathed deep.

In a line from the south, trees dipped and swayed. Something screamed and a branch crashed. Kamumbo dropped and crawled. I followed on the other side of the path. In small ferns, his muddy clothes nestled like shadows among the roots, dark and empty.

The black sweater shifted and appeared behind a tree. Kamumbo waved his hand and motioned me toward another tree on the far side of the trail. I lifted my head from the ferns and hesitated, afraid a noise would frighten them away. He jerked his head again, then froze.

In front of the tree, a young male chimpanzee stood. So quietly had he moved that even his scent had been left behind. He saw me lying sprawled on the path, one arm stretched forward. On an indrawn breath, he squeaked, bouncing into a tree. "Eeeeeek," he gasped, then took a deep breath and said, "Oo oh ooh oo EEEEK," jumping up and down on his hind legs and swinging the branch with his hands. "Hoo," he began again pitifully. "Hoo ooo ooo aaaaaaaagh." The musk of a wild chimpanzee trailed after him and filled the clearing, a sudden tang of salt and sweet fur, like all our ancestral homes. I put my head down in the ferns so I wouldn't stare, and clung to the earth in imitation of Kamumbo. My heart pounded so hard I heard drums beating, as if ancestral humans were dancing with the chimps. This was why I was born.

Like the savanna, the rain forest has no scent. The trees, always wet, release no images of themselves, and each smells only of the wet earth that clings to its bole, rotting it alive. I lay, ice-cold in the striped sunshine of the clearing, trying to find the invisibility I'd had all my life in the human world, until Africa, and wondering how to reach for my notebook without scaring them away.

Screams, hoots, and crashes erupted on the left, like a group of overwrought English soccer fans pounding toward the enemy. "Aaaaaaaaaaaaaagh," said the young chimp, all his teeth bared in a grimace of fear. "Hoo ooo ooo ooo aaaaaagh."

As the first adult appeared in a nearby tree, the young chimp screamed loudly, suddenly brave, and twisted off a branch to throw at me. It landed on the path off to the right and bounced. He hoicked his way up the tree lumberjack-style, screaming again, frightened by the noise. I let go of the notebook and settled into the ground.

Kamumbo's hand moved down to rest flat on the ground. Thinking he might be tensing to run, I watched him for a second. He was, suddenly, holding a machete flat in the cold mud. He didn't move again. Screams stabbed like knives as six chimpanzees roared into a circle around us. Branches crashed into the under-brush, each fall raising louder shrieks. Kamumbo looked back at me, and for the second time since I'd arrived at the site, my smile spread so wide and fierce that it cracked the corners of my lips. He looked at me a second longer with the fierce impassivity of any oppressed people, then miraculously cracked his old lips into a grin as wide as mine. His hand relaxed on the machete. They hadn't screamed at his movement, but as I put my head down again, they wailed in belated horror. My heart beat so hard into the mud that the poncho twitched against my shoulders.

An old female with a bare patch on her forehead walked calmly into a tree below my feet. A brief silence fell. She leaned forward to study my spread-eagled body. An infant jumped from a tree into a branch above her and leaned forward too. Their eyes sparkled as they shifted back and forth, lips pursed in concentration. Satisfied, she settled back and gave a tiny demure cooing "hoo." The others in the group answered, "Hoo." Eyes twinkling at me, she said, "Ooooo." Then, "Oooooh oooh oooo ooo aaaaaggh," her skinny chest and dangling breasts bouncing. "Aaaaaaaaaagh," her infant screamed, jumping into her arms and looking backward over his shoulder at me. The others shrieked and jumped about in the trees. Leaning back with satisfaction, the bald female smacked her lips, scratching her shoulder as the chimps swirled, defecating and tossing branches in a wild climax.

I shifted one hand an inch toward the notebook. A juvenile gave a worried "hoo," and the row started again. A male as big as a gorilla jumped on a thick tree branch. With a crack, the branch broke, and he squeaked as he fell. Two feet from my leg, the limb hit with a thud. At the last second, as it fell, he jumped to the tree trunk.

"Aaaaaaaaaaaaaaghhh." He glared at me, as if it were my fault. I shifted a numb leg, and they all broke out together, "Hoo. Hoo. Oo oo oo oo woohoo woohoo woohoo wraaaaaaaagh, wraaaaaaaagh, wraaaaaaaaagh." The following silence was deafening, as if the after-echoes were louder than the screams, or the air was so wet and thick that they still reverberated toward the ear. Then a few tentative "hoos" built up to a screaming crescendo with a great leaping and flinging of leaves. A juvenile rebounded off an adult's head onto a vine and clung, a rounded lump of fur, peering down at me. I lay still, hand flat in the mud.

Thunder rolled toward us, sparking another screaming session, and the juvenile did slow gymnastics between two vines, standing upside down, whirling about sideways, and swinging by one foot while pushing off a tree trunk. Rain pattered in through the canopy. I lifted a hand stiff with cold and told Kamumbo in sign language to go back to camp, but he shook his head. It was the first time we had moved more than a few centimeters. The bald female jumped closer and stroked her fur with one hand, touching wet fingertips to her mouth. The juvenile shook its head hard, ears flapping, and lost its grip on one vine. Upside down, it dangled in the rain.

Perhaps, like thunderstorms, movements of the earth roused the chimps to a Dionysian passion that had no boundaries left to hold fear. They danced for hours in the circle around us, disappearing into darkness and silence. I lay in the mud until they were invisible.

Kamumbo slipped silently down the path. One final soft "hoo" thrilled the wet air as I stumbled after him. He moved without sound, except for a soft padding lost in the crashes as I slid on roots and clung to branches. I slithered down the path fast, barely able to see him though he trotted just in front of me. I was suddenly afraid he'd disappear and I'd be lost within touching distance of camp. The notebook slid down inside my pants. I held it through the cloth, afraid it would slide through to my legs and into the darkness. I hadn't eaten in so long my stomach had shrunk.

A line of silver ran like mercury before us, so bright in the darkness that it floated in midair and could have pointed in any direction. It was the stream, reflecting the light of an unseen moon. As I stepped across it into the trees, the temperature dropped. I climbed, boots slipping on invisible roots through an eternity of forest. Branches slapped my face, and trees fell from nowhere into my knees. In the darkness, the path that had been so short before now stretched high and impossible above. I wondered if we were lost.

With a jerk, I stopped. Beyond Kamumbo a lighter square of darkness hung a foot before me. It moved and rustled, and behind the shadow of a tilted bush, the clearing opened before us, empty. Without humans or fire, the clearing was limp, just half-killed weeds in a sea of mud, with one small tent and a tarp.

Before I had time to worry, Simon pushed to his knees and ran to shake my dripping hand. Gabriel and Patrick crawled after him from under the table, hands icy with mud. "Memsahib, we thought empundu had killed you and wanted to come to eat us," Simon said.

Patrick studied us. "Were you afraid?" he asked.

I grinned and looked at Kamumbo. He put his head down. A noise like leaves rustling passed just at the edge of hearing. Kamumbo, faintly, was laughing.

22
Words

I opened the tent and poked my head through the zippers into a gust of cold air and smoke. A host of insects appeared, flowing over the leaves in rhythm with the water rolling through the branches. With great solemnity in the tree over our heads, a beetle trudged, huffing and whirring, still vibrating with trumpets and bugle glares from the day before. As if the earthquake had moved the whole forest to revel, the canopy stirred with shufflings and small whispers, like an audience still sitting, stunned, days after a performance and only now beginning to stir and gather handbags and chocolate boxes and scarves. The chimpanzees had gone the morning after their dance, shuffling away in the rain without touching the figs. I was afraid that they had come out of curiosity, warned the other chimps with their alarm calls, and then left forever.

The men, lined in a neat row, sat up in the clearing. Crawling out of the tent, I held the notebook above the mud.

The fire creaked and burned with a cold heat, like a painting of flames in an icy room. As I sat on the log away from the men's feet, a triangular hole puffed air from my knee. Mold had weakened the fabric of my pants. They were always wet. It was strange to have no greater memento of the rain dance. I would have given so much, and yet I had to pay nothing. Even lying in icy mud for six hours in a thunderstorm hadn't given me a cold. Days later, their screams still echoed in my memory, reverberating off the mountains.

Gabriel looked sideways at the hole in my pants.

"Me, I want to buy a suit like the WaZungu, that is blue."

"What did you wear before the WaZungu came?" I asked to change the subject before he told me I needed to buy him one in Kenya. *What do you do when you have what someone else sees as infinite wealth?* I was wondering how to record the chimpanzee rain dance. To guess at its meaning would be unscientific, but not recording the dance was an equal sin of omission. The dance wouldn't matter to science; it would have been recorded as lists of vocalizations and heights in trees if I had taken out the notebook, but one can neither leave out clusters of behavior nor pick and choose which behaviors one will record.

"We were animals then. The BaKiga, we wore skins of animals. And the missionaries, they come and they say that this is, eeeh, so bad, and so the BaKiga, they did not use their skin beds, and if they could not buy blankets, they were, eeeh, so cold and they die."

"It is so. And now" — proudly — "we have nothing from those days. All is like Mzungu," Gabriel said.

Looking at the invisible canopy, I set down the notebook. It was as if a giant vacuum cleaner had swept over the continent, tugging grass skirts and painted gourds and drums and dances and cattle-skin blankets up into the sky. I remembered Suzan's Rukiga dictionary. On the last page of the notebook, I wrote a list of words.

"How do you say this?" I held a potato in the air.

The men stood, the better to shout out first one translation, then another. Simon began. "Do not listen to this foolish man." Patrick countered. "That is not the word." Gabriel defended Simon with automatic top-of-the-mountain loyalty. "What he say, it is true. Always BaKiga say this." He paused. "And sometimes this also." Simon rounded on him. "What is this you say?" Akit muttered, "The word we say, it is this one." He spoke so quietly we all instinctively turned to him, but I could tell by the long silence that Simon and Gabriel had never heard the word he'd given, or they would have leaped into demurrals before they'd even registered it. Even Patrick, his own brother, looked a bit puzzled. "Me, I always say this," Patrick said. Simon, still taken aback by Akit's word, admitted, "My mother, she say this word," then hastily, "but she is very old." I wavered over the notebook. "Which should I write?" Each of them called out a different answer. They turned on one another. "You are a very foolish man." "You do not know what to say." "Eeeeeh." "You tell the memsahib wrong."

Gabriel sidled up to the notebook, glanced at the potato, and grinned. "There is also this word, this word, and this word." The beans hissed and spat wads of foam into the fire, where they disintegrated, wafting the smell of burnt rubber. Simon and Akit stood face-to-face, fists clenched, spitting and stammering out insults.

"So Simon's word, how is it that I spell this?" They turned and crowded round to watch me write. I had forgotten that most of the younger BaKiga could read and write some English, but Rukiga was not then a written language. The battle over how to spell the word lasted until the beans had burned.

"Eeeeh."

I left for the blind.

Mouth tingling with iron-tinted beans, tattered knee falling into the light, I sat with my notebook on my lap in the silence of the hillside clearing, where the chimpanzees could see me if they came this way. Wrapped in a halo of cold moisture by the roots of the fig tree, I watched the monkeys, who were also looking for the chimps in darts and flashes over the shoulder and sudden crouches against wet bark. The leaves were damp but overlain with dust. As I shifted, the motes rose in a nimbus of light, and glinted and ran along my legs. The tear again puffed out a short burst of air, like a breath.

"You are stupid." "Wewe, you are a bad man," I could still hear drifting in winding streams along the path up to my aerie. A fat redtail monkey climbed into my clearing, chirred in confusion, and turned its head to the south and north.

23

The Rains

Museums overflowed with skin and bones. Biologists spent lifetimes debating classification of two related species. Ethologists turned the debate from its solid foundations to the new science of behavior, instead classifying instinctive behaviors within a species. The questions that are studied determine the data found. Scientists suggested that all behaviors in animals were instinctive responses to stimuli. The behavior of parenting could be reduced to single parameters. An infant gull pecks not at its mother for food but at the red dot on her beak. It will ask any red dot to regurgitate, even one on a painted stick. The parent, with equal reliability, will feed whatever she allows near her, if it plays the right tune on her beak.

In microcosm of the combat between religions—some believing in free will, others that we are only characters in someone else's story—scientists found the dividing line between humans and other animals. Humans act with free will, they said, separated from the instincts of the body.

I left the shadow of the tree and folded giant ferns into a blind on the hillside, moving as slowly as if I breathed through my feet. Water ran down my wrists, and a beetle, funneled by the rain into a drop on the fern, struggled inside my sleeve. The stalks bent slowly. Like Robert Frost's birches, they arched without breaking until their tops brushed the mud. Carefully, hands propped in icy puddles, I gathered the stalks as Kamumbo had taught me and lowered myself onto them, rising with them from the ground.

Kamumbo had made a blind with three motions of his hand, but my bed slowly sagged apart. With a bump, I hit the mud. Fingers stiff with cold, I wove the ferns underneath me again. Ants crawled with tentative darts inside my pants, and gnats sank in clouds to spin about my hands and face. The foothills across the valley rolled from Uganda into the Mountains of the Moon in Rwanda and Zaire. Yesterday's rain still ran from the leaves, each hill swaying without wind.

I hung for a while on my ancient ferns. Icy mud sank into my pants again, and I struggled out with difficulty and groped for the backpack. My stomach, as if it had dropped too, filled with ice. Part of me had left with the chimpanzees and was traveling, invisible, in the mountains.

The chimpanzees had faded out of the forest until at last even their nests smelled more like rotting leaves than sweat and sugar, and their dung fell apart into its component seeds. The dry season was ending. The last figs dropped to the ground, the female with the red rump had led her consorts across the foothills and dispersed them there. Within the chimpanzee trails rising and falling on the mountain's knees stretched a smaller path, worn by my feet.

The savanna that was my home was farther away than ever, and the rest of the world had faded to shadow, a false hastening where no pleasure was taken in food or fire or the movement of leaves. I had to leave the rain forest soon for a supply trip, but I was afraid that in doing so, I would slowly be assuming a carapace I had shed somewhere between the two lands. This skin would no longer fit. Like clothing tried on after too long an absence, it would swell in some places and bind tight in others.

It would have been easy to let the supply trip slide away. I had lost the taste for other foods. Maharagwe heated the intestines as it slipped down, with a glow that could be felt through the skin. And I had become used to not the rain but the misery of being wet. But I needed books that would teach me to ask the right question.

In a forest so quiet that dust whispered on its path from one leaf to another, I left the blind for dinner. The clearing was empty. I looked under the table. No one sat below in the leaves, but the fire burned unchecked. Squatting, I peered beneath the dish-drying rack. Where the tarp almost touched the ground, at the back of the lean-to, the men sat together, arms wrapped around their knees. They looked at me, calm, but didn't speak.

Hovering, I waited for someone to tell me what to do, but they sat, relaxed and patient. Lifting the fariah of hot water from the ashes, I climbed to the shower corral. Standing on two flat rocks, I poured the smallest stream of water over my hair. The trees bent together into the space that the great tree had left. Green light rippled on the branches of the enclosure. Holding the can tightly because returns diminish with speed, I ran water into the laundry detergent in my palm and slapped it onto my head before it could spill. The powder dissolved into a film. Filling the can half full, I held it with both hands and let the water trickle slowly, hot, then almost instantly icy cold. A few suds washed away, and I wondered if I had enough water.

Mud ran in a river between the rocks, splashing my toes. As I dipped into the fariah again, the rocks tilted, spilling water on my feet. Stepping into the mud, I looked down. The rocks trembled again, sliding in the ooze. Shifting my feet, I bent to pick up the can and froze as the water rippled and spread in the fariah. For a second I thought I'd spilled it and seen a mirage of water left behind. The ripples settled into an infinity of circles, expanding from the center, as if the pan tapped its fingers to the beat of thunder. I dropped the can and heaved the fariah over my head, pouring the rest of the water in one great gush of heat. Pulling my pants from the branches, I yanked them on and stumbled toward my shirt, mud clinging to my legs.

The men beckoned me into the back of the tarp, and I sat and waited, arms around my knees. "What—?" I started to ask.

A wall of water crept over the hill, walking step-by-step toward us. One foot before the curtain, the forest was green light and stillness; behind the wall of rain, nothing existed except a few swirls of tortured leaves reaching out from its borders and drawing back and down into it again. We could have walked away from the cloud, it moved so slowly and steadily, but it would have had to pass over us sooner or later. A foot away from that darkness, we sat in filtered sunlight, but the air had changed. It was thick and heavy and too full of water to breathe. Strange to be so afraid of water in the air.

We sat looking out at a still valley, leaves outlined in light, while the world disappeared around us into a gray cacophony and the tarp yelped in, tearing at the edges. Rain struck upward at legs and face like knives, and we crawled back as far as we could go. I sat and shivered, head on my knees. Cold and wet and beaten by noise and bullets of mud, we waited. Time ceased to exist. All thought of past or future disappeared. We only sat, frozen and suffocated and sticky with mud in a dark world.

The wall let go its grip and eased itself down the path. We sat in a secondary storm of water from the trees, but in green sunlight again, looking out at a black and disappeared landscape. Wet trees released themselves from the wall as it passed down the hill, pulling their leaves with effort from its path and bowing there, exhausted, rivers of water running from their limbs. "What...?" I asked again, but couldn't think of a question.

"It is the rains, memsahib," someone said.

24

A Gold Watch

*Y*ou don't think, Breathe in, breathe out, *as you travel. Breath comes naturally, as does vision. But you are breathing, in and out, differently. As you move from air to air, fragments and molecules of the land and the people around you sparkle into your lungs and embed themselves there. Over time, fluids moisten the atoms and—pulling away the dust and potato peels, the clothing dye and dandruff, the infinitesimal ions that make up wood and truck—sluice them out into the blood, where, overwhelmed in water, they are absorbed. All blood must run through the kidneys, so it is here that the miniature universes, these pastiches of all the landscapes through which you have passed, and these portions of each person met, are filtered out into the serum of the body, and evacuated in urine. Your body can take any nation, and any human, and turn them into water. Polé polé, slowly. You eat the land. Be careful where you go; you are what you breathe.*

Humans breathe deeper when excited. Many parts open in the body under the influence of adrenaline: the heart, the nostrils, the pupils of the eye. The lungs expand and pull in air, preparation for pleasure or fear. Either way, we feel more intensely and react faster with oxygen and all those little bits of world pumping fast into the blood. Thus, the more excited we are, the more air we take in and the more we absorb the world through which we travel. Breathe deeply enough, for long enough, and you will become part of the world, filled to the brim and clogged with its clays and dust.

I believe that even if we pass through quickly, there are landscapes that are particularly ours, that open our lungs wide in a great gulp of air so deep and sharp that bits of that place embed themselves into the spongy hidings of the alveoli, so deep that neither fluid nor oxygen can pull them out, and we are a part, forever, of the land we have chosen.

Africa has more dust than anywhere else; it is closest to the sun. Thousands of explorers returned to Europe or America with those shards of Africa embedded in their lungs. They never settled down into their pleasant lives. Put something deep enough inside yourself, and you feel a need for more.

Branches crashed above us. I tensed and looked for Kamumbo, but he wasn't there. None of the others moved. I pulled on my backpack anyway. As I stood at the edge of the clearing, the wordless curses of a human sliding between the roots of the fig drifted down. Pulling off the backpack, I slunk back to the fire, expecting to see the officer who had come before.

Brother Odel's assistant shoved aside the last branches. He stood panting and glaring at the edge of the clearing.

Simon poured tea into a cup and walked toward him. The monk took the cup and drank without greeting.

"You are going to Kenya to buy supplies," he said.

I agreed, and waited.

He scowled. "I need you to buy me a camera."

"Well," I said, wondering why the monastery needed a camera.

"And a watch that is gold, and this bag." He described a duffel with both hands. "This bag that is black."

He didn't trip going back up the hill. Perhaps he'd grown up in mountains. Like the old man, he had taken my promise — "I'll think about it" — as some kind of contract.

In clusters of bottom- and top-of-the-mountain tribes, the men stood in a circle around me as I packed my bag. Half afraid they'd demand radios and pin-striped suits, I asked the men what they wanted me to bring from the supply trip.

Condoms, they answered. Aspirin and worming medicine and a cooking pot and a wool blanket, but mostly condoms. I wondered why they chose this problem of all the ones they suffered.

"Eh," they said. "Many condoms. The land, it is too small."

"Eeeh."

I nodded, relieved. There wouldn't be much room, with all the research books and waterproof tarps I'd bring back, and I couldn't stay long enough to order anything more difficult because the forest would change in the rains. The chimpanzees had a vast range. They could move into a rain shadow of the mountains.

Drops of water still filtered through the canopy in the morning, as greenish-brown as algae in the dim light. Humid and cold, the air pasted pants to knees, and slid mold to the back of the throat. A shred of bark fell at my feet. On a wet and rotting branch perched a dark monkey. I couldn't believe the identification book. It was a male L'Hoest's monkey, rare and almost unstudied, black underneath, white and red above in the picture, but somehow blending into leaf and shadow like a compendium of all the moisture of the forest. He watched us for a full minute, then walked down the tree and strolled through the clearing, disappearing into silhouette even before the bushes closed around him.

25

Gender Confusion

The forest hadn't been cleansed by the rain but muddied. The day before we were to leave, the rain had struck so hard it rebounded soil and dead leaves into the canopy. The trees were black with mud, and still running with water held cupped in the canopy. An invisible crop of butterflies and orchids, which must have looked from another mountain like cotton, would soon be fluttering in the light above.

Mud slid beneath my fingers as I crawled out of the tent and slithered backward to close the zipper against insects. My pants and shirt clung already with icy grip, in a humidity almost as wet as rain itself. Sliding down to the fire, I held aching fingers in flames that made no heat. My stomach still hurt with a mild throb that might turn to agony on the long hike up the mountain. The forest stirred, leaves tilting and releasing and tilting again as drops of water ran from one to another.

The rain had poured down again that night, almost beating the tent to the ground. I had waited for my shelter to fill with the rivers flowing past, but even when they bent its sides, the streams of water passed by, and I was wet only because of the humidity.

It took less than half an hour to take apart our home. Simon left the poles where they were and folded the tarps into the wicker basket with the dishes. While I struggled with the tent, the men cleared everything else into a basket.

Through dripping trees, we walked with the hushed silence of the battered. Neither insects nor birds moved in that forest, as if it had been scoured with a soap that left it muddier than before. Even as mud slid to the ground, dust spiraled to the tree trunks. We passed through the forest trails to the road, into the sunshine with a pop.

"How is it that you say this in English, memsahib?" Simon asked.

I stopped, scratched a bug crawling around my waistline, and thought. I was sure we had been speaking English.

"What language did I speak?"

Simon had the blessing of total recall, and he rolled back the conversation, labeling each sentence by language: KiSwahili, Rukiga, or pidgin French. Finishing at last, we beamed at each other, and he said, "Eh, eh, memsahib, you forget to speak English."

I had been speaking in dialects for one of the two hours it had taken to pack the camp and hike back to the village where the road began. Congratulating myself, I strode down the path. At last, I had achieved the anthropologist's dream, fluency in a different culture. And they understood me too. Gabriel found a sapling beside the path, and stood guard over it until I joined him.

"Memsahib, this tree, it is omurehe," he said. Adult omurehe trees stretched above the canopy, so I'd never been able to draw the branches, and Gabriel had suffered my disappointment keenly. I drew the leaves, explaining what I did so they could take over my work someday, and we walked on, with me clutching a small branch in one hand, all of us stepping together high over the roots and logs in the path. Only as we neared the village did we stop swapping stories and lies about our homes.

*   *   *

Simon and Gabriel walked between me and the men we met on the outskirts, lounging around with pangas and sacks of potatoes on their heads. The path grew drier, and dust puffed up in spirals, curled around my collar, and settled deep into the weave of my backpack. We trudged around a curve and into a flutter of chickens. A murmur trickled out of the huts and wound around us like spilled milk.

A single chair stood at attention in the center of the village. A different old man sat in it, a talking stick planted in the ground. He was so old he was bleached gray, as if his color had leaked out like the dye of his clothes, muttering at too many washings, too much dust, and left him with skin and shirt drooped in tatters. Even his ears sagged forward. Only the feet bulged with life, all the sap having fallen to the bottom and dried there. Standing around him, the other men leaned on one another and waved their free arms, shouting. The old man stamped the talking stick and yelled something, then beat a flat foot in the dust.

"No, no," the old man shrilled in Rukiga. "No, no." The others waited, and he talked. Then they broke in or milled around, some of the less-skilled debaters dropping out to rest under the tree in the shade. "No, no."

With one instinct, they turned and looked at us.

I froze, thinking they would pour over us, snatching the pants and plastic plates and flashlights from the baggage. Our belongings constituted more than a lifetime's accumulation for the whole village, and so, why not? We were born in different places to different people, no better or worse than any other. But the men, bottom-of-the-mountain walking with top-of-the-mountain for once, stalked on, expressionless and unafraid.

I strode as if I were stretching against invisible bonds, or leaving most of myself behind, though the sun felt good. "No, no."

The withered man stamped his walking stick in the dust. "No, no." And the roar shifted and rippled again. None of them turned to look at us. We passed them, to the bend in the road that led to the base of the mountain. A few heads swiveled. I called the simplest of greetings. The crowd fell silent. One man returned the shortest version of the Rukiga greeting ceremony for someone passing by. As we walked on, I heard a shout from the old man that silenced the crowd, brought back the watchers from the shade tree, and then blew the whole argument away with a roar of laughter. I looked at Simon and Gabriel. They tiptoed at my side, looking with great concentration away from me. The laughter followed us to the road that lifted into the mountains.

I stopped.

"Simon, what did they say about me?"

"Tindikumanya, memsahib." I don't know. He looked at his foot, dragging the big toe forward through the dust.

"Gabriel, these men, what do they say?"

"Tindikumanya, memsahib."

On Simon's face, the top creased into worry, but a grin started to flash on the bottom.

"Simon."

"Tindikumanya, memsahib."

I picked out some words I'd heard shouted and tried to link them together. "Man, woman, work, cabbage? No—pants."

Alarm chased away both expressions, and Simon dropped his sack. "Eh, eh," he muttered, shuffling back and forth. "Memsahib, it is not good. Eeeh."

Gabriel slid behind me so I couldn't see the grin that flared under the shadow of his hat.

"Oh, Simon, tell me."

"Eh, eh, memsahib."

"Gabriel, tell me what they say."

Gabriel opened his mouth but laughed before he could talk. Simon clutched his hat down and said, "Memsahib. These mens, they say, this Mzungu, it is a woman because it has breasts. This bad old man, he say the Mzungu, it is a man because it have work and a pants. He say that the WaZungu are very weak and fat and so it is that these WaZungu men, they have breasts like women. He win." Simon looked at me, holding the hat, and waited. I laughed before I thought about what I should say. His face cracked. "Eeeeeeeh." Simon bent over and hung on Gabriel. They roared until they wept.

"Eh, eh, pants and a work, eheeeeeh."

The sun burned on skin, still chill and wet from the forest, thawing my limbs to the bone. The trees were different out here, dry and light in the wind.

We passed through another village, where a man had gone crazy and run through the huts with a stick. He hit chickens and children and any man and woman he could find, and those people were laughing too, listing dead animals and small injuries.

Rain, at first welcome, washed away my sweat, and then grew into a torrent of water that rippled over my boots and pushed them backward down the hill.

"Do the chimpanzees like the rain?"

"Eeh, so much. They like the rain very much."

"So the chimpanzees, they will come back?"

"Yes, memsahib, yes. The chimpanzees, they will go so far and they will not come back."

*   *   *

The villagers ran from the crazy man; they accepted the blood and the dead chickens and the cries of the children who didn't run fast enough, and when he was done, they circled without fear around him as if he owned the village and they were all guests. There are two sides to the lost Eden—a loss of control more often throws one into madness than into light, but whether one is emptied or filled too full, the traveler has seen something beyond human borders.

The road burned dry. Vines curtained the single wall of rock to our left in a mist of rising moisture. Birds flew down from the tangle, sipped from reflecting pools of water in the dust, and fluttered back into their dark world. I had thought the mountain would stretch higher and more distant above the weight of a body that wanted to lie still. But instead, I was rising lighter and lighter in the dust.

"Eeeh, eh," someone whispered. "Pants and a work."
    "Eeeeh, eeeeeh, eeeeh!"

26

Bus Trip

A car roared past the bus stop, coughing a gray and greasy cloud that sank in a circle below my shoulders. As if a lowered head could absorb less sound, I bent to tie my shoe and hung there, aching. The bench had been set below the road next to a small flight of stairs. As the tires passed, dark dust lingered in the air. The earth shook. With my eyes closed against the sting of pollution, I could still see the camp, the only sound the fire and the distant hoot of chimpanzees, so that each car that passed roared anew into unbroken silence. Halfway back to Kenya, my eyes and ears and throat burned like fire. I was trying not to put my head in my hands when two men in suits sat with a creak on the bench.

My camp flashed still on the back of my eyes, as if it were reality, and this human world the fragmented moments of a dream, so that I saw the men through a cloud. I hadn't remembered that cars smelled, or that people moved fast, without looking, anger all around.

I swam in green light beneath a sea of leaves, looking from far away at human movement. Neither smell, nor wind, nor human distances—only mold and wet wood and the possibility of chimpanzees.

With a crash, another car shifted gears, and a black cloud sank to the bottom of the gray as it swirled back to street level. I opened my eyes.

The men in suits nodded with approval when I said that I studied chimpanzees in the rain forest. They were teachers, one said, once the most dangerous profession in Uganda. Drawing pictures with his hands, the man in the pin-striped suit told me that when Idi Amin had targeted teachers, the other had walked his bicycle around the border at night, and then ridden into Kenya. There were many teachers, he told me, who had done that; the soldiers at the borders were lazy and would rather shoot someone before them than chase someone far away in the dark.

In the Cold War, first-world countries taught soldiers in wobbling nations a path to control based on Nazi philosophy. Take power by force, then separate the population into random groups. Imprison at random within these groups, and the people will fight one another instead of the government itself. Thus, Idi Amin, an illiterate soldier of Obote's army, first threw out the Indians, saying they were bad for the economy, and then turned on the British, who had trained him. Last, before he set his soldiers free for random killings, one village at a time, he followed the lead of most dictators — those who must remove memory of the past and potential for the future — by ordering the arrest of the teachers.

A boy ran past the bench, banging his hand against the railings. "Mzungu!" he screamed, and "Mzungu!" other boys shouted, scuffing backward into swirls of dark dust. On the bench in the little halfway town, no more than a strip of buildings built on the road, ancient in its constantly renewed mud, the two professors sat telling stories of their research. One of them had an antique instrument with him, ancestor to the lyre. He traveled the villages, trying to find old songs. Lifting it from its case, he held it so I could see the strings of twisted gut, the keys that had been carved with knives of obsidian. They asked questions about my research and click-gasped with approval when I tried to answer in KiSwahili.

The bus pulled in, and we shook hands and climbed aboard. The conductor leaned out and threw luggage on the roof with one hand. "Mjinga!" he shouted, "Mjinga!" Black exhaust puffed in open windows and through the floor. "Mjinga!" he screamed as we moved away, and hauled someone in by the collar of his suit jacket.

Springs spiked through torn vinyl and stabbed my thighs like small poking fingers. Waves of mold rose from my pants, as if even in the hottest sun, they wouldn't dry.

A woman plopped into the seat next to mine and passed over her baby while she fumbled in a bag. I held my hands up away from him, thinking he'd scream, but he lay flat on my knees, staring up at me. Like Mzee, taut and firm within his flesh, he shone with all the thousand shades of brown and copper. Something human opened unwillingly in my stomach. The baby ogled with wide and noncommittal eyes. I poked a tentative finger into his belly. He arched his back to look down at nerve endings and thought about it. After a few seconds, firm lips melted into a cackle, then a crow of delight. I poked again, and he grabbed my finger with one flailing hand and wheezed into a chortle. His mother surfaced from the bag with a pacifier, the first I'd seen in Africa. In one move she shoved it in his mouth and scooped him into her lap. Then they both looked at me.

Dust swirled in clouds from the floor of the bus.

"Eeeh, Mzungu." The woman added in slow English, "Where is your husband?"

I answered her in Rukiga instead of KiSwahili. "I have no husband, Mother."

"Eeeee!" she screamed and erupted over the back of the seat. "Mzungu, anajua Rukiga!" she shouted to the rest of the bus. "Eeeeeeeh!"

A roar of approval shook the floor. "Eeeeh, eeeh, eeeeh." For a while, they told one another that I spoke Rukiga. The two professors leaned over the back of their seat to smile congratulations at me.

At the rest stop, the women crowded around me, screaming with laughter, pushing chai and sweet tangerines into my hands. Stiff with dust and spring-seat bruises, we climbed back on the bus as it rolled away. Before I sat down, the baby was in my lap again, scowling in friendly concentration. He sneezed, with one catlike contraction of his whole body, and his mother said, "Eh," and dug in the bag and mopped his face and my arm with two hard strokes. The dust sank in spirals that smelled of fuel.

The bus clanked to a stop a few miles down the road, and two Europeans climbed in from an empty landscape. "Robin Hood," I murmured, but my seatmate didn't answer. The man in front wore a forester's hat swept over blond hair, a tunic, and shorts high above his hiking boots. He walked toward me with one lip lifted in a grin. Everyone in the bus leaned sideways over their seats to look at his legs. Grown men never wore shorts, and the passengers probably had never seen blond leg hair.

"Hey," he said. "Going to Nairobi?"

I nodded. "You?"

"Two weeks, safari. If I make it back out to civilization. God, I'll be glad to get back to a place where bus drivers do their jobs and get in on time instead of two days late."

Conversation about his legs slowed. Only the wealthy would have taken the bus instead of a matatu, and most of them probably spoke English. The bus driver hit a pothole, and Robin Hood jerked and swayed.

The bus shot forward, rocking him against the bare metal of the seat back. I turned my head to the window, stomach aching from the black smoke I had swallowed in town, trying to think of a response. I lifted the baby to a sitting position on my lap and stroked his hand for my own comfort. He grabbed my fingers, and they glinted weakly next to silken, dark skin. The Belgian turned to search for a new European to meet.

Dust swirled up in a spiral behind his legs. The baby sneezed again, moistly, on my arm. "Eeeeeeh," his mother said quietly.

The matatu dropped us on the Nairobi street in the rain before dawn. I had forgotten that Kenyan money was worth less in dollars than the Uganda shilling. I had eaten nothing but samosas and fruit for three days, and I was broke until the banks opened. Borrowing money, I ate breakfast with the backpackers who had accumulated on the van as it passed across Kenya, and with Robin Hood and friend. A friend in college had told me I'd be desperate to talk to people who knew what a hamburger was, and he had been right. Tribe of WaZungu.

On the horizon, the savanna glowed in that peculiar light that is part fading moon and part rising sun, silver and gold reflected in the grasses.

The city smelled of rain and metal and car exhaust and too many humans. I could barely breathe.

It was quiet so early in the morning. The others had gone to more expensive places. I sat on the bench under the acacia by the office, waiting for the hostel to open.

Backpackers had spoken last time of the highlands, and of human travel, as if it was natural that I would be leaving this city to ride the savanna with them or someone else.

Once again turning from the cooking stoves, backpackers asked, "Where are you going?"

What are you going to become?

27

The Safari

The great transcendentalist nature writers — many of whom suffered flawed vision and thus tried harder to see — believed that only in nature, separated from human things, could we become ourselves: halted in time, and without past or future. Perhaps all moments of transcendence are ancestral flashes of Africa, seen in the light on water or wings.

We drove, all yellow and blue and scarlet fringe on a white dust road, through savanna older than mammal bones, with scallops of mountains in the distance and hot sun lighting the grasses into lamps of gold. The road passed lions musing their way home from the hunt to a favorite tree, and giraffes swaying through dust to blink at the far ends of the sky, and secretary birds, their crests rising and falling, and a herd of zebras wheeling and suddenly running, as horses do, for pure pleasure, black-and-white sparks in lighted plumes of dust. On morning spirals of air, eagles rose, like the giraffes, in simple thought. Dust sucked in under the windows and spiraled in feathers about our throats, and we creaked and rattled and thumped our way across that eternal road as guests.

The savanna seemed to have grown away and expanded, like paintings in a museum, or a lifetime of childhood memories, stretching backward and forward, but unrepeatable.

What is this light that so many disparate gods have made? Again the road had traveled through ostriches and wildebeest, gazelles and lighted giraffes. On the horizons, mountains and sky; above, a bowl of blue as if we stood on a chair at the top of the world, with nothing but air beneath the rungs. Every time I looked down or closed my eyes and then saw the savanna, I had to again get used to the singing, the uproariously singing light, the Valkyrie explosion that seemed to come from within the grasses and within the animals. Splendor.

For seconds at a time, we are lifted and spread, washing across the wind like the white dust, turned inside out with light.

"The supplies aren't going to come," the backpackers had said. "You always have to wait at least two weeks more than you think in Africa." I shook my head. Two weeks in Nairobi was too much. Even in the time I'd been in the forest, the city had crept upward, and trucks had multiplied and spread, leaving everywhere a black dust. I had to go back before the chimpanzees left, crossing the hills to the other side of the clouds. At any moment, I could be missing them, and the one sight that would open a layer of vision and earn a life on the savanna.

"Come on safari," two Australians offered. I shook my head again.

Condoms had disappeared from the stores as if they had never existed. Fear of AIDS, perhaps. I found a small box, finally, in an expensive hotel. The supplies I'd ordered had disappeared too. "Maybe in two weeks, we'll have more."

We traveled, like the nautilus, with our homes on our backs: a sleeping bag, a few shirts, one pair of pants, a piece of toothbrush, baking soda for all else, a towel, a knife and fork and plate, and one book. Everything was there on the savanna: water, canvas home, heat and light and fire. On the roads to the parks, new fences shone, and the land inside them had begun to show the signs of cattle-induced drought.

In the light of the savanna, haloed in the grasses, afterimages of the chimps shone clearer than my original glimpses of them in the rain forest. I had chimpanzees in my blood now; I was a different person in Kenya than I had been, part of me still swaying in a bed of fur and musk and salt-heat. Here, I thought, I would learn the question that needed to be asked. The savanna was my home.

Divided between the beating drum of haste—go back and earn my place in Africa—and that absolute peace that descends at the top of the world, I slept and ate and soared in a truck on the horizon, so far divided from past and future that I ceased to exist except as part of the land and all its animals.

In Samburu, all scorched dust and twisted trees, we camped. Male ostriches strutted foursquare in the dust, necks flushed red with mating anger. They attacked the car with open wings and beaks, then turned and followed the females, who floated away with their wings spread for balance, kicking back puffs of dust. The lions roared all night, and crickets chirped in waterfalls of sound. We ate beans and potatoes and chapatis baked on rocks in the fire. Three elephants strolled across the horizon toward an acacia tree set against the sun. A halo lit them into gold as they reached the summit, and an eagle followed, also changed in color.

I slept in a powder of sweet dust; the hoot of the chimpanzees disappeared into the cry of a hunting fox.

We drove through another reserve, called Mara, where the hills rolled shallow, more like gentle folds, out to the sun in the west, the mountains the other way. The people who lived around its edges sang songs of praise to their cattle, and put lobes of wood in their ears to look more like them. Their bones were so strong they shone red through the skin. No one who had heard them hum-dancing could forget. They hummed and danced up and down, shoulders jerking to some rhythm that we would never have chosen but that felt more right than anything else we'd heard before, just enough offbeat that the mind filled in the extra pulse and the whole body waited with anticipation for the next, so the traveler was always thrumming with the last hum and waiting for the next. *Hum, hum, hum, hum, whooom,* they leaped scarlet and ebony straight up into the air over the sun at the farthest edge of the place that bordered on the Masai Mara.

On the Masai Mara itself, the grasses grew green and short with the rains, and laid like a carpet of silk, brightest in the valleys, longest and driest on the crests. Through them walked elephants, rows and rows of penitent monks, heads down, gray and slow, somehow bigger than they really were. Gazelles paced glossy through the grass, heads down, eyes closed in the softest of breezes. They never walked on the peak, where they might be silhouetted against the sun for the lions who slept under acacia trees, looking about every now and then. The lion cubs leaped and played and bit, and the oldest male sat looking into the wind with his chin raised, waiting for the first smell of the lion who would come to take his place in this sleeping crowd.

In Nanyuki pink flamingos covered the shallow waters of the lake so thickly that the lake reflected pink back at them. The birds creaked and clattered their beaks and stilt-walked around one another, and a fox ran by with a corpse dragged between her legs, but a hyena saw her and crash-splashed through the water. One tug, and the hyena sat in the flamingo-fouled waters of the lake to tear off pink feathers in a shower of shakes of the head. This was Nanyuki, where the waterbuck clicked their horns together, fighting on the white mud of the shore, and baboons clutched their babies and sidled down to the water for a drink. The rocks rose high above, but the lake stretched around and about and into the pink distances. The sun set on it in a clamor of red, and the birds flew away all at once.

A leopard crept down from her branch and whisked into the acacia trees, lost in grass. She looked back once, and the tapetum behind her eyes reflected headlights in white blankness. A waterbuck startled from the bush, and a hundred more thundered forward, leaping and kicking at the air. A buffalo lifted his head, impossibly large, over the grasses and then sank back down again, without a thought as far as the traveler could tell. A dove rose from the road and clattered its wings together, very white even when it was far away.

All night a lion coughed. It was a helpless sound to come from so large an animal, just another noise in the dark. It could have been anything, branches breaking, or the creak of a tree, or a rhino digging for roots with its fatal horn. Only the rhythm was as strong as a lion, and the roar he gave when the moon sank into the baobab tree. The roar was frustration; so big and strong, and alone. The females were there, but none had answered him. I wanted to crawl out of the tent to listen, but hyenas passed by to eat our garbage. So I lay inside and listened to the cough lost in cicadas and the whisper of acacias.

Like the wailing of whales, or the chants of any monk, like drums and ocean waves and the almost imperceptible rumble from the cathedral dome of an elephant's forehead, the lion's cough is heard not with the ear but with some other organ.

Vibrations travel faster through liquid than air. The stomach fills first, as if full of calm food, then the lungs, with air. Slowing, the heart rocks the chest with its own deep thud, echoing on in the darkness.

A female must have answered the lion, because when we found him, they were lying together in short grass. They didn't seem to mind the car, so we parked near them and rested our cameras on the windows. Like any meeting of titans, it hurt. He held the lioness by the neck and shook his teeth in her when she moved; she snarled and lifted her head but crouched still. It was over fast. She turned as he moved away. He leaped from her back, but her paw hit him in the neck, hard enough to kill a zebra. Shaking his mane and licking his nose, he shuffled backward and rested in the grass with ears pricked, panting, watching her.

She ran away. One minute the lioness was lying down, and the next, running through the grass, tilting and bounding. Sun flashed on yellow eyes as she pushed up through the stalks in a last flight, then somersaulted into the dust. The lioness rolled and flung legs into the air, twisting to rasp her skin into the grass, as if cleaning the smell of the male from her fur. But then shaking the broken grass from her pelt, she trotted back to him.

He rose in one movement and waited, ears pricked like a puppy's. Rumbling, they stretched on the ground, his teeth in her neck. Both heads twisting like snakes, mouths open wide, they roared, a monstrous sound from those yawing gargoyles.

The lion broke off to bury his teeth in her nape again, and she snarled in blind whips of the head at him. At the end, this time, he leaped away so fast she missed, but she took a bound of a step and reared up to hit him again. The blow snapped his head back like a boxer's, and he jumped into the grass. The lioness lay down in the dust and tufts of fur he left behind, and cleaned her face.

*   *   *

With mane and tail and movement of the ears, animals signal their emotions. It is a kind of fire. There is a color missing in humans that other animals have: a gold color, like gold itself, lit from within. We were in the Iliad *there, in Troy and Ilium and Olympus.*

We drove toward giraffes and gazelles and zebras edged with gold. Acacias bent and swayed in lighted grass, and lilac rollers flitted and twisted in the car's wake like pieces of sky torn loose. The trucks passed with jolts and rattles over the grass. Always the end of the world seemed a short ride away, to the hill where giraffes disappeared into the seas of light, or to that other, a purple mountain floating in reflections of gold, below which the sun was rising. From a channeled dip, we looked down on gazelles and zebras and all the world.

Half the supplies I'd ordered were in Nairobi when I returned. Enough to extend the tarp of the lean-to, and to give each man a blanket. In a new duffel were a cooking pot for Simon and my chimpanzee books. To get them past a gauntlet of thieves and soldiers, I would have to watch them without rest.

28

The Soldiers' Roadblocks

*Each traveling human group evolved a religion: a myth to explain
the creation of the world and our separation from other animals,
and the blueprints for a future. Every religion answers an uneasi-
ness, William James said.*

*Ecological anthropologists show the roots of each religion in the
land and in its use. Farmers find gods that bring rain and sun; their
festivals cycle with the harvest. Islanders worship the fire gods that
move earth and appease their volcanoes. We pray to gods to bring us
things, to create order from a dangerously disordered world. In us,
the animal must be suppressed; it does not believe in the rules of our
time.*

I rode back from the savanna of Kenya into Uganda, past telephone poles lying on road-thrown mud, past shambas and banana
trees, through red, red mud in a black-scarred road, with the
chimpanzees thumping and hooting in the back of my mind, and
invisible drums beating a pulse. We almost drove through the first
checkpoint without seeing it. The bus ground its gears in panic;
we fell forward and jerked to the side. The woman beside me
made a grab for her baby without looking, then picked up a bag of
food instead and left the baby on my lap, as if everyone thought
their children safer from the soldiers with a Mzungu.

The door opened. Two boy soldiers jumped on and walked up the aisle while another yelled commands at the driver. There was silence in the bus. It was frightening; maybe that is why Ugandans usually talk so loud and fast. A zebra caught at the ankle by a lioness stands patient and silent. If it pulls, it tears the leg and lives a death of hours instead of minutes, so the zebra freezes and acquiesces, and it is over.

The Africans moved only to take their papers out of the treasured plastic fragments that kept the papers from disintegrating, which would leave them nameless and illegal. Then they sat rigid as if every sneeze would bring a shout and a gunshot, as it used to do during Idi Amin's rule.

No whites had been killed for a long time in Uganda, but I moved as slowly as the other passengers in taking out my passport. The soldiers walked down the aisle. One jabbed his gun at an old man who couldn't get out his papers. The man's hands fell into his lap; he was so afraid, he couldn't move his fingers, but his face never changed. His neighbor reached over and unbuttoned his pocket, and when the soldiers stopped jabbing and one reached out a hand, the old man gave them the papers. They walked away holding the little bag, and his head sank. The silence deepened.

Without papers, he would be arrested at the next roadblock. The soldiers strolled through the bus, slapping the backs of the seats with the old man's papers. Each person waited, unbreathing, to get his or her papers back.

"Wewe." I looked up. They leaned against both the seat and my shoulder, in a cloud of banana beer, sweat, and the smell of anger. I handed them my passport. Snatching it, they huddled in the aisle, feeling the holes on the front, the seal inside, and looking at the picture. One soldier was young, about nine years old, and the other about thirteen. If they weren't untrained killers, they would have looked like kids swapping baseball cards. They flipped through, talking about the different colors of ink in the visas, and searched around at the end for more pictures or seals.

I held out my hand, and they looked at me in that strangely blank way people have when they're deciding whether to kill you, as if you are a deer, and understanding is suddenly impossible, or perhaps they are just thinking of you as a woman. It is hard to tell the difference sometimes, even in America.

The soldiers looked for a while, then one put the passport in my hand and they walked out of the bus, chattering about the colors and the picture. On the way past, one threw the old man's bag and papers on his lap. The old man sat still. The bag and papers separated and slid from his legs to the dusty floor. With the deceptively slow stride of the BuGanda, the soldiers had almost disappeared before the door creaked shut. The old man crouched to fish the bag out from between potato sacks, and someone leaned across the aisle to put the papers in his hands. As we drove away, another long silence fell.

With an almost audible thump each time we sighted a checkpoint, like telephone poles passing an express train, the bus moved from one to the next, away from the savanna and into the green hills of Uganda, watched from above by the monkey eagles. They looked much fiercer than the American bald eagle, which scowls through overhanging brows to keep the sun out of its eyes. The monkey eagles stared straight ahead with naked eyes, and only turned their heads to look down if a car made a small flutter with clothing or paper that might be something edible.

So, as we rode in the rattling bus on the red road, we saw above the eagles outlined against damp skies, looking out beyond the horizon. Even with the sun full on them, they were silhouettes of brown on black, mottles and dabs, and black eyes with black beaks. A cutout, really, more than birds. Passing through the tunnel of ruined telephone poles, hacked down by the Tanzanian army, with those folded statues sometimes perched atop, the bus seemed to move faster and faster over the ruts, and the world creaked and bounced and crashed, with the black shadows passing and eagles folded away and the next checkpoint coming up, itself black and folded.

Lions will withdraw from an injured member, and so will buffalo. One minute a one-eyed father to be climbed on, bitten in the cheek, whose tail drifting by becomes snake or sparrow or wildebeest leg. In the next second, if the injury gets worse, dripping from the eye, head held stiff and at thoughtful angle, he is, to them, something evil, and they slink away if he comes near. If he was less large, or more weak, they might cuff his face or bite at his neck or legs to chase him away. Weakness attracts predators. Hyenas, like vultures, can smell corruption from miles away, and will come loping with eager anticipation down paths of scent. Then the cubs and the lionesses will all be at risk, under siege, tainted by smell and proximity. There is a reason why they turn from their loved ones with fear.

At the second roadblock, only one soldier stepped on and shouted, waving the submachine gun at the driver. Lifting their bags, the passengers climbed down the stairs. Some of them carried things out, where the soldiers could take them, and some of them left their things in the bus, where the soldiers could steal them. I took my day pack because I wanted to know what happened to it, and abandoned the supplies to the roof of the bus. There was nothing in the books. More ecology, more hierarchy that could refine the data I had into a hypothesis. But the tarps, green and already dusty, I had wrapped tight against the longing glances of conductors and border guards.

*   *   *

We stood behind the bus, and the soldiers shouted and waved their guns until we faced them, like an execution line. Then they started at the far end, shouting and jabbing. As they finished with each person, he or she melted back to the bus, so there were only a few passengers left when the soldiers gathered in front of me. I held out my passport, open to the first page instead of the photo, and they shouted and shook it in my face. I took it back and opened the book to the picture.

One of the soldiers held a jug of banana liquor, and they swayed, red-eyed. Holding the passport upside down, the smaller one, with knobby knees, read aloud slowly. I didn't turn it right side up for him until he shoved the passport in my face, shouting fumes at me, pretending there was something wrong with it. They laughed and slapped their knees and held the jug to my mouth.

"No, thank you," I said in KiSwahili, and they laughed again and repeated what I'd said.

"You stay with us," they said.

I laughed and took back the passport. The chimps were drifting across the mountains. "No, I have to go. Thank you, though. Good-bye." And they said good-bye as I got on the bus, which had already started creeping away, as if eager to leave me as a gift to the gods for an easy passage. And yet people in the next town told me the buses before and after us were robbed.

We passed out of lighted dust and onto red roads, where banana trees hovered temporary beside mud huts. In the distance, a black mountain shone in clouds.

29

Chimpanzee Dung

A strange thing happens here during these luminous tides. The phosphorescence is itself a mass of life, sometimes protozoan its origin, sometimes bacterial, the phosphorescence I write of being probably the latter. Once this living light has seeped into the beach, colonies of it speedily invade the tissues of the ten thousand thousand sand fleas which are forever hopping on this edge of ocean. Within an hour the grey bodies of these swarming amphipods, these useful, ever hungry sea scavengers (Orchestia agilis; Talorchestia megalophthalma), show phosphorescent pin points, and these points grow and unite till the whole creature is luminous. The attack is really a disease, an infection of light. The process had already begun when I arrived on the beach on the night of which I am writing, and the luminous fleas hopping off before my boots were an extraordinary sight. . . . This infection kills them, I think; at least, I have often found the larger creature lying dead on the fringe of the beach, his huge porcelain eyes and water-grey body one core of living fire. Round and about him, disregarding, ten thousand kinsmen, carrying on life and the plan of life, ate of the bounty of the tide."

—Henry Beston, The Outermost House

A different forest closed behind us, trees darkened with water into solid walls of shadow. From the ground rose a fine dust, washed from the canopy and still falling from bark and leaf in halos of thicker air. As we walked into this new darkness, handfuls of bark crumbled from the trees and clung wet and cold to our fingers like flies holding on with all six wet feet. A drop landed on the back of my neck and ran down with its skin of sharp dust, and then another, until I was wet and dusty, as if a clown had thrown pails of water and sawdust at my back. I had waited at the gorilla research center for Dr. Tom to come back, miserable with a sore stomach. Then Olin had gathered the men and sent them down with me to the chimp research site.

In all deserted homes, the wind seems to blow through with a gray air. The clearing was empty of all but crushed ferns and the log we'd used as a fireplace, and a few columns of burnt wood standing from the mud. Gabriel clicked his tongue.

"Eeehh. Poachers." He pushed the wood with one foot and said, "Tchah." Then, looking at me, "The chimpanzees, they will go."

The chimpanzees had gone. The valley was empty and flat, smaller than I remembered.

"Memsahib, we must to go back." A murmur of anger swelled to a Rukiga shout. "Wewe, you are a bad man," someone said into the air.

"Eh."

I turned and saw a L'Hoest's monkey. Thudding like a horse, it galloped through the clearing past us and into the leaves without looking around.

In the L'Hoesti's wake, as if pulled forward by a vacuum, the canopy chirped and rustled. Almost silently, as though in small groups, redtails lost the joie de vivre that flung them from branch to branch with a great crash; a few landed near camp and sat quietly for two minutes, then jumped after the others. I sat hunched on the wet log, sweating. The doctor in Kenya called it typhoid fever, though I'd had the vaccination. Air as thick as cotton wrapped around my face, cold and clinging.

"Memsahib, you must to go to Kagote. The chimpanzees, they will be there."

"Wewe, it is that they are here."

Monkeys chuckled in a diminuendo ripple. Three redtails sat nearly touching on the end of a branch at ten meters. Two ran up out of sight when I raised the binoculars; one stayed and fed on leaves. Thunder rolled with a sudden shock that shook the earth. A hidden blue monkey barked, and rain fell without movement. Slowly, a L'Hoesti strolled across the valley and hopped into an omufa tree right below camp. I watched flashes of black arm and yellow fruit among the leaves, then she chirped and jumped down to the ferns, invisible.

Trees dripped and swayed, and the mud ran in rivers of dull reflections. Startled by the silence, I looked up. The men had stopped arguing.

"Kamumbo?"

He looked expressionless at Gabriel, and Gabriel said, "He say we should go to Kagote, memsahib."

"Simon, what do you think we should do?"

Simon set dishes and cups on the drying table, untouched under the rotting tree. "Eh, memsahib. The chimpanzees, it is that they will come. We must to stay here," he said halfheartedly.

Gabriel pushed at his arm. "No, memsahib. It is that we must to go to Kagote. Kamumbo, he say there are many chimps there, where he live."

I looked at Kamumbo. He stood without expression, neither looking at us nor looking away. Gabriel had always wanted to move up to the top of the mountain, away from the poachers and smugglers.

"Akit?"

He shrugged.

Patrick elbowed past him. "No, you must to stay here. The chimpanzees will come back, you will see."

I thought of the hike up the mountain, of the shouting crowds, and of Batuko's hills. Movement isn't easy for the flawed of eye, and my stomach ached like a stubbed toe. Chimpanzees had slept beside this camp.

"This man, he say this because he want you to stay in this place," said Simon, reversing himself.

"Tchah."

"Wewe."

"Maybe we should stay here until we can find another valley with fruit trees up there?" I said.

It was a question, but Akit and Patrick stretched the second tarp over its branches. "Wewe. Come here and help us with this!" Akit shouted. Simon and Gabriel climbed over crushed bushes and leaned their weight on the poles. Kamumbo stood with hands in pockets, disappeared from sight.

We put our bags on wet bushes and unpacked, enough for the night. Gabriel and Simon tied one of the new tarpaulins onto stakes, and stood back to admire it. "Eeeh." "Eeeeh, eh."

The tent pole bent into a triangle and flattened the tent. I pulled out the pole and looked at the loops. I tried the pole in both directions, over and over again. Suddenly, without reason, it popped into an arch and lifted the tent into shape, streaked with mud on its sides like stripes of dried blood.

Simon leaned over the branches that had been a poacher's fire. Blank-faced, Akit and Patrick strode into the forest to collect firewood. "Can I do anything?" I asked, staring at the tent as it lifted with a whoosh of air. "No, memsahib." "No, memsahib," they said together before I'd finished. Notebook in my pants, I poked the side of the tent, waited, and then wandered off to look under the fig trees. The fruit hung green and hard, unchanged in size.

Dark and crumbled, a lobe of chimpanzee dung sprawled beneath a branch. Squatting on the path beside camp, I poked it apart with a stick. One hundred twenty-eight entero seeds, one omusingati, and two very small seeds that had begun to sprout sprawled in the black mud. Kamumbo stood over it with me, looking down. I asked if it was about a month old. He nodded his head once — up, down, up.

"Eh, memsahib. This say that the chimpanzees, they come and see this poacher, the bad man. They run run away and do not come back," Gabriel insisted.

"But this chimp was standing still." If a chimp had been frightened by the poacher, it would have shot out liquid scat while running and screaming; the dung would have scattered. It had come, marked the place we had stolen, and left. The chimpanzees were just gone, eating fruit somewhere in the rain shadow. Entero and omusingati probably grew on the other side of the mountain too, where figs would flow as ours had ebbed.

30

Chimpanzee Socioecology

The American transcendentalists, though religious, wrote about nature as it was seen, unfiltered through gods, with the precision of Fabre or Pliny. The world was miraculous in itself. Every now and then, if one watched long enough, in the right place, the eye would open and time would halt. Changes of light operate upon us, opening and closing the pupil, sending firings of electricity to the visual cortex.

As if the rain had washed away all life, or dissolved it into the particles flung back as mud and dust twenty feet above the floor, the valley lay as empty as a sieve. The forest, during the rains, drifted in a haze of dried mud and insect parts like any desert.

Gabriel said he and Kamumbo would go to Kagote to look for ripening trees. As they left the clearing, Kamumbo high-trotting over the roots and his friend striding at half speed beside him, a group of monkeys chuckled and grunted in the short tree near camp. I looked up. Two sat in a crotch a few inches from the ground, one walked beneath them, and another perched in a bush two meters from Simon. They sat there, looking out into space like Kamumbo did, with absolute peace. I unwound the notebook from my pants carefully, but the monkeys didn't move.

I sat unbreathing on the wet log. Green light filtered through the canopy and sharpened into separate columns on each monkey, a rare burst of pure light. Their heads bowed as if in prayer; they sank into their perches like Buddha rising and spreading into the air from his bodhi tree.

"*12:34 H female unknown tree ½ m sitting. H female unknown tree ½ m sitting. H male unknown bush 1 m sitting. H juvenile ground sitting.*" One of them looked at me and looked away. I sat on my backpack and waited. For half an hour, gray monkeys sat without eating, then stood and strolled away. "*13:04 H f1 unknown tree sit end. H f2 unknown tree sit end. H m unknown bush sit end. H j ground sit end.*"

The monkeys might have been the last of a migration from the foothills. The forest quieted into stillness again. Sighing, I set the notebook on the day pack and crawled, aching, into the tent. In a small stationery store beside Nairobi's market, I'd found a green notebook with a grid of columns and rows, and a softer notebook to fit in my pants. With a strange reluctance, I pulled the plastic bag of books from the backpack and crawled backward out of the tent into the mud settled on the log.

The log burned with cold through my poncho. The books looked like an optical illusion in the rain forest. In the plastic bag they'd been safe from the dusts of Kenya and the mud of Uganda alike, and they perched on my lap as glossy and clean and chemical-scented as if I were browsing in a bookstore, seated on a stepladder, and only imagining myself in the rain forest. The fire crackled and spat. I touched one new cover with fingers that looked dirty, and creaked the book open. The men hushed their laughter and receded, as if I were only now doing important work.

The splintered box and Tom's accumulation of papers on the

forest monkeys had already shown me how to take some kinds of data on height, vocalizations, foods eaten, and age/sex composition of groups. But I must have been looking for something more because I now hunted from beginning to end of Ghiglieri and Goodall. Setting the books carefully on their bag, which was already condensing inside, I sat for a long time without thinking. The men stirred and murmured, stricken with too long a silence and needing to comment on what I was doing or perhaps arguing again in subvocal protest that we should leave instead of hiking in aimless search after the chimps. Ghiglieri had found a fruiting fig, and sat before it to wait for them, so my disinclination to move had served me well.

With a few additions from Ghiglieri's work, and some from the wooden crate at Tom's site on vocalizations, I had a full research program. I hadn't realized that in socioecology one needs no thesis and no questions to prove; one can simply record facts to show a trend. In ecological theory, if foods are limited and several species eat the same high-demand foods, they must separate their feeding techniques. Often, smaller animals can feed higher in the canopy than larger species that might otherwise force them away from the food. I guessed that the redtails would feed highest and the chimps lowest in the trees. I would study competition for food among the chimps and the blue, redtail, and L'Hoest's monkeys by recording the foods they ate and where they found them.

My stomach ached with a steady throb. Holding it with one hand, I breathed in shallow bursts. The typhoid medicine hadn't helped. Rain fell as hard and as cold as poured buckets of ice. As the trees dripped with a secondary rain, sheets of water rolling from one leaf to another, I rewrote the sentences from my old orange notebook into the graphed columns of the other in data form, to see what would happen. The books lay on my lap, hard and shiny, so clean that all the forest looked dirty. For a long time, I thought, afraid to continue with something missing, watching droplets of water sliding down the trunk of our tree. Flames lit them gold and white and with small flickers of shadow. The tree shimmered as if swaying. If I found a question I wanted to ask, nothing could be added after research began. I could only write, in the margins, ad libitum stories of behaviors I wished I had included. If the primates came back.

Setting the books, still open, on the day pack, I pushed both notebooks into my waistband. They dug into my stomach as I bent to crawl over the mud and into the tent again. Inside the big backpack, under a few other books, I found a box. Worm medicine, aspirin, and the condoms the men had asked for first.

Folding the dirty notebook inside the one with graphed pages, and sliding that into the day pack, I stood and held the cardboard box toward three men in clothes dyed brown by river water. In a formal triangle, the men stood facing me. The tallest accepted the box with the palms of both hands, bowing slightly. Behind us fell the canopy of the rain forest, dark green and glittering with water. Captured in oil, the exchange could have been Queen Victoria accepting a gift on some state tour, or Dr. Livingstone shaking hands with Stanley. The box, like most symbolic presentations, was small, the only one I could find in Kenya.

31

African Wives

We developed agriculture first, from nomadic gatherers to settled city-states, with new government and laws and rules of trade. Already there was less time to spend with the children, but the women carried the babies in slings on their backs for years while they worked. Infants learned the chores by heart long before they emerged from their chrysalis, by the movement of muscles in rhythm. Bend, chop, pull, move on. And they slept in one bed together at night, safe from lions.

Wet pants clung to ankle and knee. Too tired and full to wash, I sat on the log, staring at the fire. My stomach hurt with a pure, unending throb. Water fell from the tree and exploded in the fire. I leaned forward to duck the smoke, eyes burning, and the pain suddenly eased. Tilting forward, I rested my forehead on my knees. The stabs of pain ebbed away as if bipedalism itself had created them. The notebook bent in my waistband, pushing against my chest. I held my breath as if holding time still. The chimpanzees hadn't come back. It was too late to study anything else. I had been wrong again. But for the first time in my life, I wasn't sorry. It was as if I had eaten of one food and had no need of another but was starving still for the first. I could have existed on air, if only I saw them again.

Simon looked at me. With his bare hand, he poked the fire, a quick slap into the white embers. A column of flame and falling sparks burst like fireworks against the ghost of a tree. I was afraid he was going to argue against the bottom-of-the-mountain men again that we should leave and go back up the mountain near his home, though Gabriel and Kamumbo hadn't found anything, but instead he pushed his lower lip forward in storytelling pose.

"Me, I was like a girl."

The men settled into the grass mat, and Gabriel lowered the kerosene lantern to a glow. Simon wrapped his arms around threadbare knees; the yarn poked like whiskers from his elbows. He had allowed himself to sit with me because he needed a place of honor to tell the story. Full of beans and potatoes — scorching away the day's rain — and sorrow for the chimps, I straightened, set the notebooks on the backpack, wrapped my arms around my own frayed knees, and listened.

"Me, I was like a girl."

The forest stirred with water, dripping insects and still-held dew into cups and pools.

Simon thought he was born long before Idi Amin's war, well into the British reign. In those days, Uganda was rich. Every man was both farmer and cattle herder; every woman had goats and chickens, and her own garden.

Simon's mother lived in a mud-and-branch hut that her husband lent her when they married. It was on the side of a hill in a slashed-and-burned clearing inside the forest. She farmed the land and sold the extra food at the market. Her husband took the money, as do most BaKiga men, and gave her back a little for kerosene, cooking oil, and clothing. When Simon was born, she was very happy to have a son to take care of her in her old age, since a wife must leave her hut and land when her husband dies. For three years, she carried Simon on her back in a sling of red fabric, and fed him milk and beans with potatoes. When he was old enough, she gave him work. So Simon, because he had no sisters, carried water from the river every day, and fed the chickens, and cooked food for his father. In season, he climbed to market with his mother and helped her sell beans, potatoes, yams, squash, and sometimes peas.

Simon's father married a second wife. The second wife had no children, so she told Simon's mother that Simon had to help her too. For more years, Simon did these chores. Then his mother divorced her husband. Leaving Simon behind, as BaKiga women must, she took her cooking pot and two dresses, and walked home to her father's village. Simon stayed and was both son and daughter to the second wife. As he grew older, he helped his father with the garden too, cutting down trees and pulling out roots so they could turn over the soil and plant farther into the forest. Finally, late in life, Simon married, either because his father paid or because he had a small salary from helping other people. With the wife, he became a man. BaKiga men cannot touch their wives' pots or make their own food, so Simon stopped cooking, and carrying water, and feeding chickens, and did only men's jobs. He cleared the land, carried sacks of potatoes to market for his wife to sell, and worked on other farmers' lands for money to buy her a dress and cloth, and plastic dishes. "And now," said Simon, throwing his head back and laughing, "me, I have two girls, but I must to be a good cook for the WaZungu."

"Eeeh," the others said. Then Gabriel told a story about a man who had too many wives, and how Gabriel had tried to help him by becoming a second husband to the youngest one, and Simon laughed and said, "Wewe," and even Akit smiled a bit.

Water hissed and sizzled in the fire, and the tree above burst seeds with a pop. Small green balls, heated in the steam, pattered down and themselves disappeared in the fire with noise.

32

The Fig Tree

Since the first cave paintings documented migration and family structure, humans have studied animals. These studies have always been divided between necessary fact and unchecked myth. While Aristotle, Pliny, and Aelian, then Linnaeus, Fabre, and Darwin, recorded the world with few mistakes and settled it into an almost-unchanged order, other naturalists sat in cages in the wild and wrote about their own families, as if animals had evolved from weaker versions of ourselves.

When the behaviorists took over science, it was in reaction to the anthropomorphists. Only facts could be recorded, and only those facts that held true across the species. We were not interested in behavioral variation—only in the essence of a species. To eliminate extraneous detail, the behaviorists conducted experiments.

Primates have always been a focus of study; their followers cross academic lines, from animal behavior studies to anthropology, sociology, and psychology. It is difficult to study instinct in an animal with so much variation. No one can say which behaviors an infant learns from its mother and which are instinctive to the species. A scientist named Harry Harlow took infants away from their mothers at birth and raised them in a cage.

In his keynote film, which persuaded the scientific world of the 1950s that animals need love, a white man in a lab coat walked down the aisle. He was the picture of his time, in black-and-white film, *the eternal father figure, rigid with power. Like a Norman Rockwell subject, he was severe but pleasant. In his world, children behaved with eagerness within their respective roles, the boys idealistic about sports and America, the girls about boys and motherhood. Harry Harlow explained the experiment's origins and said that the original study had been expanded. Scientists were interested in learning how lack of socialization affected animals.*

Harlow rested his hand on a cage and said, "And here we see the result," or words to that effect. It was a pleasant picture. He beamed a benign, controlled smile at the television. Inside the cage, a young monkey sat with its back to a wide-eyed wire doll. Arms wrapped around legs, it stared at the floor. It ignored the scientific singsong above but seemed to be listening to something else. Harlow told his listeners that the infants were depressed. As he stood there, the monkey began to rock forward. Arms clasping its flashlight-size body, the monkey knocked its head against the mesh of the cage.

The television panned slowly past Dr. Harlow, down the lab. It was a cozy room, simple and well lighted. In some cages, the infants sat still; in others they stirred as if pulled by a voice into different rhythms or put a body part in their mouth. Some were missing a finger; others a hand.

Rain poured down, ten inches, then fourteen. The coffee can in the bath enclosure filled with dirty water, then overflowed, then ran a fountain of dark water into the air that crashed down the hill long after the rain had ended. A lone blue monkey, chuckling softly in threat, foraged through the trees toward camp. "We must to go, memsahib. It is that we must to go up the mountain." The valley hung motionless. Kamumbo neither glanced at any compass point nor left on his mysterious errands, so I sat in camp as the light filtered through, crouched with hands in the fire.

There was no way to know when the primates would come

back. No one had ever studied the seasonality of fruit trees in these mountains; most of them hadn't even been recorded, though they were as old as the dinosaurs. Kamumbo might have known only the trees in his section of the forbidden forest. He shrugged when I looked at him. I sat shivering on the log, notebook in my hand and nothing to write in it.

Branches crashed and shook. I tried not to jerk upright but did anyway, as if pulled upward on strings. Chuckles and coos and screeches of rage echoed in the empty valley. Redtails poured through the canopy toward camp. They leaped and swept and swam through the leaves, blue monkeys following behind in syncopation, bass drums to snare. A group of L'Hoesti strode through at a diagonal, unattached, and passed by without fuss. The fruit trees were peppered with hard green fruits, but the monkeys reached for them in a hysteria of jumps and threats and screaming-runs-away. Kamumbo disappeared without looking back.

A L'Hoesti male jumped into the fig near a blue male, as if all the laws and social contracts had dissolved. He grabbed a handful of fruits and dropped them before they touched his mouth. Chuckling, the blue monkey lunged at him, and the L'Hoesti dove into the tree beside the fig. As if patrolling, the blue monkey faded in and out of the canopy, ducking its head. Facedown, a L'Hoesti female climbed into the fig. Sliding up and down the trunk, she reached with nervous hands to pick and pluck. While she ate, she cowered and turned her face away from the screaming crowd. The blue monkey sat with his back to her and all her darts and rushes. He climbed out of the tree without eating, but she scrambled silently away when a male L'Hoesti jumped in.

Notebook page filled again, I waded through roots to the south fruit trees and saw clusters of the figs suddenly round and light, sour pebbles grown to green Ping-Pong balls again. They weren't edible yet; only animals separated from their group's food finders would have been hungry enough to try. I didn't know how long the fruit would take to ripen, but under the fig tree, with the redtails staring down at me, chirring a warning, I let go of the earth and tap-danced with arms in the air for the first time in my life.

"Raf, raf, raf, raf," they shrieked, and clattered the branches like castanets.

The redtails followed me back to camp as if checking the trees themselves, and then passed on, too fast for the ear, into the distance. Quietly, a lone blue monkey walked through the canopy to camp and sat without eating in a tree. A black-and-white colobus growled, making a *wak-wak-wak* sound in the south. Thunder rolled through the clearing, then drizzle, then the rain stopped with a click.

"The empundu, they will not come back. They go far, far away. They do not like to stay. We must to go."

"I will watch the monkeys, because I know that they are here. If the empundu come, that will be good."

"Eeeeh," Gabriel said with doubt.

Pulling the yellow notebook reluctantly from a wet waistband, I read through the notes, correlating first with last sighting of each monkey into lines on the grid of the green one. One line for each tree entered by the subject, neatly pigeonholing chaos into simple data. Height in tree, time, date, species of tree, age, sex, species of primate, foods eaten, if seen, time at each level of the forest.

The tree lifted over the fire, branches wide, engorged with rain and new seeds. It swayed, bent, and dipped in a stray shaft of air from the valley. Trickling through its leaves, smoke rose.

Kamumbo shifted, and we looked across to the other hill. In dark glimpses, a chimpanzee moved across the valley, away from the fig tree, seen more in the turning of leaves and the corner of the eye than as a shape. I heard my heart beating. Breath seemed unnecessary. Without sound, the shadow disappeared. The wet air burned like fire on my legs.

33

L'Hoesti Lost

There was nothing in the morning. No chimpanzee call, no scream of excitement near the fig tree. I climbed the mud to the toilet pit through a gauntlet of monkeys that crashed and sprayed water and chirped and warbled and chuckled threats. Swaying in the branches, a group of redtails ran and play-fought and pulled fruit down and ate with nervous hands. Leaves scattered as they screamed and bit at one another's tail.

Outside the pit, a group of blue monkeys squatted in quiet rows, thumbing their chins and watching me, close and calm while I was separated from my notebook. Leaning forward to peer at me, they muttered in quiet discussion among themselves.

As I left to find my notebook, they chuckled in mild threat, and crashed after me through the trees. One by one, discarded old males crept into the tree above camp and onto the stump beside it, and foraged through the moss, alone. Infants crawled to the edge of their branch to look at me, and mothers tugged them back. As I slid down to the fire, males chuckled and barked. A group whirled into battle, then slowly, without conclusion, settled into the dusk of morning. The men looked at me but didn't say anything about leaving.

Kamumbo stood at the edge of camp, visible for once. I realized he was waiting for me. Without my backpack, I followed him north through a rain of leaves still sifting through the canopy. Branches shifted and invisible male monkeys leaned forward to chuckle a sleepy warning at me. *Mzungu coming*—member of the tribe who changes things.

On a log by the path lay another old chimp scat, as if a chimp had marked the territory against us or the poacher. I pulled it apart with two sticks and found forty entero pits, six figs, and one ombakumba. It would be easy to live on these fragments of the wild; many doctoral candidates, after months without sightings, had switched from behavioral studies to fecal analysis. But scat in the rain forest usually fell between roots or washed away. Only ones that fell on the path could be seen in skeleton form, by the seeds they left behind.

"One month?" I asked in KiSwahili. Kamumbo nodded his head once and disappeared. Sprawled from their original oblong into the path, the entero lay, orange and lozenge-sized; the figs tear-shaped and fibrous; and the ombakumba oval, smooth, and gray, with a point on one end, all of them clean, with only the faintest smell of chimpanzee fur and sugar.

I squatted in the path and bent forward to wrap the scat and seeds together in an envelope. Leaves dropped and swished in the south as quietly as if a chimp were gliding through them. Standing with a gasp, I scuttled along the south trail for a few meters. Something barked at me. I froze, then backed up, turning my eyes to the ground.

Calm and unhurried, with no exuberant leaps, a red-tail climbed a tree next to the fig and disappeared. Something chuckled and then crashed away. I walked on through the rain. Chimps ate redtails; the monkeys wouldn't have stayed near the fig with a predator in it. My pants gaped in front, letting in cold air. I was losing weight. Through columns of light, torn leaves spiraled, gold, then black, then gold again.

A L'Hoesti climbed into the fig tree near camp and picked at green fruit, chirping in a metallic undertone. As if her stomach hurt, sitting with that unripe fruit in her hand, she lowered her face and groaned. Patrick said the chirp was her way of calling her family, and the moan was a sound of distress or pain. He had seen a L'Hoest's monkey in the field of a farmer he knew. A group of monkeys had been eating the beans, so the farmer had set a wire snare. Patrick and some friends heard the moans and, thinking a child had been hurt, followed the cries through the garden. The monkey sat groaning as they watched, until the farmer found it. It must have looked like a child still, because the farmer touched its arm though the machete was raised for a killing blow. As fingers reached fur, the L'Hoesti bit him. With one blow, the farmer killed it. Before the farmer had touched it, Patrick said, the monkey had been crying, arm raised to its eyes.

The female left her tree and wandered into the mists of the canopy, the still, mechanical cricket cries drifting back, then muffling into silence.

Yellow beak with scarlet tip, black-crested head, white tail with a black band around its end, a turaco sat in the fig tree as if none of these primates could eat it.

34
Old Chimp

Before the 1950s, a firm hand was taken with human babies. Hospitals put the babies in nurseries, in rows like potted plants. "Don't pick them up when they cry," doctors said. "It's just reinforcement." The babies lay silent after a few days. It was normal for premature babies to rest in isolation boxes for months, until a doctor found that infants touched a few times a day grew faster. Emotions evolved to push us toward behaviors that would help us thrive and produce reproductively successful offspring. Science believed that once the need for these emotions dissipated, the emotions themselves would disappear. Infants were warm, safe from predators, and well fed in the incubators. They should have had no need of their mothers. But we evolved in the rain forest, held close to our mothers' bodies. Lions lurk before blind eyes, jackals wait behind trees for a moment's inattention. We were born with the desire for warm arms.

Into this hygienic world, Jane Goodall wrote In the Shadow of Man. A chimpanzee mother raised her sons and daughters with tickling and laughter and a daily grooming.

"Anthropomorphic," the scientific world called Jane Goodall's book.

Our clearing shone with mud. Beans burning on my knee, I turned to listen to crashes in the southwest. When I looked back, a blue monkey sat in the fig tree across from camp, eating a pale red fruit.

A small female L'Hoesti ran from top to bottom of the tree as the blue male walked nervously out and then back in. On opposite sides, they sat like bookends, holding one fig each, and eating fast. The blue monkey barked.

Without beginning or end, a chimpanzee screamed from the northwest. I jerked upright, blotching the notebook, and the monkeys scattered. Turning, the L'Hoesti ran back, snatched a fig, and jumped out of the tree. She hovered, outlined against the sky for a second, in one of the only clearings in the forest, a curled silhouette with one black hand clenched into a fist; then her body fell into the shadows.

Six leaf shadows changed themselves into blue monkeys and crashed away through the canopy. A knotted twist of branch unfurled into a redtail. From the north, chimpanzees called, very close, like foghorns in the mist.

For an hour I sat before the fire, peering into the dark morning. At last, with a sigh, one hand on an aching stomach, I hauled up the sodden backpack and stood, a failure in some elusive way. Kamumbo told me the chimpanzees sounded like they were near, but they were far away. They would be here tomorrow. All this without saying a word, just pointing and shrugging and waving one arm, but someone translated anyway as I left for the north fig, stomach pounding with a gentle pain.

An echo of silence fell on the valley. The last bird sank down out of its flutter into the canopy. The monkeys must have slid away. Even the trees seemed to hold their drips of water, and rested one-dimensional, glossy with unshed rain. Or perhaps the world had slowed enough for me to focus my eyes.

I sat at the fig, alone and silent, with the great tree arched over me and sunshine filtering into its clearing through the skyscraper-high canopy like columns of light through stained-glass windows onto a stone floor.

My fingers were frozen in the morning, locked into claws on the sleeping bag. I crawled past the men to the fire. They sat with hands folded, waiting. After breakfast, I sat on, waiting with them. At fifty minutes past eleven, when I was sure the chimps had passed the foothills, a tree dipped, then flung its leaves upward. Bowing down again, it accepted some weight and, rising, held its breath for a hushed moment.

For a second, the hillside rested. I shifted one sleeping leg and leaned my weight on the other without moving a leaf. Lowering itself, then soaring again, the tree flung a dark bundle into the sky. Fruit rattled to the ground like rain. The men sat, quiet. Two chimps called from across the valley. "Waaaaggh, waaaaaggh." The call spread from one hill to the next, so quiet an echo it seemed merely an afterprint of memory.

35

So Many Cars

With the production of Darwin's elegant proofs, the study of human separation turned dramatically. Scientists could no longer say that humans differed from animals because the former have souls and the latter do not. Science wanted concrete proof: beaks and orchid leaves and wingless birds. We are animals, he had proved, with hearts and lungs and genitals; we were evolved from fur.

Refuting the genes of turkeys and giraffes and chimpanzees that we carry in us, scientists then cut us off from other species by saying that humans are the only animals that use tools. Even though several species use tools by instinct, with unvarying similarity, this argument held until Jane Goodall followed chimpanzees in Tanzania's Gombe Stream National Park. A famous archaeologist told her to look for the use of tools by the chimpanzees. Goodall climbed hills in the rain forest for months before she saw a chimpanzee walking to a termite mound. The chimp carried a blade of grass to the termite mound, scratched open one of the tunnels with one fingernail, and pushed the grass stem into the hole. The termites clung to the grass as they attacked, and the chimp pulled the blade out and ate the termites. The chimpanzee ate not only termites that day, on its spoon of grass, but humanity's definition of itself.

Perhaps, science responded, we are the only animal that makes tools. But that group of chimpanzees gathered moss to use as sponges, *soaking water from narrow crevices in trees. They trimmed blades of grass to the size of termite holes, and tore branches from trees to throw at hunted prey.*

And in Mahale, other chimpanzees carried rocks to set in rows beneath trees of nuts. They'd search, sometimes for miles, for hammer or anvil, testing the smoothness of a rock's surfaces, its graspability. If one had not seen the chimps eating, one would think this residue a sign of religion, rocks in rows with their hammers laid within hollows, the scattered offering of shells brushed aside into a thick carpet below them, one primitive statue after another, in a circle.

Icy water trickled up from the ground through the waterproof poncho, by some sort of osmosis soaking the seat of my pants and gluing canvas to skin. The tree, as lighted as the savanna, let small curtains of slanted sun fall to the bushes below. Its roots must have gripped the hill like a corset, holding ground as wide as its farthest leaves. Nothing grew near the fig but bushes and tree-high ferns. An ant ran up my legs and hovered busily by my knee. I shook my foot and squeezed the ant down and indignantly out. Trying not to move, I clamped a finger on the hem to stop the insect from running back up as it turned and huffed over my boot.

Like the beating of a heart, the foothills rose and fell behind us without sound. Out of the shadows, a chimp climbed, looking over its shoulder. Something had fallen heavily through the leaves in the south. The fig tree blazed in the sun above the canopy.

Narrow and dark, the old female drooped on the trunk, lower lip sagging. A bald strip shone black on her head as she tilted to peer to the south, then down at us. Staring over her shoulder, the old chimp walked up, then down the tree. I hid my eyes and my breath. Silently, she pulled herself into the canopy. Leaves dipped and shadows altered and she was gone. Chimps called in the distance, a long, calm wail. The air smelled of sunlight and ashes.

I folded my poncho and sat down to wait, eyes held down on the ground. The tree beside the fig didn't stir this time. Two chimps slid quietly from it into the fig tree. The one on top jumped out again, and the other slid down. Hunched and hasty, she picked figs with both hands. Balls of fruit bulged in her mouth. She climbed down, dribbling bits of fruit from stretched lips, and the other disappeared with her, empty-handed.

Redtails crossed the valley, chirping with suppressed emotion. Another group crashed out of the leaves with screams and great leaps and followed them. A redtail from each group chirped, then fell silent.

Like lava boiling in a volcano, the tree dropped its seeds into the fire with a sequence of hisses. Kamumbo had told the men about the chimps. "Eh, memsahib," they said as I crashed through the trees.

The tree over camp dripped dark water with a steady liquid sound; it bent and gnarled overhead into sprays of parasitic ferns and water-killed moss. The path shone beneath it, twisting into the undergrowth in a river of footprints smoothed by mud. The forest gurgled like a stream, millions of trees releasing the rain in slow afterthoughts. Speeches flowed in celebration, nothing about animals, just essays on a theme. Africans fill in the color of their lives for one another until a whole village has the same experience. They always, as in any poor country, tell of great plans for the future.

"Chimpanzees," I wrote with a star, in a column in the back of the notebook, where I'd listed the men's workdays and the daily weather. All the primate hours logged added up to less than a quarter of an undergraduate thesis.

Graduate school was receding farther and farther from my reach, but something was here, only a fingertip away.

"Me, I want a suit like the WaZungu," Patrick said, looking from the corner of his eye. He repeated it twice because the clearing was as blurred and indistinct as a subway across the world. I didn't want to talk while the chimps' bright eyes still flashed in my memory, but he was about to ask me to buy one for him. Firelight flickered across his face and vanished into darkness past his arms. In our bubble of light, he glowed without movement, vibrating even as he sat. The other men hushed into the stillness of a BaKiga honoring a scam.

I said, "Me, I do not like the WaZungu clothes. The suit, it is very uncomfortable." They sat up straight. Sacrilege. BaKiga would slave longer to buy a suit than a wife. "I like these pants better." I plucked my army pants, and the men subsided, shaking their heads. Patrick tucked his hands behind his neck again.

The forest settled into its nighttime silence. Even the leaves stilled as air chilled and sank down again, clouds dying to be reborn.

"Me, I will go to America and buy many clothings."

"Eh, Patrick, you would not like it. The city, it is so big. You walk like this." I set the notebook on my knees and mimicked rush-hour stop-and-go walking. "These people, there are so many that you walk like this." Clearly they did not believe me. Why would people walk only in one place? "There are so many cars here, and houses here, you can walk only in a space so big. Here, you have three cars or four, but in America there are many thousands, and, eeeeh, it is so hard to walk."

Patrick cocked an eye at me, and Akit stayed tactfully silent. "Eeeeeeeh, there are not so many cars."

Simon jumped to his feet. "It is s-s-so, as memsahib said." He was so angry with Patrick that he stammered. "Me, I go to Kampala. The army, they come to my home and make it so that I walk to Kampala, eeeeeeh, so far. And...and me, I see, I see cars, so many cars. Eeeeeh, so many cars. Even fifty cars, I see in Kampala."

Patrick-the-educated stuck out his lip. "Me, I think there are not so many cars. Kayonza, it has two cars only. And the motorcycle of the gold smuggler." Silence fell for a second, like the ebb of tide between one wave and another.

"Simon, which army took you to Kampala?"

"Eeeeeh, memsahib, I do not know. Eeeeh, but I was scared. There are so many cars, and"—he glared at Patrick—"so many houses."

I tried to describe a city, but the three men who had never seen anything larger than a village didn't believe me. Even Simon shook his head a bit when I spoke of skyscrapers. In awe first, then in disbelief. With a shock, I realized that Patrick, who spoke English as well as I did and worked like an insider trader for profit, was picturing sixty huts piled one on top of the other.

Akit interrupted. "Memsahib, how much to buy a wife?"

"Ah." I swelled. "In America, there is no price for the bride. The woman, she chooses the husband." A moment's silence fell.

"Memsahib," Patrick said with reverence, "I must to go to America. Me, I will take so many wives that I will drink beer all day."

"Eeeeeeeeh."

The fire flickered and silenced us, and it was a while before Patrick, perhaps because I had been glad to write down some of their traditions and Rukiga words, told me about the dead.

"One must never disobey one's parents. A parent who is constantly disobeyed will return after death and kill the offspring by suffocation. This can be cured only by holding burning onions or bicycle-tire rubber under the nose of the undutiful child. The spirit asks through the afflicted one, in the voice of the dead, why the bad smell is being held to its nostrils, and then is gone."

The fire hissed and released its own smoke, and we watched the flames rise and fall. Neither book nor voice was needed at night. The events of the day flowed past in the movement of light through gases, and released into the air with them, leaving the sleep free for other dreams.

36

Warning

The visual cortex is a thin, two-dimensional sheet of neurons, and the neuronal activity across its surface is a fairly faithful projection of the neuronal activity across the retina....

"Only when the eyes are jointly fixated at exactly the same depth as a given object will the two images of that object be in exactly the same relative position on each of the two retinas.

"[Fixation cells are] liberally peppered across the surface of the visual cortex.... Any given fixation cell is maximally active only when the spot of cortex where it lies is receiving identical input activity from each of the two eyes. [Fixation cells inform the brain when] the left and right images match perfectly....

"We possess not only 'fixation cells' scattered throughout the visual cortex, but also 'near cells' and 'far cells.' These latter are cells that respond, respectively, to left-right correspondences slightly in front of and slightly behind one's current fixation depth.... The near and far cells give notice of objects just fore and just aft of that primary planelike locus. This allows us to have a simultaneous awareness of the presence of several objects at several different depths simultaneously. This is what finally brings us the full-fledged stereo vision most humans enjoy."

—*Paul Churchland*, The Engine of Reason

*   *   *

Sweat and dead insects crusted my shirt and scratched my skin as I walked back to camp. The bald chimpanzee had never returned. In each direction of the compass, nests and feces had melted back into the forest. I walked the east path in a fury of search, staggering and slipping and wrenching my ankles between roots.

I slithered and almost fell and caught myself and fell anyway, then paused, panting, on hands and knees, with beetles struggling between my fingers. The blood thumped furiously in my skull.

I lifted my head to plot a new course of bipedalism. A small silver tree twisted in a patch of sunlight before me. Fragments of figs lay piled about the bulbous roots. I slithered upright on loose vines and held on to a bole, staring at the tree. The scent of rotting figs rose as sweet and unmistakable as the smell of one's own home. Faintly, the scent of feces wafted upward from the ground on which I'd fallen.

A column of light fell on the tree and its grasping roots. The tree must have been the offspring of some fig so large that the decades after its death hadn't filled in the clearing yet. The young tree was winning the battle for light. My sore stomach wrenched with a pang that stopped my breath.

While I had been sitting without hope beneath the tree in which I'd last seen the chimps, eight to ten hours a day staring into empty leaves for the smallest movement, this tree had filled, ripened, and spread its figs across the forest through animal intestines. The men had left camp every day "in search of fig trees." Instead of walking this path, they must have been disappearing into the forest on errands of their own.

A sprawling bush tore at my pants, flinging me forward. I grabbed a tree in a reluctant embrace. Dust dropped from its leaves in a talcum of mold, dead bugs, and dried mud. Scratchy things filtered through my shirt and melted into sweat. I let go and slid forward onto a clear patch of trail. As my knee pushed back the last fern before the camp, an ant clung with a few legs to my ear, stung, and dropped to the ground. Though I stood still, I felt as if I was crashing on, thumping through the forest on a head-long career. A pulse pounded in my stomach. Looking up, one hand clinging to the last tree at the camp's edge and the other to my burning ear, I saw men standing completely still in shadows on the far side of the clearing.

Some said language was the wall that lay between us and other animals, but all the great apes could learn human sign language without much difficulty. Then they said it was abstract ideas — but one of the "ape scholars" defined death; another categorized birds. An orangutan picked the pocket of a keeper and held the key to his cage in his mouth for days until an outer door was left ajar. They found him eating chicken at the concession stand with a laughing group of tourists who thought his stroll was one of the zoo's attractions. Later, with all keys removed from his reach, he stole a screwdriver and unscrewed the poles of the fence and again strolled out to his charmed public.

Humans find the roots of all their actions in the scale model of other primates, Frans de Waal said. We have forgotten that we are animals, but all our sins of war and crime came from the ancient bond of the social group, without the peacekeeping that is part of community.

Chimpanzees are capable of deception, evidence of tertiary awareness. They understand what other chimpanzees know. But they must fight their honest physiological responses to lie, pulling lips from a fear grimace into a threat with their fingers, turning their eyes from the hidden fruit that will evoke a food scream.

Humans are the only species that can both mask and simulate their emotions without difficulty. Maybe, as we came to depend on spoken language rather than visual to communicate, we stopped learning to see. Or perhaps we stretched so far from our animal roots that we forgot what we had once wanted.

In the firelight, faces once friendly, obsequious, alive with mischief, or blank seemed to be retreating without moving past the campsite. They seemed to pass through the clearing and into the forest, so deep and dark that they shuttered themselves into one of its secrets like the bird that called once from above the canopy and was otherwise silent, or the fire ants marching in their thousands, frightening the forest into immobility. These men who had nagged me, begged for money, laughed at my worse-than-a-baby helplessness, who had fed me and protected me and brought food and told me stories until late every night, had suddenly vanished, and I was alone in the forest with four strangers. I wondered how they knew that I had found the tree. Had they never walked that trail, so close to camp, at all? Or did they want me to fail so we could all leave? Too tired to listen to the argument that would begin of whose fault it had been, I turned away and flicked a beetle from my hair with one hand. The men didn't move, and at last, reluctant, I looked up, wiping my neck with a dirty hand.

Without expression, Akit stepped forward. Bowing, he handed an envelope to me with both hands. Inside, his father had written a note in faint ink.

Dear Miss Memsahib,

This note, it is to tell you soldiers, they have escaped from the army and want to come to kill you. They are beating up schoolchildren for their money and want to find a guide

to come to kill you and to take your things to sell in Zaire.
Please to send medicine for worms.

Sincerely, Stephen

The BaKiga shouldn't have needed deception—cheating was done with laughter. Still protected by the invisible arms of whiteness but no longer friend or memsahib, I stood in the center of the ring. They knew already that I was not going to understand the threat. The BaKiga had grown up knowing their children might be taken out into the dust, where pieces of them would be removed until they were dying, and then they would be stamped upon and kicked and hit with sticks like toys in games of skill. BaKiga had an extra eye that was always kept open for soldiers' feet.

Whiteness in Africa would mean nothing unless the soldiers killed the men and kept me for their safe passage through to Zaire, and then killed me. Still, there would be a nation of strangers trying to save me because of the whiteness of my skin, and no one to help my workers.

They were wrong about what I thought was coming, though. I knew the sound of soldiers' feet. I was one of those middle-class Americans who had been listening all my life. I knew from history that holocausts can happen to anyone, and that I had no eyes to see good from bad in humans. I would always, if I trusted, be easily tricked because I didn't understand my fellow Americans' need to live for display. I had been expecting human disaster. Humans look most like animals when they are consumed with a single emotion, and it is then that they are most likely to be hiding something. We are creatures of ambiguity, so imbued with language that we cannot see an emotion clearly without it.

Still, I had sense enough to know that the men were more likely to die than I, and that I, flawed and weak, was more likely to let them die to save me than I was to save them. When people reach a climax of misery, it becomes a relief to kill others. If the soldiers were coming, so was death.

Firelight twisted on halves of faces. I was as alone in the clearing as if they were gone already. The fire burned hot—it had been a dry day, and the air didn't set a solid barrier of water between us and its heat. I shivered with the itch of drying sweat. If we left that night and walked up to the research site, I would have guns and friends, and a cement floor upon which to bathe.

Strange, though, that Akit's father gave me no advice, such as leave now and go to the gorilla site or to some other village out of the marauders' path. Who is to say, if I left the forest, I would not meet the soldiers somewhere else? The letter could easily be a trick. Perhaps the expressions on the men's faces, those granite-carved fireside statues, were those of BaKiga honor, refusal to expose a cheater.

Stephen could want me out of the forest so he could force poachers to bribe him, or the gold smugglers might have threatened to kill Akit and Patrick if he didn't send me away. Perhaps the men were tired and cold and wanted an honorable escape from this part of their job, or maybe Stephen needed his sons back for something else.

It was impossible to believe anything bad of Simon. And Simon broke first. From silence to stammered shout, he swung round to Akit and Patrick and accused them. He listed reasons for lying that I had missed. "These are bad men," he said. "These men, they want to kill you." Akit and Patrick stood silent, still immobile, still hiding something.

Kamumbo faded backward out of the firelight and out of the clearing, to the edge of the world of humanity. He might have been smiling; he, at least, was not worried. He must have known more than any of us. The WaButi nations seem to hone everything that is animal in us with human intelligence until they are, to us, like gods who can smell emotions and see past and future. There is always the forest to protect them.

Turning away from the human masks, I watched the rain forest. Where the clearing ended, a few bushes clung to the mud and, behind them, a tangled wall so thick no one leaf could be seen. There were chimpanzees in there. In forest so deep, elephants could be watching us from ten feet away and we wouldn't know until they'd passed and the smell of salt and wild things had spread to our clearing.

Over our heads, the canopy pressed in, a roof as wet as a sponge. I breathed in, inhaling deep.

I knew I should leave and come back some other year. It wasn't worth our lives. But I wasn't finished—not only with the data but with a still-unseen question.

These soldiers were BaKiga or BuGanda. Both tribes had been kept out of the forest for thousands of years by Pygmy folktales. Before that, they had migrated in from the plains as nomadic cattle herders. They had never lived in the forest. No Pygmy would teach them how to live in a home they would destroy.

The soldiers would be afraid of the woods, and noisy in them. I could escape and be invisible before they got near camp.

"It is that we must to go, memsahib. These men, they want to kill us." Simon flapped his chin at Akit and Patrick, who scowled. None of the men looked at me. Simon somehow made packing gestures without moving his hands.

37

Soldier Decision

volution moves in small steps. Our ear evolved from the reptil-ian hollow, slowly convoluting itself into a maze, just as our brain folded itself into infinite curves, expanding the electrified surface layer. Where evolution is not random, it operates in response to a stress. Moths evolved echo chambers in the only empty space available, between the muscle attachments of the wings. Even the faint whisper of a bat's wings could be magnified here, and the moths rose, in response, above the arc of the bat's flight.

Whatever the men's motivations, I knew Uganda was still a shattered, forbidding country. Between the roadblocks on the way back from Kenya, in the bus station, signs for ruined towns had hung lopsided over cars and trucks and matatus surrounded by men shouting names to the east and west. One man sat in a car seat perched halfheartedly in the dust; another walked by in a polyester double-knit skirt suit, pink at the collar where it was cleanest. Two families had moved into the bus terminal, and there was no one to tell them to leave. The windows were shattered, and one cluster of bullets had gone all the way through the walls. Smoke from the families' cooking fires whispered out of the holes, gray.

A boy swung by with watches on a pitted Styrofoam board. He thrust them in my face, grinning, and the multitude with him, emboldened, pushed closer, grabbing my arms and jabbing me with their goods. I tried to sidestep toward the matatu, and the boys blocked me. "Sitake, asante," I said over and over again, while the crowd watched, laughing. The matatu sent out a jet of black air and coughed. Music roared to life. I knew if I pushed back, they'd let me through, but I couldn't do it. Finally, the conductor shouted in some language, and they stepped back, screaming with laughter. Shouldering through them, I felt a few last jabs and tugs. The little backpack hung slack as I put it on my lap. Two zippers had been opened, but nothing taken; the pockets had been empty. I'd closed the main pocket with a paper clip twisted twice. The fabric smelled of dust and fear and fury.

There wasn't much color left in Uganda then, after two decades of the kind of war we would never understand in America, where the president tells his soldiers to go and kill a village for no reason, no reason at all, and they go and jab the people with their guns and burn their huts and kill their animals, and then, in the center of the village, cut the silent people apart with their machetes, taking each limb and putting it in a pile until there is no one left except a smashed baby that is still crying until they throw that in a burning hut.

Even after a hundred thousand of these quiet deaths a year, the land was still stretched under too many people, people who'd been raised when factories sold shoes and health organizations came with vaccinations. Now there wasn't enough clothing or food to go around. A shirt worn for three years turned gray or red, the color of the dust, dyed by the mineral pigments seeped into the river. Seams stretched and then frayed, buttons disappeared, stains sank in and mottled the back like mold. People walked slow in the village, in their flapping shirts, gray after gray, like prisoners in uniform, or like extras in an overly organized play, bowed down under the knowledge that death is certain.

They were still in shock, helpless, six years after Idi Amin, piles of bones always a possibility, children in flames accepted too easily. It was hard to love a child who would grow up to be taken apart in the red dust of the village center, piled in pieces under the baobab tree, nibbled at by the marabou storks.

In the corner of the wasted station, framed in a dirty window, a group gathered to laugh at a baby. She took her first steps and clapped her hands when they roared with laughter, cheeks bulging up to her eyes. "Hee," she said, and sat down, and all the people in their gray shirts and browned kangas bent over and slapped their knees and told one another what she said. They drifted away, laughing, as her father scooped her up and held her in the air.

The men still stood in the shadows, not as if they were waiting for an answer from me, but as if they were each making separate plans. Simon nearly blocked Gabriel from view. Without his mischief, Gabriel had shrunk to the width of a teenage boy, windmill arms rigid at his sides as if they had never moved.

"I'm not going," I said in some language to Simon. "I'm sorry." He froze and looked at me. I thought of blank-faced men with submachine guns and pieces of uniforms, standing in the clearing. The other men too looked at me, waiting for an explanation. It wasn't courage. It was just that, without depth perception, a fall into a hole that could have been a shadow was as likely to cause death as a soldier with a machete. And there was nothing to go back to, just a whirling world, without elephants or flashes of monkey tails.

I didn't like the image of the men being killed because I hadn't believed in danger, like some gin-soaked antihero from Graham Greene who destroyed the best before he destroyed himself. I said, "I will pay your salaries and you will go to help Dr. Tom or Stephen if you want to stay in Kayonza. Go home and take a few days' vacation, then take a letter to Tom, telling him to pay you." I was certain that I could cook the beans, keep the fire going, stay dry, and find my way back to Ruhizhia if there was trouble. And I'd have the chimpanzees, alone...

A small fire sparked in the lump in my stomach. If I moved camp even a hundred feet from the path, I'd be invisible. There would be no arguments, no shouts that chased the chimpanzees away, no demands for money or tickets or cameras. Just silence as holy as that of any cathedral and a single focus unhindered by other people's needs.

The men stood around the clearing, silent, expressionless. I poked the fire, trying to imagine making one with wet wood. The top log crashed down into the coals, and the whole fire blinked out in one second, from roaring mass to shadow. The sudden darkness narrowed the clearing to a single circle of light. The men disappeared in the new shadow, except for fragments of lighter clothing.

I had brought a camping stove. I could cook on that. My clothes were wet most of the day anyway; they were cold again as soon as I turned from the fire. Laundry didn't need to be done. The clothes never dried and smelled of mold within a day.

"Memsahib." Simon stepped forward into the glow of the embers. Six lines pushed up the skin of his forehead. He walked slowly across the clearing and squatted next to the fire. With a hand under one end of the log, he held it in place, then pulled another log forward and let the first crash down. Sparks flew up, ashes traveled, smoke spiraled in a cloud with swirls of cinder.

"I must to stay here. It is that you will kill yourself."

The log underneath sizzled and, with a crack that startled me into a crouch, a low line of flames spread across it. The men watched, silent and unsmiling.

Without a word, Simon filled the fariah with river water and set it in a triangle of logs in the fire. I stood, too prickly with dust and sweat and a dozen dead insects to make another move. As if time had slowed, or the fire had lost its heat, the water lay still and cold. I shifted from foot to foot, slapped a black beetle out of my collar, and pulled an ant from my sleeve, then finally reached out and took the fariah. Three bubbles popped to the surface as I lifted it. "Memsahib, it is that it has not boiled for three minutes, as it is that you say."

I shrugged. He drank it unboiled from the stream himself. The stream ran straight down from the top of the foothill. The morning's cloud turned to water. Liver flukes could only live in standing water.

Naked, with only branches between me and the path, I bathed too fast, hearing soldiers in every creak of waterlogged bark. That night, as I sat before the fire, ghosts of the insects that had crawled on me ran in prickles up and down my skin until at last I took the towel and bathed again.

The clearing hung dark and silent as the fire struggled. By contrast, suddenly visible out of the moving shadows across the valley, a young chimpanzee climbed into the fig tree. It looked at Simon and Gabriel, turned its head further and saw me sitting inside the tent. Silent, it trotted back into the canopy. Another chimp crashed onto a branch near the fig and whisped out a quiet *hoo*, the delicate woodwind breath always followed by a whimper, a pant-hoot, and then a long, drawn-out scream, as if the chimp were having a tantrum because if it came out to eat, I would see it. The chimp screamed in a high-pitched voice and threw some leaves into the canopy. I saw a glimpse of it near the top of the tree, and it faded back, squealing. After an hour of this standoff, it swooshed downward and hooted. The chimp screamed for almost ten minutes like the high note of a trumpet, screamed until the whole forest sat silent, and the birds had taken roost, and it was choking with every indrawn breath, visible only in the movement of lighted leaves.

38

Photos

S t. *Teresa of Avila and St. Paul, with their migraine visions of light; epileptics and their great moments of clarity; the dying who see a tunnel of light and are never the same; Buddhist enlightenment; nature ecstasy; blindness and sensory deprivation; the seeing of angels; and the act of dying — the flashes of light are all the same, as if only one physiological response answers to any step taken from the human road.*

The highest fig tree hung empty in a haze of shadows. Neither chimpanzees nor monkeys wandered through. As if the leaves had grown closer or the sky had lost its light, the rain forest darkened. Trees hovered within shadows of moving clouds. Above and below, mist drifted, rising from roots to hover under the canopy, filtering through spaces in the leaves where a tree had died and rising zigzag from one level to another. Against the night sky, in open patches, those diffused clouds reflected the moon, lighting the forest they had blackened during the day.

If the men left, I'd have to spend most of the remaining time stoking the fire and cooking the beans on the stove. But there would be silence. And perhaps the chimpanzees would come back and let me enter their world.

*   *   *

Late into the dusk, I sat hidden in the silver light, arms around my knees, watching the leaves. At last, I slowly rose and slithered down the path, reaching for familiar branches that had disappeared. At the edge of the clearing, Simon's voice drifted with the scent of smoke through the leaves. "These men are bad men." I froze for a moment, shivering but not wanting to squat in wet pants. Someone quietly left the clearing, and after a moment I pushed through the last bushes.

I sank onto the wet log and held frozen hands to the flames. The men stood, silent and blank, facing one another, so alike in the dusk I couldn't tell who was missing. Rain had beaten the clearing flat. Broken bushes lay stretched in long fingers toward the stream. The men sank finally onto their log. I wrote the data about the chimp into columns and rows and wondered if the men would be there in the morning, and how much the soldiers might pay for a guide.

The next day, they still lay asleep in their neat row on the mat. Mist crawled flat along the ground and rose in trickles through the trees. Wreathing about their feet, it passed along the rain grooves of the hill and spread into a gray floor. Wet stalks of what had been bushes poked through like islands in a sea. Instead of relief, the quiet brought a surge of loneliness. Just so, humans have lain throughout all of history, child and mother and father lying still on their backs, arm to arm. A Masai warrior, trained to fight lions with a spear, almost died of loneliness when his chief sent him to Germany to study law. The first night, he tried to crawl into bed with his roommate as he had always slept with family or friends. "These barbaric people," he wrote home to his father.

*   *   *

Branches crashed in the northeast, and a L'Hoesti walked into the fig tree. After it left, a redtail male sat in one side of the tree with his back to me, shifting nervously. The men stirred and threw off their blankets and separated to opposite sides of the camp, bottom-of-the-mountain and top-of-the-mountain. "Eh," someone said. Setting down my breakfast, I wrote in the notebook, then took a picture, but the redtail stayed, without eating, until a blue monkey had barked four times, and then it jumped away. The film clunked and tore as I wound it forward. Rewinding the roll, I tried to open the camera. Akit, Gabriel, and Simon crowded over my shoulders, after days of silence, and watched. "Eh," they said when the door creaked open. The camera was wet inside, filmed with something colorless that smelled like insects and feet. A blue monkey called.

With the corner of my shirt, I wiped the inside of the camera. The men hovered, watching with their first emotion since the soldiers came to Kayonza. I remembered the pleas of strangers in Kenya, to take their picture as I walked by. An official whom Dr. Tom had taken me to meet for research clearance had shown us his cement home with its clean floor, the single lightbulb hung from a cord in the ceiling. As we crossed the threshold, he turned the generator on and, throughout our visit, left the bulb burning there like a firefly marooned in daylight. He'd shown us two snapshots, himself in one, people he'd never met in another.

Now was the first time bottom-of-the-mountain and top-of-the-mountain had stood together since we'd heard of the soldiers. Not certain whether I was breaking some taboo and itching to go back to the blind, I asked, "Do you want me to take your pictures?"

As I loaded in new film, they rushed over to sit in the chair of branches and vines built into the far side of the clearing. No one had ever sat in it before. Perhaps they had once meant to build me a separate fire before this throne. Gabriel and Patrick reached it at the same time, and I waited. For one second, I thought they would sit for the shot together, then Patrick shoved against Gabriel's back. Patrick was a game guard in training, and Gabriel had no title at all, but Gabriel pushed back, grinning, and held on to the seat. "Wewe!" Patrick shouted. Gabriel clutched the seat, waving one leg in the air for ballast. Patrick pushed with ferocity. Grin fading, Gabriel froze, then braced his feet and shoved harder.

Simon hissed at him to sit down and not make a loud man of himself, and Akit waved to his brother. "Wewe. Sit down, you are a bad man."

Swelling in the face, Gabriel and Patrick planted their feet and, back-to-back, pushed until they rose out of the chair. Suzan and Charles would have made a joke and laughed at them, and that would have ended it, but I didn't know what to say or why they were so angry, except that they all knew something they weren't telling me.

"I will take one picture of each of you," I said, in case they thought there would be only one. They sank into the chair and leaned against each other. "Me, I will be first!" Gabriel shouted, and with one surge of his behind knocked Patrick off the seat. "Wewe!" Simon bellowed. Patrick pounced back and at a loss, I lifted the camera. They shuffled against the chair and sat up straight against each other, scowling like Victorian fathers. I waited for them to relax. Patrick and Gabriel held the pose until I lowered the camera, relaxed, and snapped back into straightness as I lifted it again. "Me, I want this picture for my wife." "Eeeeeh. Me, I want this picture for my girlfriend. My wife is not good." "Eeeeeeh!"

"Eeeeeh!" They laughed and slapped their knees but separated again into their subtribes as soon as the photos were taken.

Simon strode through them to the chair made of vines. Scowling with a ferocity I had seen in none of them, he sat straight and rigid, frozen. I took one picture. As he relaxed, I lifted the camera again. Simon froze into the same immobile hostility. Gabriel pushed him out and sat again on the chair. I pretended to take a picture of him, rigid and angry. He jumped up, beaming, and I clicked the camera shutter, capturing him limpid with pleasure. "Eeeeh!" he shouted. In the silence, I wondered whether it was an insult to take a picture without permission. The men gathered round him and slapped his back and laughed. "Eeh." "The memsahib, she take your picture and you do not know it." "Eh, eh." And Gabriel leaned over, helpless with laughter, and I still didn't know if I had done something wrong.

In the distance, some primate roared with territorial rage, and small things squeaked and rustled, dropping shreds of bark.

I took Akit and an embarrassed but still visible Kamumbo, then Gabriel pulled the camera from my hands and took my picture in the green light as I stood by the tent with the wall of the forest behind. I thought there was no need—I would never forget the rain forest or this camp—but I posed as awkwardly as they had, though without the scowl.

A combined group of redtails and blue monkeys rioted through the canopy. Turning from Gabriel, who was still poised behind the camera, I whipped the notebook from my waistband. Heights, following order, sex/age, species, vocalizations.

In the silence the monkeys left behind, a tree bent, bowed, and dipped. Still without sound, it ruffled itself straight and then bent and bowed again. In the distances of the rain forest, size is impossible to calibrate. No land is level and no background is marked in anything but an eternity of leaves, one mass of shadow. It seemed to be a small chimpanzee that climbed from one branch to another, but she could have been any size.

"Eeeeeeeeh," the men said.

> 6:42 <(F)> 2 *empundu, AF/v young I. Mom has v. grizzled hair, anxious eyes, and badly scraped left leg ~ 9m.*
> 6:44 *b. black skinny one at bottom moved away from tree and sat for a second.*
> 6:45 *1 enkunge arrived. AF/I moved down to tree on left N.*
> 6:47 *She moved farther down.*
> 6:52 *enkunge ran to perpendicular branch on S side then E. Many crashes close in E.*
> 6:54 *chattering and brief scream from E.*

39

Famine

Carol Zaleski studied these transcendent moments of light and said that they might be caused by several factors, especially sensory deprivation in times of danger. In Otherworld Journeys, she writes, "The central nervous system, while hyperaroused by stress, is starved for stimuli. Obeying a biological imperative—for unless it is fed it will die—the brain turns inward in search of substitutes for its sensory nourishment. It must make do with emergency rations, made from random blips in the visual cortex mixed with the stored goods of the memory." The mind left abandoned creates its own lights and colors and emotions.

I set the books on the backpack and, from between two smaller volumes, a tiny photo album slid out. I put it back between the books and sat on the log. Flipping through some of the hardbacks, I found nothing else to do research on and opened the album.

Into the silence of the clearing, I said cautiously, "This is my father.

"And this is my mother."

I hadn't shared this picture before because each part of it showed more wealth than had all the villages of Ruhizhia. My parents stood smiling against distressed-pine paneling by the fireplace. Two brass lamps flanked them, lighted and glowing. On the mantel, there stood a painting, some pots, and a stone sculpture. I thought the men would snatch the picture from my hand and talk about it and laugh. From their separate sides, top-of-the-mountain and bottom-of-the-mountain, they peered over my shoulders.

Their anger toward one another had been worse since President Museveni devalued the Ugandan shilling that month. A million became worth the equivalent of a hundred US dollars overnight. Without newspapers or radio news, most people didn't know what was happening, only that they'd been ordered to line up and turn their money over to strangers and soldiers with guns. When he came back from Ruhizhia, Akit said that people stood in line for days, and at the end the bankers sitting under the shade of a tree took whatever they wanted of the people's savings and gave them a few new bills. Refusing to return to the barter system because the missionaries had said that only animals did that, the BaKiga stopped selling their food at market and ate what they had.

Then a storm had knocked down the banana trees of Kayonza before the fruit had grown. Their main crop wasted, the people in the valley ate their beans early. The wind that flattened the valley had barely rippled the leaves of the rain forest, where the dirt was covered with trees like blankets, but money couldn't buy us food.

"Eeeeh," Patrick said. "Your father, how many years does he have?"

I looked at the picture. My father's temples were barely gray. "He has fifty years."

"Eeeeeh," they said as one. Silence fell.

"He must be very respected in his tribe."

"Eeeeeeh."

"How old are you, Simon?" I asked. I had thought him fifty at least. "Me, it is that I have thirty-five years, memsahib. I think," he added. They turned and trudged back to their separate sides of the clearing.

A thin, sour smell rose from the fire and clutched at the back of our throats. Simon thrust his hand into the steam of the boiling pot, lifted a handful of beans into the green light, and squeezed his fist shut. A trickle of gray suds ran between his fingers and frothed on the ground near the sleeping mat. The hand opened. Empty hulls clung to calloused skin. "These beans, they are bad. The worms, they eat them." Wave after wave of pinworms and dysentery left me numb to a worm that ate beans.

"What do we do?"

He shrugged. "If memsahib can get more beans, we throw these away. If memsahib does not get more beans, then"—he shrugged again—"we eat these beans." Dropping their bodiless forms back in the pot, he added, "And these worms."

Beans tucked into the back of a hut, or gathered and left wet, grew these invisible worms like spontaneously generated flies.

Digging deep into my camping backpack, I found a plastic bag of soup mixes that my mother had put in before I left. There were enough packed for a few days' meals at least. I showed Simon how to make a packet of tomato soup. The men looked away, uninterested. "Look," I said proudly, "you just add boiling water, and you have soup." Simon put a finger in the soup and tasted it, then spat it out. The others tasted and spat and wiped their tongues with dirty sleeves. I watched them in disbelief. I loved this soup. Raising the mug to my lips on the untouched side, I took a long drink. The men watched me. I didn't spit it out, but I would have if I'd been alone. I drank the soup to see if it got better, but it didn't. I had eaten beans and potatoes from the ground near me, untouched by chemicals, genetic modification, or artificial fertilizers, for months. Every chemical in the tomato soup stood out, plain and bitter.

"Memsahib," said Gabriel, fingering the empty soup envelope, "it is that I would like to have this bag."

"Memsahib, it is that I must to go home. It is that I must to go to the research station, and if they do not have food, it is that I must to take some from my wife." I wondered if Simon had told this story to leave behind the camp, and the coming soldiers.

He took my hand in both of his. Eyes that were honey-brown and yellowed with age looked through mine, and my own dropped to the ground. If the soldiers did catch him, Simon, I knew, would walk back on broken legs to give us the food.

"Memsahib, this is very bad. The worms, they will make you sick." He went over to Gabriel and shouted him into seriousness. Spoken in anger, Rukiga sounded like the spitting of watermelon seeds. Simon left, and Gabriel came to thaw by the fire. Too shaken to think up a well-fleshed-out lie, he told me Simon was sending him to the monastery to beg for a bag of beans. "He say that me, I must not eat the good beans and give you these bad ones."

Gabriel stalked off, without asking for money, to the village where the soldiers had beaten children. Patrick and Akit and I ate the bitter beans. With the spoon Simon had cut from a branch over his head, we tried to skim the soapy scum off the top. There was nothing underneath but more soap, so, passing the gray bag of salt, we drank the broth and ate the beans that hadn't dissolved. I didn't eat much. My stomach hurt so badly that it tightened against the beans, and they sat in a lump below my throat.

The crippled female chimpanzee who moved so slowly that monkeys sat with her in the fruit trees had left the valley, the last of the chimps.

*   *   *

If Simon had really thought the bottom-of-the-mountain BaKiga were helping the soldiers, he wouldn't have left me alone with them. But the men sat, still unsmiling, silent. I wrote in the orange notebook, straining to think.

Akit sat at a distance, rifle cradled in one arm like a baby, both of them glowing in ripples of reflected firelight. Between his feet, a leather bag rested half buried in dead ferns. In it lay three bullets, the game guards' allowance, but only one held gunpowder. Someone had sold the powder in the others to smugglers who blew trees out of the river for the grains of gold in their roots.

Leaning over the bag, Akit opened the bullets, poured some of the powder from the full one into his hand, and then tipped it back in.

He looked up and frowned at Patrick, who sat with his feet in the fire. "Wewe, take the memsahib's plate and wash it." Simon had left all the jugs full of boiled water. Scowling, Patrick dunked each plate once in cold water, sticking them half dirty into the slats of the vine table. Recovering his good humor, he bounced over to us and, ignoring Akit's frown, shouldered past me to push his feet almost into the fire. He inhaled deeply and leaned back, arms behind his head. I listened with one ear to my stomach rumbling and wondered if Gabriel would come back that night.

The path above crackled and swayed. Akit reached for the rifle and searched through the mat for the good bullet. We sat unbreathing, and waited.

Blue hat at a tipsy angle, Gabriel strode through the last bushes, holding high a plastic bag of peas. We exclaimed, and looked at them, and hefted the bag in our hands to feel the solid healthy rattle of them. Akit set the rifle and the bag of bullets carefully on the mat. Gabriel ambled to the fire and flicked a few sticks farther in, placing the peas in honor on the sleeping mat. Brother Odel, in the midst of famine, had given us a two-day supply of food.

The day was as dark as night. Simon hated the forest and once had already been chased by policemen in the evening. I thought he'd wait till the morning to come back, for fear of the soldiers, and after a while, I leaned forward to put the pot on the fire. Gabriel and Akit jumped up and moved it to the side, forcing another branch underneath the one I'd loosened.

My stomach ached. No matter how far I leaned into the fire, the flames only seemed to pull cold drafts closer. I wrapped my arms around wet legs and put my forehead down. The stomachache grew from a throb to a constant stab, an alternation of hunger and nausea until I wasn't sure I wanted to eat at all. The forest closed around the clearing, damping the fire to a silent sheet of flame.

With an unending sting, the chemical tastes of the tomato soup curdled my tongue. I wondered, with a sudden chill of panic, whether that clarity of taste would disappear once I was surrounded by man-made products. Or perhaps just knowing that that display of chemicals existed, was it too late? That almost-forgotten world, at home where I had never been more than a guest — it could be seen only dimly now, through a tang of artifice. I had been right to not belong to it.

Someone slithered down the far hill. Akit hunched over the rifle, loading the bullet in the black of early evening until he saw Simon's face. The burlap sack over Simon's shoulder was a fraction as full as it should have been. I thought for a second that the top-of-the-mountain had had a famine too, but Tom's volunteers had two cars to buy groceries anywhere in East Africa.

Simon tripped over a root. Bowing, he handed a note toward me but held one end. With the bag clutched to his shoulder as if he were there only temporarily, he looked at the ground. His mouth trembled, and I realized he was trying not to cry.

"What happened, Simon?" The loudness of my shout surprised me. "Did the policemen beat you?" I was afraid to mention the soldiers, for fear of what they might have done.

We held on to each end of the note. The bag sagged over one shoulder, but he pulled on the paper. He wanted me to hear it from him.

"This man, he say I am lying, that we do not need food but I want to sell it, then he say..." Simon choked and shifted the bag up so he could hit his eyes with the back of that hand. "He say that he send some beans only and some margarine and some of these bullets." His hand slapped across his eyes again, and the note shook in our grasp. He breathed in and looked at me intently. "He say that I am lazy, and like to lie." It was an exact imitation of Ted, but I knew that Charles was somehow behind it.

Simon let go of the note and I read it by the fire, keeping my body turned toward him because he looked so alone. The letter was from Charles, saying that Ted had refused to send food and bullets because we'd already had some and they didn't have enough, but that he and Suzan were going to send some after the jeep came back with supplies. They hoped they'd sent enough until then. I could see as clearly as if I'd been there: Ted handing a small bag of food to Simon, with Charles laughing like a beautiful flame and Suzan standing with her hands on her hips, glaring at Charles and making him undo his mischief.

"Oh, Simon. He had no right to say that to you." But I pictured Charles laughing as he sent the cattle herders with their spears into the bedroom to wake Ted.

Simon dropped the sack and stood, twisting hands and body

and panting. "He, he…" He paused. "This man, he is a VERY BAD MAN."

But it was plenty of food.

Redtails and blue monkeys slid chittering into the clearing. A quarter of an hour after the monkeys silently crashed away through the valley, a female chimpanzee—without entering or leaving the tree, just suddenly sitting in it, one leg crooked at a polite angle—crouched in the fig. Her shaved leg set upon the branch, she looked down and then away. Poachers set wire snares for any animal that came by. Chimps were strong enough to break the rope with which the wire had been tied, or to break the branch the rope was tied to, but they usually tore their skin off too, and sometimes cut through tendons. This female's leg looked as if it had been neatly shaved and was still being held, bent, by the barber. Perhaps because of the old injury, she had stripped herself of all the signs of chimpanzee dominance, making herself small by hunching her shoulders and holding down the fur that, if set on end, could have made her loom as large as a gorilla.

40

Mama Shaveleg

Species prepare themselves for the tasks of their land. Remove them from it, and their generations will still pace eternal distances and press to the edges of their cages when the time for migration comes. We replaced birdsong with music, horizons with paintings, and the movement of hands in dirt with shopping. Cage us too long, in too small a place, and we ease one stress with another, biting our hands or banging our heads against the bars. We are not meant for walls.

The afternoon rain rose from the back of the hill, dissolving the trees into a dark blur. The canopy glowed silver, but underneath, humus, leaves, and dust torn from the trees circled in a dark cloud as the rain moved on, thunder behind a curtain. In the icy air, I bent my head over the notebook and held it clasped to my chest under the poncho, farthest from rebounds of rain, still falling from the canopy, that burned face and legs.

There are times when we are so cold and wet that movement stabs as sharp as a splinter and we pass over a boundary into an acceptance that brings peace. The stiffness that had been part of the pain retreats, and we accept the cold without shrinking. My stomach throbbed in a body so still that it no longer had boundaries of flesh between itself and the world.

In the sudden silence of the passing of the rain, the forest hushed. I had to look twice to believe that a chimp sat in the fig tree. She had again climbed into the tree in silence. The old female sat hunched without motion, shoulders rounded up behind her ears like the wings of a bat. If I hadn't seen other chimps on that branch, I wouldn't have known she was big. On that gnarled limb, she sat as if hiding. No conqueror this. With the water dripping all around, flowing and twisting and layering itself down trunks and dropping from weighted leaves, she squatted, gray and strangely dry. Eyes moving fast under scowling brows, she watched not me but the trees, as if afraid to look down.

Another thin chimp, darker than the old female, at the bottom of the tree moved away. Silently, a redtail monkey jumped into the fig, and without a glance or threat, the old female climbed slowly out into a nearby tree. I had never seen a monkey jump into a tree with a chimpanzee. The chimpanzee shifted on her branch, turning in one stiff heave. Scraps of black skin dangled over her lower leg, scraped to long-healed pink flesh. Hair from the knee and thigh fell over the scar, covering it until she moved.

The redtail monkey ran to a perpendicular branch and out. A group of animals crashed away, and something chattered and screamed. With a graceful crouch, the old female crossed the tree, carefully not looking at the new monkey. I lifted my head to look. Dripping diarrhea through the canopy, the chimpanzee crashed into a thicker tree, then ran. The second chimp leaped after her, and crashed away with a scream that faded into the leaves.

With the wicker basket filled with food, I had lost my appetite. I breathed in slowly and smelled mold and rain and something else.

41

Rafiki

A tap and patter of bark fell on the tent's fly. I unzipped the door and knelt in a flood of sunshine. From a twisted branch over the tarpaulin, a redtail male sat in a column of light over a patch of moss, flicking his fingers through its glowing fronds as if grooming another monkey. Gabriel stood beneath the tree, staring into the branches, but the redtail fed as if basking in the sun. "Rafiki," Gabriel said, beaming at me. "He is my friend."

"Good morning, Rafiki," I said in Rukiga, and Gabriel laughed with delight, slapping his leg. Crawling from the tent, I looked carefully away from the redtail, but without glancing at me, he strolled away into invisibility.

With a strange absence of noise, a confusion of monkeys passed through camp — blue monkeys both alone and mixed with redtails. For ten minutes, a neat line of colobus monkeys crossed through them, like sedate office workers passing a group of soccer fans rioting home from the bars. The colobus leaped and crashed and climbed in some predestined order, equidistant from one another. White tails flared behind them as they stretched their hands in midleap for the next branch. While the redtails and blues swirled and called and quarreled in primate tornadoes, the colobus walked in order from one branch, soared to another, and without pause walked on. It was regal, the colobine march, and if I hadn't been waiting for the chimps, I would have tried to follow them.

The notebook overflowed with notes and side notes.

After two hours of monkey havoc, a young chimpanzee screamed in the south. With a crash, a redtail jumped into the fig tree and sat next to a lone colobus monkey, watching me. Two more redtails ran by and a baboon screeched, but the colobus didn't move. A wave of baboons swept in on the ground, eating omufa leaves and digging up roots as big as sweet potatoes.

Strolling toward camp, a female baboon picked figs off the forest floor with her right hand. A male followed her with nonchalant interest. Her behind bulged with the massive swelling of an old female in heat, as red and shiny as burnt skin. I reached for the notebook in my waistband, and they both jumped into the bushes. It was the first time I had seen baboons in the forest, one of the few times I'd seen colobus monkeys, and the only time such huge intermingled groups of redtails and blues had followed one another through the valley. So much color.

Rafiki Redtail came back and fed near Gabriel for two and a half hours. The monkey sat peaceably on the branch for a few minutes after I returned for lunch, then, without distress, left.

Sick with fever and stomachache, I sat alone in the rain in front of the same fig tree all the next day and tried to make sense of the frantic recordings. The female with the shaved leg didn't come back.

The rain ended and the trees ran with water, but though there'd been no less rain in this storm than before, the secondary streams slowed, then dried and disappeared, as if we'd been raised closer to the sun. An old chimpanzee climbed hand over hand into the fig tree but jumped out and crashed away when she saw me.

"It is that we must to go to this tree there, memsahib." Gabriel led me to the fig tree in the south. On the trail, we saw a L'Hoesti sitting low in a tree, basking in the sun with that Bahamas vacation ease of the species. A redtail climbed into the tree and sat by the top. The L'Hoesti continued to sit in the sun, hunched over a plush belly, until the redtail saw me and hopped into the canopy. Like an echo, the L'Hoesti left. Gabriel and I walked farther and saw the redtail eating entero fruits. Hiking on, we saw another large male redtail sitting in a fig tree with green fruits. Redtails had strung themselves on the trail like beads in a necklace. After half an hour, I moved closer to one to see what it was eating, and it left.

A L'Hoesti climbed into the tree and put out one slender hand to eat unripe figs. Shifting in my squat to turn a page of the notebook, I fell onto hands and knees. The monkey looked at me, jumped into a nearby tree, and ate the fruit in his hand, in the shadows.

That night, one blue monkey and one colobus roared in rhythm. My tent vibrated with the after-hum of each challenge. *Wakawakwakawaka*, then *bleah-bleah-bleah-bleah-bleah*, as if they were either competing or agreeing.

42

The Blind

With a panga, Gabriel built a new blind—a Batwa hut— on the south trail; he put it by the fig tree where we had watched the L'Hoesti and redtails eat unripe fruit.

For floor and roof, he carried back ferns, and he drove posts into the ground, then lashed them together with a rope of vine and branches, with leaves braided in as walls. He knotted three sticks into a triangle, then tied these onto a longer pole and wove ferns into the mesh. With a tilt of the arm, he showed me how to move the door up and down to give a slanted and clear view of the monkeys.

I knelt inside. Green light filtered through the ferns. The air was already less wet. The ferns, like sponges, soaked the moisture from my knees and separated me from the wet ice of the forest floor. From above and below, all human things were hidden; the hut was bush and fern, invisible in the earth.

"Why didn't we build this for camp, Gabriel?"

He looked at me with an open mouth. "It is that the house of the WaZungu is good, memsahib. This house, it is for animals like Pygmies."

"It is a very good house," I said, and he laughed at me, eyes sparkling. "Eeeh, eh, WaZungu."

*   *   *

Unfolding my rain poncho, I settled in the soft ferns. Silence fell, but of a different kind. I was invisible to scent and sight and hearing, wound about the forest as I was, woven into its fabric. For the first time, I felt alone in the forest, on the edge of a stairway, as if climbing down from a tree that inhibited motion toward a lighted lake. Animals couldn't see me watching them. The forest lay still and silent, as if waiting for something. Water trickled down off the roof in plops and short streams. On all sides, mist rose but drifted away in flecks of light. I sat for a long time, feeling warmth reflect back from the walls. Within the rustle of water and shift of leaves, I had disappeared. The valley lay still and hushed, the tree lit with the spotlight of its solitude. But there was no hurry now. Something would come.

My stomach throbbed, surprising me. I'd forgotten its pain. It stabbed again, so hard I bent forward and gasped. Holding my watch to the light of the door, I read the time through thin etchings of glass, a fungus that had left delicate tendrils. I'd been in the blind for hours. I looked out at the lighted valley, so ripe with rustlings and thumps and insect grumbles, and then slowly packed my bag.

The ache in my stomach would reach a level of pain that would stop my heart for whole beats if I didn't eat. Water fell like rain on my pants as I set aside the fringed door.

The valley hushed and fled, emptying of everything but the trees. I breathed wet air for a minute, then slung the bag on my back and slithered down to the path. The hut sat straight and obvious behind me, but a few steps along the path, it blended into a small hill, then nothing, and I wondered if I'd be able to find it again. My stomach throbbed once more, and I pushed through the last bush to camp without listening for the soldiers.

Simon walked toward me. A letter lay on both of his hands.

Heart pounding, I stopped at the edge of the path. Five of the seven escaped soldiers had been captured and taken away by police. Two had attacked and beaten a few children for their month's school fees. I looked at Simon but couldn't tell what he thought.

"Memsahib, it is that we must to have these bullets."

I woke with a start from the half sleep of a soldier watch. For a second I thought they had come. *Clang*, like a bell, something rang. Then, after a pause, again, *clang*. Fast and thickly together, the bell was rung. I opened the tent carefully and called to Simon. In a rigid row, as if posing for photographs, the men slept, arms straight at their sides, feet pointing upward, like all children who sleep in family beds.

"Simon?" I called again. He snorted and turned and at last said, "Memsahib." Even then, he didn't understand what I was saying, though the small timpanist was closer to him than to me. *Clang, clang*, the bed of the forest rang. After a while, he looked down and then looked up at me, confused. "It is an animal, memsahib." I crawled from the tent into wet air. Our fariah pan had filled overnight with rainwater. In its iron depths, the smallest of mice, just eyes and whiskers and tail, was swimming. Round and round, frantically paddling, then *clang*, into the sloped side. Colors were rare in the rain forest, and this was the closest I had come to a wild animal. I squatted beside the pot and wondered what to do. Silver-gray, impossibly small, the mouse spun round. *Clang, clang*. When he saw me watching it, Simon lifted himself from the mat. He put one giant hand under the pot's edge and tilted water and mouse alike onto the muddy slope. Like a leaf rolling, the teaspoon of fur disappeared in a steady rush beneath the rain forest floor, alive or dead.

43

Sensory Deprivation

Perhaps the light that is seen by epileptics and religious converts, by worshippers of nature and autistics, by the near dead and the sensually deprived, this incandescence that stops time and empties the body like dust into the wind, perhaps it is seen only by the flawed of eye—those who cannot properly see the world before them. Emerson's tubercular lesion, Muir's factory damage, Dickinson's light sensitivity, St. Teresa's migraine blur, the near dead's loss of peripheral vision, autistic hypersensitivity of vision, the epileptic's misfirings of the visual cortex—they all focus the body onto its flaws. Wordsworth and William James and Paul Churchland and Buddha and Emerson and Voltaire and Dante and Pliny, a common thread runs through all, a moment of separation from time.

Monkeys and rain had disappeared; only rats came at night and chewed, not on our food but on the pillars of the tarpaulin. Something like an insect had crawled into my tent, and I slept with flashlight in hand that night to catch it when it attacked. Swirling with the colors missing from the forest, in a sudden dream, were blue and scarlet and yellow things, and flowers and fabrics and a dozen human places that I had never seen. Hands relaxed on the sleeping bag, I let go of the watch for soldiers, insects, and leaks in the tent, and slipped down, in a dizzying spiral, into sleep. One after another, houses and rooms appeared; humans swirled in and out. I became different people and experienced new emotions. Sometimes I walked for a long way, in a story, sometimes danced, which I could never, with my flawed eyes, do awake, and sometimes I waited for people to return. The savanna hovered in the back of everything, not in pictures but as a freedom that had become part of me.

They floated back at the end of the night, fading gently in and hovering there, sweet-smelling. Like guide dogs, they led me up out of sleep again. Could I do it without them, or would I lie in the lowest level forever? Sensory deprivation, removal of stimuli to eyes and ears and nose, can change the chemicals in one's body. We are what we see and what we breathe. If we don't fill our eyes and our lungs, and feel our species' touch, the brain will manufacture dreams to its own requirements. I breathed in the rain forest air, and watched its dark leaves, but always, in the back of my mind, the savanna flashed forward, recapturing itself again and again in memory, changing the chemicals of my brain.

I sat by the fire, lions glinting behind my eyes. The insect had bitten me again in my sleep, and a wet bump grew on my shin, larger by the hour.

"Memsahib, we must to go to Kagote." The chimpanzees had gone, long enough for their feces to rot and crumble and grow small green sprouts from seed. No one had ever studied the patterns of the chimpanzees in the last of the Mountains of the Moon. With a sea of forest before them, they could have gone to any paradise of food and light, out of the dark valleys.

I thought about going back to safety, to human villages, and about an end to the silence at the blind. It wasn't worth it: I wouldn't have to look over my shoulder for soldiers, but I wouldn't have something to look toward either.

"I think I should wait for the chimpanzees here, Simon."

"Eeeeeeh."

44

A Multitude of L'Hoesti

We see reflections and mirrors, reversals of the world, and all its colors in opposition. The ocean is blue because it has no blue; a tulip has no yellow. We see none of the patterns of ultraviolet light that lead insects to pollen like maps of the oceans' currents, nor even suspect their presence.

Upside down and turned back up, the eye sees nothing. The scene before us is sent on its wayward course through lens and mirror, straight into storage cells. From there, the picture is memorized, altered, and flashed upon a screen.

"Memsahib, come quick. Kamumbo say many monkeys."

With his lips, Gabriel pointed up a trail I hadn't noticed. I set my beans on the log and, panting, with a backward glance to the Mutwa hut's trail, climbed to the ridge of the hill. Kamumbo squatted in the leaf litter, lighting his pipe with the embers from a fire stick. He inhaled once, then pointed with the pipe. Down the hill, dark bodies slid into the undergrowth on a hidden path. Gabriel began counting in KiSwahili. "Hamsini, memsahib." "Fifty, he say, memsahib," translated Simon. "Tchah. The memsahib, she speak the KiSwahili."

I'd counted only fourteen and wondered if he was trying to please me. Kamumbo sucked on the pipe with a popping sound and shook his head once. He said something, and a moment's silence fell while we looked at him. Gabriel translated. "One hundred." I leaned forward, straining to see, notebook clenched.

Halfway up the hillside on a rotting log, I saw a sudden white flash. A L'Hoest's monkey stood watching us with his feet curled around the old log. White cheek patches stood out in puffs against his black body. Ready to threaten but not yet feeling the need, he tilted forward. Suddenly, I saw Kamumbo's legions behind him, an endless line of monkeys slipping without haste through the bushes. With their heads lowered over their white tufts, they were no more than shadows until they turned to look at us.

In faint trembles of the bush, the monkeys stretched invisibly forward up the foothill, at least a hundred, if they walked as close as the ones still seen. In none of the papers had a large L'Hoesti gathering been mentioned, only small family groups. But they'd been seen so seldom that no one really knew how they lived.

We followed them up the hill. As we stood at the top, watching the last casual shadow, the rustles quieted. The final monkey's tail disappeared, and we were alone. Near the log I found one lobe of dung, possibly the first L'Hoest's ever studied. Dissecting its curls of steam with a stick, I wrote the color, texture, smell, size, and names of the seeds inside. A leaf bud had passed through intact, though wilted and damp like old lettuce in salad dressing. I marked the spot so I could find the seeds after the rain had washed them clean.

As we pushed through the bushes on a ridge, Gabriel saw another L'Hoesti, and we dropped into a crouch. A large-shouldered male sat in a column of sunshine. The air was so thick with moisture that the light glowed in visible lines and wrapped sleepily about him. We moved, and he glanced sharply at us, then put his head down again to muse some more.

Two young monkeys rolled, biting, in a small tree behind him. One climbed high, and the other jumped to catch its tail. They tumbled with a thump to the forest floor and leaped up again. Pushing off, one jumped down onto the old male's head, then flounced its legs and kicked off back up into the tree. Gabriel shifted and laughed and made some remark. "Sh," I said. The male lifted his head and stared not at Gabriel but at me, and then sat on in the sunshine like a sun-dazed Buddha. He looked quietly at his stomach. The longer I looked at the monkeys, the larger they became, until they were a whole world of stars and slowly turning galaxies. For seconds that could have been infinities, I sat watching them.

On a low branch only inches off the ground behind the male, two females groomed each other, sagging to the side, drugged with pleasure as fingers slid through fur. Forty-five minutes of data in one day.

All primates groom. The merest infant is licked and sucked and examined inch by inch. If it is female in a female-bonded species, it will be groomed for hours every day for the rest of its life. This grooming is its greatest pleasure. All primates slide down in their groomers' arms as if they've lost bone and muscle.

Scientists identified two kinds of grooming: the pick and slash techniques. In the latter, the groomer slides one finger through fur and lifts it to peer underneath. Anything found—flake of skin, fleck of dust, insect egg—is eaten. Pick grooming passes faster. Quick pokes, with long probes. No one knows the value of the different techniques. Their uses seem unrelated to blood or friendship or reconciliation. But it is the slash grooming that slows both animals until they breathe deep and half close their eyes with pleasure. A tame monkey will part human hair, searching stroke by stroke for parasites or crumbs of salt and then lie flat itself, back ready, in unspoken demand.

I tried to sleep, with grooming monkeys and echoes of chimpanzees and white envelopes swirling behind my eyes, but as I spiraled down and dreams danced like colored flames, the prickles spread. Insects swarmed on my skin. Outraged, I threw off the covers and turned on the flashlight. Nothing. I ran shaking hands down my legs, but there was nothing there. Every hair on my body was pilo-erected, standing straight up. The dreams disappeared.

45

Fire Ants

Asia spread across the steppes, through the arctic snow of a land bridge and into America. From igloo to pueblo, the Asians passed, broadening their rib cage, bringing humans to the last empty continent. The trade routes had already brought plant medicine and acupressure. The Asian immigrants built canoes and fields of corn.

A small line of dark leaves flowed toward the garbage pit as if my itches had been insect precognition. I sat for a while, elbows on knees, hunched around the pain in my stomach, and watched the ants. They climbed in step down into the pit and foraged, grunting, among the plantain peels, climbed back up, still in their perfect lines, and marched, straight as a Roman road, up the hill. Nature's disposal system in a land without visibility for vultures, and in which most mammals had been shot.

Simon came and also watched.

"Maybe we should cover the garbage with dirt?" I asked.

"It is not good, memsahib." He didn't explain. The fire roared as he built it high.

Bending ferns in the nest that Kamumbo had made on the north slope and wishing I had a Mutwa hut here too, I sat on the rain poncho, backpack perched between legs prickling with the memory of the ants.

Something urinated for a long time in the fig tree. Then it hooted, low and thoughtful. Three crashes, a squeak, and more water drifted down, then another hoot. I heard swishing and crashes in the northeast, like those of a small monkey. It was Shaveleg, sitting hunched in the middle of the tree, shoulder, ear, and one leg in view. I stared too long, and she urinated and moved back into hiding. A few minutes later, the tree thumped. She peered out, looking miserable.

The infant misted into sight on top. Shaveleg hooted quietly to herself and urinated again. Something else thudded. The valley smelled of feces and fear. Monkeys climbed into the tree above me. I bent my head and tried not to look at her, but without volition, my eyes lifted and swiveled toward her. She hooted and huddled herself closer to the tree. Forty-six minutes had passed since she'd climbed into it.

Gazing through the binoculars at the ground for a long time, I slowly, haltingly, raised them to her. Pretending to forage on ferns didn't work. Chimpanzees were too good at reading human body language, and I still hadn't learned how to breathe when watching them.

She peed again. Something chirped. After sixty-eight minutes without feeding, she vanished. I didn't know whether she was still in the tree or not. *68 min, adult female chimp in fig.*

A shiver spread from earth to leaves. In air as damp as ice, rain thundered down the hill. For a second more I stared into the dark branches, hoping to see rebellion against the stings and arrows of weather, but nothing moved except the canopy. Like cymbals crashing, rain struck the mud, carrying an applause of broken branches and leaves ripped loose. Amid the timpani, trees cracked and leaned. Head down, I stumbled back toward camp. From under the rain poncho, my pants poured water. Squatting in the path, boots washed with a torrent that slid me sideways, I unzipped my backpack, hands shaking with haste. My plastic bag had a hole in the bottom corner, but I wrapped the binoculars and notebook in it anyway. Mud shot stinging pellets into my face, and the rain slapped my legs sideways on the path. I slipped and fell. With another rush of water, a branch the size of a tree broke off and fell nearby. Holding one hand in front of my face, I staggered, head down, along the path. Camp was invisible until I had spun past the last tree. Rain fell in vertical sheets, but the ricochets spun in all directions, so we huddled at the far edge of the tarpaulin, against the slope of the hill, and waited.

Within the buzz of still-falling water, the forest trembled with a vague roar. Insects and birds settled into silence, and the thrumming came nearer. Simon bent down to the fire and scraped some coals to the edge with a stick. A rumbling slowly grew until some hidden tumult shook the ground. The black mud dulled and turned brown, as if rusting before our eyes. Fire ants roared in a solid swath across the clearing, in no order this time, swarming over leaves and trees, rushing across roots, toward camp.

The ants poured down the hill like Ugandan rain. Inch by inch the humming deepened; the ground sank darker and darker under their bodies. Simon picked an ember out of the fire with bare fingers. Sliding it onto his palm, he shifted the coal into position and lifted his hand as if releasing a hawk. An arc of light sped across the dark clearing, spattering a meteor shower of sparks that hovered and then collapsed. Slowly he built a circle of fire around us, throwing coals at the dark gaps in the circle, where the ants had smothered the flames with their piled corpses. The ants paused, hesitated at the edge of camp by the tent, then moved in a carpet up the stakes and fabric, over the tarp, into every dish and spoon on the table. Swarms dangled and dropped from the edges like bunches of grapes, reabsorbing into the army as they fell to the ground. Always they moved forward, downhill, toward us. Simon tore an ant from his ankle and flicked it, still snapping, into the fire, where it crackled and exploded into nothing.

Holding the notebook, I tried to code entries for the data book but couldn't take my eyes from the ants. Simon sat next to me on the log for the first time, as if in crisis he would allow us to be equal, and said, "Ehh."

Through the twisting masses below us, a mouse jumped from hiding and ran. It beat its head with small paws at every step. Four ants weighed the mouse down, in armpit and neck and the hollow of the back leg. A stream switched direction within the flow, moving toward the mouse. If it had run without stopping, it might have made it, but probably not. Like liquid flowing downhill, the ants overtook and covered the running mouse. It reared up twice, pounding the air with its paws, yellow teeth bared up at the sky, then sank into the swarm. The carpet of ants heaved once, and then a new stream formed, carrying its meat back uphill to their home. Insects we hadn't seen before climbed to the top of ruined ferns and fell, invisible again beneath the ants' bodies.

Simon froze and watched, then with haste threw coals at the ants crawling over their companions' heated corpses into our circle. "Memsahib."

"Yes?"

"Memsahib, it is that we must kill these animals."

I hesitated. "We'll ask the game ranger what we should do." I hadn't come to the forest to make it comfortable for humans.

Simon leaped to his feet. "Tchah," he said and, picking a handful of red coals from the fire, threw them into the ring of ash. As each coal in the circle flickered and darkened, with jerks of the wrist he sent new ones thumping into place. I stepped carefully through the stream of uninterested ants to the blind, leaving Simon standing by the fire, a coal glowing in his hand. Redtails traveled by, silent.

Patrick passed the nest without seeing me and exclaimed, "Ehh, dudu wengi!" to himself. Voices ebbed and fell, and the forest listened. There were too many people in camp. I sat below the fig, sick and wet.

L'Hoesti walked on the ground through camp, moving in the ferns. One male leaped into a small tree, ate a leaf, then jumped down. An infant hopped into a tree, looked at us, then let itself drop to the ground. Its fur was plastered down, and it sat awkwardly, as if it didn't want to feel its own skin. Something thumped, crashed, and chuckled in the tree above me. More thumps, crashes, chuckles, then a swish, and I saw a redtail behind me. Fruit dropped. Monkeys ran on branches and chuckled.

Just as darkness fell, a chimp, fat and unfamiliar, shifted into the fig tree, its leg pale and scarred, and I thought at first there must be two chimpanzees with shaved legs in these foothills, even though I knew how much chimps could change their shape with their hair. But it was Mama Shaveleg putting all her hairs on end, either from fear or as protection.

Chimps screamed in the distance. Redtails chuckled. Shaveleg moved around the tree slowly. A vine swung near the fig tree as if an animal had climbed in or out, but I couldn't see anything.

The redtails chuckled and grunted. Shaveleg and her infant sat on in the tree. Something swished closer in the near west, and the opposite side of the valley echoed in a crash. The fig tree shook, and vines moved beside it. A minute later Shaveleg and her baby left. They must have gone far away to make their sleeping nests, because we heard no crashes of branches broken or moved.

46
Outside the Ring of Fire

Simon sat backward on the log above the fire and threw coals and hot ashes as the ants swarmed in a smaller flood that night. Unlacing the broken ties on my hiking boots, I pulled both feet out and placed them carefully on the tongues while I unrolled once-white socks. My big toenail shivered as I pulled off the first sock, twitching into the air after the cloth, then settling back onto the toe. The ants clattered and swished in rivers around the circle of fire. My socks blazed dry in a wave of moldy air as Simon poked the fire.

It was something to be surrounded by even such a small piece of nature as an ant. Like a thousand machines, they ran down the hill with their single passion. I longed for the Mutwa hut by the smallest fig. Silence and peace. Early in the evening, I stepped through the ants and crawled into the wet sleeping bag, listening to the murmur of small feet magnified by infinity.

The tent pulled down at the corner tentatively, then more firmly ducked and sank. A rattling, thrumming shadow spread itself above my face. Slowly separating from a dream, I shone the flashlight upward. Inside the fly, a thousand ants ran, dipping the tent roof inches from my face. Through the fabric, I could see pincers probing, searching for a hole. If they found a way in, I could have opened the tent and run away from the horde. Ants can kill only insects or small mammals that can be caught by surprise and weighed down or pinched in awkward places. I would have had to lie down in a swarm and fall asleep to be killed, unless the swarm was so wide that I fell down in shock before I reached its edge.

Simon woke, with someone else. They said "tchah" and threw coals at gaps in their ring of fire. Against the green wall of the tent, I saw lighted shadows arc with a hiss, and on the other side of the fabric, its antithesis, a mirrored darkness passing by like a comet before the sun.

The ants found the hole where I had dropped the tent on a sharp, pointed bush. The tent-repair kit a salesman persuaded me to buy sat in a duffel I'd left behind at Tom's cabin, but I had crisscrossed the slash with duct tape. The ants buzzed in excitement around the ends of the tape. Feelers waved double time and legs scrabbled under the edges. But they left at last, both duct tape and tent proving insect-resistant. I came out the next morning thinking our camp must have been wiped clean. But they hadn't eaten our food, except one bowl of rice, though lids now sat beside pots of flour, and bags of beans gaped open, and they had walked a thousand small tracks of mud across the bananas.

47

Poachers' Dog

7:42 saw a squirrel moving in 1st bunch of omurehe. The fruit is almost gone, but there must be some higher because I heard it dropping after the squirrel moved up.

8:48 crash approaching from W.

8:52 thumps.

8:55 crash, growling <(v)> [vocalization], crashes still occurring at 9:22.

left at 11:00, feeling sick, runs, fever, headache, v. cold.

returned at 2:15.

2:42 heard hoot. Quite a bit of thunder in S.

2:46 chuckles <(v)> very near me.

I left 3:30, dizzy, nauseous, general feeling of utter misery, and headache.

We ate a bowl of beans from Tom's site, clean and fresh. Rain slanted down through the leaves and into our faces.

Like a secondary plague, fire ants crawled out past the shimmering, still-rocking pools of water that lay about our camp, and foraged for food in plastic plates and cups half buried in mud.

"Memsahib, we must to kill them."

"We can't. This is a wildlife reserve."

*   *   *

Kamumbo sat silent, out of the ring of fire. As the ants poured down, he slowly moved to a corner of the clearing and squatted again, smoking his pipe. Without a glance to ask permission to join the circle of fire, he left after a while, trotting through the flow of ants with that high-stepping gait so smooth and fast that no ants attached themselves to his feet.

One by one, the other men found excuses to leave. Even Gabriel left for food. Lying alone on the mat, Simon said, "Tchah," about the others, without explanation.

With that ache in the stomach of internal organs beginning to press too tightly against ribs and vertebrae, I lay sleeping, one ear turned always toward the path, listening for soldiers.

At night the fire should have ebbed and washed in yellow and green light onto the walls of my tent. On other nights, over the hours as it murmured down to a throb, one of the men would mutter and kick out a foot, and the fire would flame again, roars and flickers and hissings of raindrops. With the fire dying, the forest hung over the tent like the lid on a pot, pressing chill upon the sides. The silence filtered into my dreams as a breathlessness, and I sat up in the sleeping bag. I shivered in the wet air, then froze. So high-pitched that I was afraid before I heard it, a wail lifted and rose and fell in the distance, detached and anguished.

Soldiers, and death. I leaned back my head to loosen the muscles in my throat and gasped.

"It is that you hear a tree that is falling, memsahib." Simon's voice was shaking, but I didn't say anything. That was no tree. I sat in the sleeping bag and listened for a while, then, without knowing it, lay down again.

Simon must have stayed awake to watch for the soldiers. Perhaps he couldn't sleep with the others gone, or believed what he'd said about Patrick and Akit, that they made excuses to leave because they knew the soldiers were coming. For the first time, only the embers still burned in the fire.

Wrapped in my dream, I turned away from Simon's footsteps, and he said instantly, even as my sleeping bag settled down around me with puffs of moldy air, "Memsahib. You are awake."

I sat up and coughed, still half dreaming but trying to prove I was alert. "Is something wrong?"

"No, memsahib. It is just that I hear that you are awake."

"Oh." I lay down and sucked back into the dream, with my mind half working. Maybe he just wanted to talk. This might be the first night he had spent alone, going from his mother's bed to the army, to his wife, to this quarrelsome mat.

He shifted around and clanked pots together by the fire. My eyes popped open, with irritation at first, then with focus. If Simon wanted me to wake, he had a good reason. I sat in the bag. Simon listened.

"Memsahib, you are awake?"

"Yes. And you?"

"Me, I am awake. I to watch the soldiers."

"Oh. Thank you, Simon." As I lay down, my stomach churned. I knew I should help Simon watch, but I couldn't stay awake all night and watch the monkeys all day. I got little enough sleep as it was, with the soldiers coming.

The BaKiga fell asleep each night as soon as they stopped talking, telling one another the events they had all seen. I lay awake longer, with all those lighted eyes flashing from memory and vision. And with the soldiers coming to kill us, every crack of a branch woke me.

Simon had never listened to the sleep of someone who had slept alone since the day of her birth, tossing and turning in vast expanses of dreams. BaKiga, like most Africans, slept bundled together without movement. He thought each turn of mine was a waking, when it was really a deeper slipping into sleep. This habit of sleeping separate from our children is recent, a by-product of wealth. For warmth, for comfort, for safety from predators, for all the animal needs, babies have slept with their families in almost every country, until we replaced ourselves with heat and locked doors.

I slept for a while, semiwaking every time Simon coughed or muttered. In my dream, I heard two men laughing.

Slapping aside the sleeping bag, I shot up straight. Simon didn't ask me if I was awake this time. I had forgotten that, in Simon's English, "I to watch the soldiers" could mean either "I am watching for the soldiers" or "I am watching the soldiers." My fault, because I didn't concentrate when Simon asked me to correct his sentences. By that time too, after five months of pidgin, I was forgetting how to speak proper English.

The two men laughed again, and I sat in the tent, surrounded by the light of dying embers, and listened over the tapping of my heart. Branches bent and cracked with whooshes of water on the ridgetop. "Simon," I said, low.

"Eh, memsahib. You are awake." This time I heard the quaver in his voice. It was very cold with the fire gone. I sat with the sleeping bag clutched around me and shivered in long spasms. I should have left the tent, but Ugandan nights are colder than the days, and as wet as air can be. It was easier to die in the tent than sit in the cold on wet wood over a dead fire.

"Is it the soldiers?"

"Eeeeh, memsahib. Me, I do not think so."

The men laughed and called to each other, going slower now on the muddy slope. *Crash, whoop, crack!* One of them skidded off the path into a branch. I always slipped there too, in the sudden ditch and bend of the roots. He cursed in Rukiga, and the other laughed, tripping and stumbling too. I heard a rustling in the ferns and whipped around as if I could see through the tent. Simon was searching for the bullet bag with our new bullets. "Eeeh," he whispered under his breath. It wasn't there.

The rifle clinked as he opened it with shaking hands. One of the old bullets that had been stripped of its gunpowder was still inside. Simon slid it quietly home and clicked off the safety. Then he squatted in the ferns. The men were close now.

"Simon, what do we do?"

We should have run into the bush. Lost as I was in the trees, I could still move faster and more quietly than those two. Reluctant to leave the warmth of my bag, I waited.

"Eeeeh, memsahib, I must to shoot them." The fig tree by camp rustled, and Simon stood up and roared, waving the rifle in the air. Silence fell. We waited a few seconds while the embers hissed and turned in the wet air, and then Simon shouted something in Rukiga and snapped the bolt home on the rifle again, more loudly.

The crashes, mutters, and curses rippled back up the valley, onto the slope and along the ridge.

"What did you say?"

Sheepish, he muttered, "Me, I say that the Mzungu have many guns and is very angry."

"Eeeeeh. Bwana Simon."

"Eh, eh, eh, memsahib." He laughed and poked the fire. My tent flickered in yellow and green in long stretches up to the roof. I thought it was over and lay back.

Thwack. Someone laughed by the fig tree across the valley where the chimpanzees had danced. *Thwack.* The tarpaulin cracked like a bomb, and water crashed onto the tent. Something mammalian screamed a protest in the distance. *Thwack.*

"Simon?"

"It is all right, memsahib, it is that these bad men, they throw stones because they are angry that they cannot hunt."

"Do you need help, Simon?"

"No, memsahib. It is that they have lost their dog and are very angry that they cannot look for it."

Cracks and crashes ebbed back up the hill, and again a lone animal shouted a warning.

On three long notes, a wail echoed over and along the hills, up to the mountain. Dispassionate yet containing an emotion I'd never heard, the howl passed beyond the range of the human ear, first high, then piercing, then gone, except in vibrations of the air. Something prickled on the back of my neck. I put up a hand to touch it and jumped when my palm hit neck hairs so rigid and stiff that they felt like beetles' legs. Gooseflesh washed in one long shudder from my legs to my scalp, pricking through my hair. We are an animal like any other. Our fur rises with fear; we enlarge with our own chemicals and electricities like any startled cat.

"What was that?" I asked with artificial calm.

"That was the dog of the poachers, memsahib. These bad men, they lost their dog."

That was no dog. That was part wolf and part jaguar. I heard the voices crackling from the ridge across from us.

"Simon, they are coming to the river."

"No, memsahib, they must to look for this dog."

The hill across from us cracked as the men slid down it. I heard Simon kick the fire with his foot again, and I wanted to shout at him for making such a clear target but didn't. A stone *thwocked* into our tarpaulin. Two pots fell into the mud.

Thwack. Something again fell from the sky.

"Eeeeeh, they are bad men. Very bad." Simon roared again,

and the noises stopped. I unzipped the tent to keep him company, wincing back from the shower of dew on the fly. Then, at a loss, I sat in the opening with the sleeping bag wrapped around my shoulders and watched the fire with him. Simon's hair was wet. He must have splashed water on his head to stay awake.

As soon as it was light, redtails ran across the valley to trees near us. Blue monkeys came and sat near the camp, as if it had become a safe zone in the forest.

In my sleep I had lain back in the wet bag again. With the tent open, icy moisture hung inside, clinging to my skin and darkening the flannel shirt I'd borrowed from my brother. Climbing out of the bag, I crawled backward into the mud and zipped the tent, shaking drops of condensation onto the sleeping bag.

With another shiver and stopping of breath, I felt that howl begin again, almost silent, then rising to a calm statement of some unimaginable emotion.

Simon looked at me as I froze. "It is the dog, memsahib." I tried to laugh. "This dog, it will not hurt you, memsahib. It is that this dog, it is lost."

No Ugandan dog stood higher than my knee. I couldn't explain to Simon that it wasn't the dog I was afraid of but the sound it made, because I didn't understand it myself. Ashamed that he had seen my fear, I gathered my toothbrush. The dog wailed again like a demon lover passing from one world into another in search of something lost. As I walked to the toilet pit, trying to breathe, I was afraid for the first time since I'd been in the forest, not of animal or man but of things outside some ancestral campfire and of the silence they left behind.

48

No Chimps for a Week

Redtail fights.

L'Hoest's monkeys eat orange fungus. I asked Kamumbo if it was good to eat and he nodded, then shook his head when I stretched one hand toward the tooth-marked frill. Perhaps he'd been making a joke.

11:22 colobus begins bleahing <(v)> near omurehe, and redtail begins <(v)> wrak wrak wraking back.

12:23 something is <(v)> squeaking, a jump and a thump.

12:28 more jumping.

12:53 incredible <(v)> roar, followed by clucking <(v)> from redtail, and 2 colobus monkeys <(v)> bleahing in N & S, there also seems to be a blue <(v)> barking somewhere. Rain all afternoon.

5:40 <(F)> [Feeding] Rafiki (Gabriel's redtail friend), male, returned and began feeding on entero leaves and kakoba leaves at 24?m.

5:49 moved to omushasha 26m to eat moss and leaves.

5:53 jumped.

5:54 blue barked wrakwrak <(v)> in S.

5:56 colobus <(v)> began bleahing in S.

5:57 *Rafiki jumped to 18mm in omusheshe.*

5:58 *down out of sight colobus cont. [enkunge male 28 min,
omushesha 18–24m].*

6:05 *enkunge moved down (still there) to 17m.*
feeling sick.

49

Black Magic

Redtail monkeys paused in the circle of trees around the fig. The chimps were gone again. Slowly and with long rests, I walked beneath them to the blind, holding on to mildewed bark, forehead pressed against a tree. The fever was worse, and my feet felt strange.

The air hung heavy and hot in the sunshine, and they leaped with screams into the fig, each jump raining fruit with noise to the ground. Some couldn't even eat yet; they had to chase one another and scream and chatter about their fortune until they could sit down and, panting, force figs into stretched mouths with both hands. They ran, searching for the best place, fighting with yaps and chatters and squeals over one bunch or another, then cooing over the red ones, chewing fast and dropping most. Wasps and drunken flies moved over the heaps at the bottom, licking up sugar from the broken figs ripe enough to ooze.

Noises trickled back into the grove on the rivers of scent, and the redtails ate faster and fought without moving, glancing over their shoulders and giving little cries. Leaves and water crashed to the ground in a leap of sound as blue monkeys surrounded the tree, talking loudly. With a few last shrill cries and snatches of fruit, the redtails crashed out of the tree in a shower of figs and water, and the blue monkeys ran in.

The blind was hot in the sunshine, with wasps crawling swollen through the vines to rest and the figs fermenting with pulses of wet air into the opening. The whole valley throbbed with the smell, like a headache. Drowsing in the branches, blue monkeys rested their stomachs with legs stretched out or dangling, picking a fig just to hold it in the mouth or to eat a drugged fly. Redtail monkeys darting in for a handful got nothing more than a cluck or chuckle of irritation. But even in that air, in the sunshine, with full stomachs and the buzzing of the wasps, they all watched and waited for the chimpanzees, looking back over their shoulders at each noise. There was a crash across the valley, and then a hoot, a quiet and gentle sound, but the monkeys screamed and leaped out of the trees, and ran back in to snatch one last fig, then screamed and crashed away through the forest until it was quiet.

A blue monkey barked near the west fig tree. I heard a colobus *bleahing* in the north, and a redtail clacking back. The redtail clacked toward the fig tree. On the way back to lunch, I waded through a stream of fire ants. Rafiki sat in camp with Gabriel, eating entero and kakoba leaves, then hopped to another tree and rummaged through the moss. A blue monkey barked *waka, waka, waka* in the south and a colobus *bleah-bleahed* in the north. Rafiki jumped out of sight. I pulled the ants one by one from my shoelaces.

They clung single-mindedly, releasing only as the fabric tore. The ants twisted, not to bite my fingers but toward the shoes they had left behind, opening and closing their jaws on empty air.

I pulled off my sock to reach a last buried ant and a toenail came with it, stretching in the air between foot and fabric. A piece of skin at one corner tore with a pop, though the rest had lifted without a pang, and the nail dangled like hardened wool from the sock.

Leaning forward, I peered at it with a feeling almost of pride. Then I looked down at the toe. The skin was damp but thick, not like the throbbing bulge that wells from a nail cut too short.

The fire ants, in their explorations, carried away all organic material from the garbage pit. If they found the nail, they'd float it up the hill past the men. I could flick the toenail into my backpack and bury it the next day as I sat under the fig tree, but I knew that I would forget about it and someday hand someone a canteen with a toenail dangling from the strap.

In the end, as humans have always done, I burned my leavings. The fear that some black-magic-practicing poacher might find it, or that the damage wreaked upon the toenail by insects and predators would be visited upon me, moved some instinct, and I flicked the nail into the fire.

The fire ants came back as I sat on the log, waiting for my beans to cool on my knee.

50

Lost

*Like any American expatriate in Europe, Emerson was passed
from one artist to another, and shown the sites of extinct cul-
tures. The land beneath his feet was layered with mythology, thousands upon thousands of years of gods. Coleridge and Wordsworth
spoke to him of grocery lists and the price of coal; human history
encompassed one mistake after another. Emerson wrote in despair
that no great thinker had more answers than anyone else.*

Kamumbo led me to a small hill, so gently sloped that I would
be able to sit, shoulders against a straight tree, without a hand
propped below. In the clearing above, one small fruit tree stood,
half lighted by the emptiness. The leaves all around it were black
and shadow, rising skyscraper high, but in that inexplicable hole
of the canopy, the omusingati tree shone green and gold where it
reached into the light. Vines as thick as birches rose in twisted
strands against the forest wall, releasing waterfalls of leaves into
corners of the clearing. But their roots halted there in the shadows, so the ground was as bare and clean as that of the ridges,
littered only with mulch.

Without visible movement, Kamumbo sank to a squat. I squatted too, thinking he was pausing before bringing me to a fig tree.

He had never stayed with me at a tree before, except when we all watched the chimps across from camp.

Kamumbo pulled two sticks out of ragged pants. Settling the short one into a notch in the larger, he twirled it between his palms, moving his hands up and down, until a wisp of smoke came out of the hole. Lifting the leaf below it, he tipped the glowing sawdust into his handmade pipe, as smoothly as a movie star lighting his love's cigarette.

We didn't see any monkeys.

Blue monkeys crawled out to the ends of branches and sat hunched, shaking their heads and licking their lips. They never sought shelter, even when the rain came down in a solid curtain, like water poured from a bucket. A mother in front of me crouched over her infant and wrapped arms so tightly around it that ten minutes later, it emerged dry, along with the sun. Her older daughter, mourning the loss of that warm stomach, huddled next to her on the branch, eyes shut in misery, still running with water. I squatted with ankles wedged at an awkward angle in my hiking boots, rain poncho covering my backpack, binoculars in their plastic wrap. With the hood pulled down to my chin, only my hands were exposed. They felt wet all the way through, like sponges immersed in cold water. Water rapids leaped around my boots. With the rain over, I was still wet inside the poncho. The trees' rain rebounded off the ground onto my face and neck, along with bullets of decayed leaves and dead insects.

Kamumbo had let Gabriel lead me to the clearing this time and had disappeared again. I breathed in, waiting, certain that something was going to happen. The tree stood above the hill, lighted like an altar. Its fruit, a narrow skin of flesh over bright beads of stone, was ripe. Almond-shaped and as red and shiny as currants, omusingati had few vitamins, but since they usually grew beside the figs, dropped in primate feces as seeds, monkeys ate them often, while waiting for their entrée to the fig trees. With that strange clearing on the hillside slope where growth should have been thickest, monkeys sat outlined like cutout silhouettes.

The monkeys shook themselves, sneezed, and brightened. Infants bounced into the branches, and some adults reached for omusingati. I watched until dusk, then slowly, reluctantly, moved my stiff clothes up the path. Careful not to let them touch bare skin, I creaked up the hill and halted on the crest. For the first time, I was coming back from a new blind by myself. I had learned the forest. A monkey sneezed at me sleepily, and another roused itself to *yarp*. I turned left. The path dwindled into a solid wall of forest, barred with vines, knee-high roots, and bushes. I hadn't crawled through this. Gabriel had taken an easy path that morning, never one that would muddy his suit. I walked along the path, then back again. Five times I walked back and forth, looking for the side trail that led to camp. The clearing lay east and downhill a few steps away, but I was afraid to leave the path. Hills turned into valleys in the Impenetrable Forest, valleys fell as ditches in mountains, and rivers ran through both. The civil wars of Rwanda and Zaire lay a few hours away.

I heard Simon and Gabriel talking and thought about yelling for help. Until it was too dark to see any trail, even with a flashlight, I walked back and forth on that short strip. Simon's murmurs were louder. I heard, "Memsahib." When Simon was upset, his hands flapped. The spoon hit against the pot with a clang. If I waited any longer, I knew, he would stir so wildly that beans would sizzle out into the fire and burn. He yelled at Gabriel. "You, where did you take the memsahib? Why is she not back?"

Gabriel mumbled something.

"*You*. You go and to find the memsahib."

Beans crashed into the fire and it roared a protest. Gabriel mumbled something else. I knew, as if I sat there, that Kamumbo, on the outskirts of camp, was standing without a word to come and find me. I cleared my throat loudly, then again. "Er, um. Oh, Simon, I'm over here." He didn't hear, so I said louder, "Over here, Gabriel, Simon." They thought they heard something and fell silent.

"I'm over here, on the hill." They told each other it was the memsahib. Then they sat down again. I waited a second, then realized they thought I was coming. I cleared my throat again.

"Simon." "Memsahib." "Simon, I am lost." "Memsahib?" "I cannot find the path." "We are here, memsahib." I couldn't tell where the voices were coming from. The rain forest had closed around the trail, wiping out primate footprints as if a hundred years had passed since the last step. "I don't know how to come back." Long silence. I thought I heard some muffled sounds. "Simon?" "Memsahib, Gabriel, he comes to get you." Gabriel crashed up the path with my spare flashlight. The lantern would give more light, but the flashlight was a novelty. "Memsahib, where are you?" I cleared my throat. "Over here." Feet climbed toward me, then stopped. "Where?"

I shouted, "Here," so they could follow my voice. A fern rustled ten feet away. My voice wavered, and I bit my sleeve to stifle a giggle. "We are come, memsahib." Gabriel and Kamumbo stepped over a small bush, and I suddenly saw the path beyond it, clearly marked by chimpanzee feet, except for that one plant. They panted forward, eyes wide. "Memsahib, you are ill." Dropping my sleeve, I thought briefly, then discarded all the lies that came to mind. "No," I admitted. "I couldn't find the path."

They looked at me, then at the trail leading down to camp.

Kamumbo stepped backward and grinned. Gabriel's mouth opened slowly, and a strangled "eh" came out. He repeated, "The path, you do not find it." I nodded. "Eeeeeh, eeeh, eeeeh, eeeeh," he roared. "Eeeeh, eeeeh, eeeeh, eeh."

"What is it?" Simon called from camp.

"Memsahib, she cannot find the path." They turned and walked back to camp. Kamumbo's back shook with suppressed laughter. Gabriel gasped for breath and wiped away streams of tears.

A few steps down the path, I saw the blue tarp through the leaves. Simon came up the hill to meet us. "Memsahib was lost?" "Memsahib was lost." Gabriel told him how close I had been to camp.

The fire snapped and turned burnt beans on their sides in its ashes and lifted white smoke to the trees. All through dinner, one after another of the men said, "Eeh, memsahib, she was lost," and they laughed until they cried, snuffling and wiping their eyes on the edges of muddy shirts. "Eeeeh, eeeeh, eh."

"Memsahib, she was, eeeeh, so close to this path, and it is that she did not see it." Word by word they repeated the story until it was agreed upon and honed into the shape it would take over the next decades, an echo of myself left behind and spreading through the land like the tale of my gender and of the measuring of nests.

51

Shaveleg's Son

Gorillas travel within large home ranges. Females rest several years with a male in his territory, raising an offspring with him, then usually leave, often when two groups meet at the farthest limits of their routes. One researcher found dozens of lowland gorillas in a small swamp in Zaire, each male with his accumulated young and the females that had chosen to live with him, one group resting or passing by another as if blind. In the water, gorillas waded, backs straight and arms filled with water plants, plucking one here, one there. The gorillas walked on their hind legs in the dark water, longer than any primate has been seen to walk on two legs. Perhaps because the water took their weight, they didn't sway as they walked but traveled straight and slow from one patch to another.

Kamumbo carefully led me to the omusingati. As I sat on the wet ground and leaned into the base of a sloped tree, a few redtails passed. With a subdued crash, they jumped four-legged into the branches on the side farthest from me. Hands reached from the leaves, plucked a few of the fruits, and moved on, leaving the omusingati still glossy, like a Hanukkah tree with red fruit.

We think of animals as adapted to their environment, with an instinctive knowledge of where to find food and shelter and water, but they are not. They learn and are taught where the ripe figs are, when to hunt, and when to sleep. As in our culture, knowledge accumulates over the centuries, so that a chimpanzee is as deeply embedded in its place as the place is embedded in it. It is not easy to find food in a rain forest, where sight and smell and sound are blocked by a canopy so thick that wind itself cannot enter.

One can hold to a small range, as the redtails do, and compromise on the quality of food eaten, taking more widely dispersed, less nutritious food and the occasional fig. Or one can, as the blue monkeys might, keep a wider range, overlapping across redtail territories, using their more intimate knowledge of the time and place of openings to find the better foods. The redtails often travel with the blues—no one is sure why, since the former are chased away from the figs and have to steal them from the edges. Either the blue monkeys piggyback the redtails against their will, or the redtails use the blues as cover from predators, their one chance to travel loudly, noisily, high up in the canopy, where the monkey eagles watch.

The chimpanzees spread over vast forests, traveling in separate groups, a mother and her children, or perhaps a group of males. When one of them finds a ripe fig or a cluster of lesser trees in fruit, she calls in a voice that lifts over the canopy with screams of excitement, and the other chimpanzees rush in from their far lands. But chimps must also follow the excitement of the monkeys in the area. I rarely saw chimps arriving at a fig until the monkeys had been there for a while. It is hard to see what the monkeys gain from this intrusion. Even the most sated of chimps rarely lets a monkey gather much fruit, and indeed it would be unwise to venture so near those grasping hands. Chimpanzees prefer meat to fruit if they haven't had meat for a while. Perhaps when leopards and lions lived here, before the war, monkeys preferred to sit near an animal that could chase predators away, and resigned themselves to eating their protectors' leavings. The monkeys didn't hush their noise after they heard the chimps call their greeting, until they were close enough for danger.

So there are those with small ranges, and the users of their knowledge, the migrants who taste the face of the earth. Within each group there are also divisions. Female chimps seem to have a more stable range, while males check the perimeters of the territory more often. Thus females — the older the better — are more likely to know the patterns of the area and to possess knowledge passed on to them by their mothers. A son is often served well if he abandons the disputes of the male groups and travels with his mother to the best foods, building strength and size.

Kamumbo skimmed up the hill toward me, and I stood. As soon as he saw me, he turned and left. I followed him back through camp to the west blind.

"Empundu," he said, and left it at that.

A black-faced juvenile sat in the fig tree, scratching and watching us. After ten minutes, he moved up and was enveloped into the canopy, bending branches into what looked like a day nest. A balding, grizzled head poked out near us, then withdrew. Small things dropped into the undergrowth.

A small infant climbed up high. It had a very gaunt face and long cheek hair, like side whiskers on a Victorian gentleman. The infant climbed farther up, and Mama Shaveleg's grizzled head poked out again. She looked at us and hooted quietly. She sat in the same place for a while, eating omutuunda fruit. A stream of froth and saliva poured out of her mouth as she rolled a hard green ball between her lips. She watched us. Once, she twisted on the branch away from us, and I saw the scar on her leg, near the knee. She moved up, still watching us. I heard a quiet hoot, then another, and three more. Kamumbo and I sat, fully exposed. One of the animals barked and moved. I didn't see any of the others but could hear them still there, feeding. A blue monkey in the south chuckled and clucked once, then said *wrak, wrak, wrak*.

I thought the chimpanzees had left, but when I looked down at my notebook to add some details and then looked back up, I saw them. Shaveleg sat with a young male and her infant in the omutuunda tree, grooming, about ten feet away from me. She saw the difference in my attention and, gathering herself and her infant, left the male bereft, still stretched on his branch. With an almost invisible hush, he disappeared through unbent branches.

Another toenail came off, then a smaller one. I held them in my palm. Snakes must shed their skin to grow larger. What size can one achieve if the remnants of a carapace too are sloughed away? I had expected to pay with limbs or life for this year in Africa; toenails were small coin for what I had seen. But I dropped them too in the fire.

52

Machete Cut

The chimps were gone. I sat on my poncho and watched the trees for signs of them. Someone crashed and slid down the hill, quietly, as if he knew the forest. I lay in the bushes, hidden, and wondered if it was the soldiers. "Memsahib," Gabriel said from the trail, and I climbed slowly off the slippery stems and came out. "It is the forest ranger. He has come to speak with you."

The forest ranger stood when he saw me. "Give me your papers," he said. He had come back to order me out of the forest because I'd applied to his superior for permission rather than to him. Like most officials in Uganda then, he was as wide as any two other BaKiga men, nostrils flared in a scowl that had cut deep grooves in his forehead. In that clearing, so populated by men as slender as saplings, swaying now toward the edge of the trees, he stood out like a dragon guarding the treasure of tent and tarp and fire. More at home there than I had ever been, he waited. I glanced around. Simon's face was gray and twisted; the others had disappeared without motion.

The forester asked to see my papers or letters of recommendation. I pulled them out of the big backpack, and he said I wasn't supposed to be in the forest without his permission. I stood, heart thumping, not sure what to say. It was still too soon to leave the forest. Breathing in, I agreed that he should've known about my presence, but as I had arranged to see the forest ranger at the Kayonza meeting and he didn't show up, and two forest guards were also supposed to come but didn't arrive until I had left, and the entire district of the Ruhingire officials knew why I'd come, for how long, and with what authority, and I'd come with two game guards who had every right to be in the forest and take anyone with them, I didn't see why I should have stayed for weeks in Kayonza on the chance that he would pop in.

He agreed that game guards could enter the forest as they wished, but everyone else had to get written permission. I told him I knew that anyone was allowed to enter the forest with a game guard or forest guard, and it was ridiculous to expect tourists and project volunteers to wait in town for him. Then I said Tom had permission from the president to work in the forest, and I was working for Tom.

"Oh, I didn't mean you, your papers are in order, I like the project. I mean the monks and the Mzungu, they can't enter without written permission."

"The monks came with forest guards both times they visited. Are you saying that anyone but the brothers can do that?"

"No, they can come, I like them, I live near them, but the Mzungu can't stay." A few of Tom's volunteers had come down to help, but they had long since gone back anyway.

He told me to visit the DFO in Rukingini — a week's journey away.

We sat in silence for a while, my stomach aching. Then Gabriel burst into the clearing, shouting in a recognizable language for the first time in three days, "Akit, he has chopped himself, and the blood, it is come."

Joanna Greenfield

The ranger sat on as calm as a Buddha, and I stood up to get my bag of Band-Aids. Akit limped in like Johnny Appleseed, with a hand-cut walking stick and his regulation boots hanging around his neck. I was in no mood to humor Gabriel, who danced around the clearing, shouting, so I was short with Akit. The slash on his foot was deep enough to show muscle, but it was only an inch long.

Akit was too dignified to mention the cut. He sat down by a pan of water and slowly splashed the mud off the wound. Without touching that dignity, I suggested that he use some boiled water instead, and explained about the problem of infection. He boiled the water himself while I checked the wound. Then he splashed it, still bubbling, over the cut. It didn't seem to do any harm, so I kept talking to the forest ranger and didn't say anything when Akit thrust his whole foot into the pan. After the sterile water had turned brown, he decided he'd humored me enough and wiped the cut dry with one rough stroke of the rag that he carried in his pocket to clean the rifle. Excusing myself to the forester, I stood and found an antiseptic ointment. Kneeling slowly in ice-cold mud next to Akit, I bent over his foot to spread the salve.

The forest ranger squatted nearby to watch, and within a few seconds, everyone was peering at the operation, murmuring "eeh"s of awe and shaking their heads. When I pulled out a Band-Aid, they all reached out to touch the plastic with a middle finger while I held the lips of the wound together. The forester watched, expressionless.

Gabriel slid the sleeping mat under me, distressed that I was kneeling in front of them in the mud. I borrowed a handkerchief and wrapped the foot. They sighed and sat back. I suggested that Akit rest for a few hours, then put on his shoes and walk to the village so the doctor could put in a stitch, and they nodded and clicked their tongues, though I suspected the witch doctor was cheaper and better supplied with medicines. But Akit could stay with his father until he felt better. Patrick agreed so fast that I was afraid he would force Akit to stay behind until they'd both had a weeklong paid vacation, leaving us alone without the gun or its guardians.

"Why weren't you wearing your shoes, Akit?"

"Me, I did not want to spoil them."

"Will you wear them now to keep the wound clean?"

He pointed his palm to the thick bandage. When he set off on the hike to the village with the stick in his hand, the shoes dangled neatly over one shoulder. Gabriel danced beside him. Patrick sulked on the edge of the clearing, afraid to sit by the ranger. I wondered why no one was afraid of going through the village where the soldiers had beaten schoolchildren.

The forest ranger climbed to his feet and loomed in the clearing's dusk. I thought he'd order me from the forest, and I looked at the men, who hadn't left after the show. They stood, laughing and telling one another about the bandage. I inhaled in preparation for a forgotten battle.

He reached for my hand with both of his and held it with a warm clasp that had me twisting with guilt. I had done so little, and with such bad temper. He smiled, said thank you without specification, and left. I climbed to the blind, sure the chimpanzees had come and gone. I had forgotten to ask about the fire ants.

53

Mama Shaveleg's Return

S ome primatologists have returned to the richness of untested theories in Darwin's work in their exploration of the evolution of the human smile — a filament of research stretched from Darwin's The Expressions of the Emotions in Man and the Animals into whole cloth. Monkeys laugh with lips closed over the teeth in statement that they mean no harm. Only the apes pull their lips from their teeth in delight, though they still laugh with lips down.

Like the primatologists, Elaine Morgan wove an idea from Darwin. Humans, she said, evolved from the ancestral primate when it left the dying woods to cling to the riverbanks. All the differences between humans and other apes are most typical of species that have passed through an aquatic phase of existence. Humans have several characteristics of aquatic species: we grew a cartilaginous nose, developed fat beneath the skin and an oily layer on top of it, and shrank the hair on our bodies. We are primates, but like elephants, hippos, and pigs, we lived for a time on food beside and within water, where naked skin and unimportant claws mattered less than a nose that held air and legs that could swim.

The rains had merged one into the other in those last days, gathering speed and falling more heavily to the ground. One could dry neither clothing nor one's skin — only wait under plastic for the worst to end. Living trees crumbled to the touch, spreading bark and pulp as liquid as silk on wet fingers. Fungus bloomed on the dead trees like flowers. Kamumbo stopped and looked at one yellow trumpet. I mimed eating, and he shook his head once to each side — *tick, tick* — and trotted on.

Thunder shook the trees. It had been late when Akit and the forest ranger left. Water sprayed and trickled through the leaves, etching a cold line down my back. A smell of mold lingered under the poncho, stinging my eyes, but I didn't move. The rainstorm had been light enough to sit through, so I had put on my raincoat over the backpack, wrapped my binoculars in plastic, and squatted with my notebook under my chest.

Nothing had appeared during the storm that day except a half-drowned and surprised beetle from my sleeve when I moved. I stretched one leg, then hastily pulled it back. Better to suffer pins and needles all at once than piecemeal.

A gray curtain of rain crept by, then out of the foothills and into the valley, and as the steam left behind cleared and settled into mist, a shape in the fig that could have been shadow or leaves or absence of leaves changed itself slowly into a chimpanzee sitting on a branch. Feeling very small and very wet, with my rain poncho pulled down around my ankles and my head bent over, I squatted against a giant root, next to a fern as tall as a house. The mists rose and swirled, and I lifted my eyes into a wall of rain. Shivers ran from my ankle to my neck. Water had boiled up from the ground, rebounding six feet into the air from the mud, and I was wet underneath, and chilled and bruised above, by rain striking like icicles. I had been thinking of sliding back to camp to thaw my hands.

As I lifted my head, the fig tree wavered in the still-crawling mists from base to hidden tip. Steam moved by in slow, thought-ful patches, and water drizzled what light there was down in refractions through the leaves. The canopy poured water still, like a faucet left open. A hole in the mist cleared again into a female chimpanzee. She sat in the top of the fig tree, just below the last rising cloud, and an infant ate figs above her, still shadowed.

54

The Fruit Tree

We are made of electricity, random firings and rhythmic pulses, all music and thunder. Every sense changes with alterations of current. We see with tunnel vision, more clearly and with more light; we smell single scents that burn into memory. Hearing sharpens to a pinpoint, and the primeval hairs on our skin rise, as if enlarging us to face our fear or pleasure. The lungs fill with air, though they have stopped moving, and the eyes, with their narrowed gaze, see a thousand shades of color and the clear outlines of light, transcendent.

They hadn't seen me. The shy infant son of Mama Shaveleg was frisking with slaps and hops on the branch before the others. Light glowed through leaves above them, illuminating pieces of the chimps in green columns. The fruit tree was empty of monkeys and other chimps but filled with omusingati, perfect for a slightly crippled female who couldn't range far in search of larger foods. This was my first clear look at her son. Holding the notebook tight, I leaned over its bright cover, afraid that they would see me before they started feeding. Mama Shaveleg stopped, half leaf and half animal, at the end of the branch.

The little fruit tree stood in a small clearing on the hill, exposed from all sides, and had to be jumped at from the nearest tree. The infant stood and whimpered, looking at his mother next to him. She crouched slightly to jump the gap, grunting, then shot across. Fruit pebbles sprayed the ground like bullets, and the whole tree bounced sideways. The infant shrieked. Mama Shaveleg turned on a swaying branch and looked back at the baby. Gathering knobby limbs beneath him, he shoved off like a kangaroo, all his teeth showing in a grin of fear. With more noise than his mother, he landed on all fours in a cloud of loosened leaves and clung chattering, arms bent, as the branch rose and fell. Looking around, he gathered his limbs into a hop, then a leggy leap, and swung to the branch above with one hand, only his white-haired rump poking out, then swung down one-handed, holding the end, whizzing past his mother.

She looked around just as the branch pulled him, chuckling, back up into the canopy. The top of the tree bounced as he hopped straight-legged from one end to the other. His older brother, who had been hanging back in the other tree, leaped into the fruit tree near Mama Shaveleg. The infant squealed, clutching the tree limb, wide-eyed, until the swaying stopped, then gave another straight-legged hop and bounced off his brother's leg back into the top of the tree. His mother leaned against the trunk, buttocks perched on a thick perpendicular branch. She was fourteen feet away from me and fully visible.

My pulse pounded so fast that I choked. I had never been so close to a completely wild animal. She smelled of salt and musk through the perfume of the crushed fruits, and every motion was audible, even the shifting of her rump on the wood. I breathed in air as sharp and cold as glass. Sitting beside her, I had lost my human skin and become part of the wild. Only two months ago she had run, screaming. I recorded the ecological and behavioral data, then, staring hard at the notebook whenever I could look away, I wrote down every move or noise the three of them made, as if I could still find what I was looking for in heights of trees and foods eaten.

The older son climbed away from and behind his mother and stared at me, hair puffed so he looked bigger and blacker. I lowered my eyes and turned away again. His fur rose and fell, then he reached for fruit.

The forest, strangely, seemed to become more colorful as the light disappeared. During the day, everything was uniform in its dark green, but in the hour before darkness, leaves sparkling with rain shone gold against black trunks, moss, and the dusty canopy.

The infant jumped onto its mother's stomach, jerking his head back to suck on a long flaccid nipple. Mama Shaveleg cupped the back of his head with one hand and flicked through the smooth hair on his round head with her lower lip, leaning forward to probe any flaws in the exposed slash of skin. The infant leaned back against her knees, still sucking, gazing up. I could barely see his finger in the gloom as he gently scratched at her face.

As the evening insects creaked and swelled, Mama stood, and the infant jumped before her to the end of the branch. Without hesitation he leaped into a tree above me. As Mama Shaveleg and her older son jumped after him, the infant shimmied up the trunk to a vine and, clinging there, like a ball on a string, stared at me. Carefully, the grown son turned his back to his mother. Even with shoulders hunched, waiting, he loomed higher than she. Head bowed in humility, he sat beside her, lower lip sagging. Mama Shaveleg reached out a hand and rested it on his back. She stroked through his fur and, slowly, he sagged onto her knees. Brown eyes stared, fixed on the canopy, in an agony of pleasure. Mama sat on a thick branch with her older son stretched across her lap in a column of green light and searched through his fur. His arm dangled below her; he relaxed into a coma of bliss.

Shafts of light fell through the canopy, slanting under the leaves with the last of the sun's angles. The chimps sat high in the canopy, resting in a separate day above my evening. Moisture hovered in a lighted halo about the groomer and the groomed, a yellow light, reflected off eyes and wrapped around shoulders and the palms of curved hands. The notebook rustled as I lowered it to my lap.

Mama Shaveleg sat for a while after she'd stopped grooming, narrow shoulders hunched over her son, lower lip and ears sagging tiredly, until he swung up along the branch, then out of sight. Her infant climbed into her lap and pressed against her stomach, suckling again. The older son shimmied down to stare at me, then moved to the right and out of sight in the canopy. I thought that he'd gone and that they'd follow. A branch cracked, then another, but it was a while before I realized he was building a nest above me. A musk of salt and sugar and wildness drifted down.

A sodden notebook fell from my knees onto a wet fern and hovered there in midair, brushing my hand. Staring up at a dark, still hump on the branch, I reached for the book slowly, then let it sway on its fronds of air. Circles of water sank and darkened on the cover. The paper relaxed from the curve it had taken from my stomach and rested there, limp. In the dark, the forest narrowed into single trees against an infinity stretching backward and forward as far as the mind could remember. Seconds lasted years. My eyes saw a world so clear that everything before and everything that would come faded into memory. This was the world, and all else was theater. Perhaps that is transcendence: that one can put oneself in the way of a moment in which one will stay forever.

The shape moved and separated into a large and a small darkening of shadow, slipping up the tree. Branches rustled and snapped as Shaveleg bent them into a platform for the two of them, below her older son. A soft, throaty sigh drifted down, and silence fell.

55

Bitten

Each culture has rules to overcome the animal in us. Marriage regulates sex; jobs are split by gender and level of hierarchy. When we seek food, we seek it alone. In exchange for the reassurance of grooming, we wear masks of politeness and bare our teeth often in smiles: I mean you no harm. *We neither carry our babies all day, nor lick our families clean. Religion, which has taken our animal selves away, replaces what it can with song and gold walls and a new search for gathered goods — pebbles for a soul.*

Fire ants swept the camp in a horde that filled the clearing from one chimpanzee trail to another. I waited in the little blind for the chimpanzees, but they were gone, then walked back to camp, pulling ants from bootlaces and pants.

They washed down and through the camp, then receded invisibly back. Like the chimpanzees, they left a stunned silence behind. I sat in front of the fire that night, arms wrapped around stomach as if holding it together, instead of transposing the day's small data into the research notebook.

The chimpanzees had been gone for two weeks, but I listened for their nesting coos in the dark as I duckwalked the slope through rustling leaves to the toilet pit. As I bent to pull the branches of the gate closed, something pinched me lightly on the shoulder. I slapped and felt another pinch, then a third. The flashlight swung in an arc and lighted the ground, then illuminated a black ceiling of ants, swarming so thick on the trees they hung like moving stalactites. Clusters climbed as if on ladders down a hive of other bodies and dropped in a last flare of the light onto my shoulders. Dozens of legs grasped my shirt and felt for flesh. Slapping and gasping, I ran in the dark down a path slippery with crushed exoskeletons. With a thud that didn't hurt, I hit a tree and stopped. Looking up, I saw shadows dropping again. Something burned on my neck, and I ran through the trees to the edge of the clearing and stopped.

I stripped only a few feet from the fire, in the shadow of a bush, to pull the ants out of my shrinking flesh. It took a long time. So that they wouldn't see me naked, the men doused the flames in a shower of sparks and sat in the darkness as I searched with shaking fingers for one striking body after another. Bites and stings prickled with fire, so I was still slapping with both hands as I stumbled back into camp. The men watched with concern as I pulled the last few ants from wrinkles in my shirt. "Eeeeeh, memsahib." "It is that this insect, it is very bad." "Aargh," I said, as I pulled another from my boot with a shudder and another one struck for my collar. Someone snickered.

Most of the ants had clung, hoping to weigh me down, but some had bitten and fallen. So bits of me had been taken and spread through the forest in wind and now earth.

Simon said the next morning, "These bad insects, they must to die." I told him I'd write to the forest ranger to ask, but I thought perhaps we should cover our garbage to take away their food supply. "These insects, they must to die," he said, pointing with his lip to the fariah, and I realized he meant that they had been killed. He held up the fariah to show that they had tracked the morning remnants of the horde back to the mud mound they'd built, and poured boiling water down the entrance hole.

One after another, the figs bloomed into fruit, and the monkeys came back in screaming, leaping hordes, but the chimpanzees had gone so far that the mountains blocked their calls. I sat hunched on the log, too weak to stand, holding my stomach. Gabriel strode down the hill, shy and proud. "Memsahib," he said, "it is that this Pygmy, Kamumbo, he has brought you dawa for your stomach." Kamumbo held out his hat to me with both hands. In its crown, coiled like a snake, lay a long branch. "He climb, ehh, so high, so high I cannot see him." But I had taken worming medicine and could eat nothing else.

I wrote to Tom, asking if I could stay another year. For a while there was no answer, then a single page. Simon handed it to me on both hands. He looked sad, though he'd neither opened it nor spoken with the guard who'd brought it. Some osmosis of body language had told him we were leaving before I looked up from the letter and explained it to him.

The government had revoked the visas of all volunteers in the country. In one week, those remaining would be declared spies and arrested. It didn't matter. I had an answer to the question I hadn't asked, though I couldn't understand it. Perhaps it was only that for the rest of my life I would see a chimpanzee mother grooming her son at the bottom of the canopy in a column of light while I sat among their family like mouse or monkey, ignored.

56

Soldier End

*I*f *water plants were harmful—too sweet with too few nutri-ents—or if the water was filled with parasites, like the liver flukes that cycle from snails to anything else they can catch and then pass out again through urine, then the gorillas that spent the most time in the water would reproduce less and their genes would die out, along with any other traits unique to them. If the water plants were nutri-tious and the water safe, the species would change.*

As the animals eating the rich diet reproduced, if their offspring grew large and fast, their genes would spread. The semi-aquatic apes with the most erect posture, who could stand for long periods of time, would gather more food than those straining to straighten. Perhaps fur would then disappear; it impedes movement and is slow to dry in cold air. But what did we do when we became naked, and the lions came down to drink?

The men and I left the clearing barren and trampled, and walked the dark path up and down the hills out to the red dust of the road. With a shock of electricity, we stepped into sunlight so hot our pants steamed dry. The rain forest closed with a thump behind us, the path invisible two steps away from its end. For a while I stood, eyes closed, while the men talked. My senses returned threefold. The dust was as red as a blood orange; I felt the wind and heard the calling of birds.

My stomach ached as we walked, as if a lead ball were swaying inside. But it seemed only minutes between leaving the trails that I knew so well and walking down the road to the village. I braced myself, but the huts were empty.

A different old man walked through the dust to shake our hands and say good-bye. He asked me for a job, then a radio and a watch. I told him I was leaving, and he said I could send them from America.

"I'll think about it."

"Thank you, memsahib." He shook my hand with both of his, and I wondered what I had promised.

Simon asked him for news.

The old man said, "No news, just these soldiers. These men, they shot a man with six shots in the chest. This man, he had six million shillings with him in his shirt, so the soldiers, they take his money and his shoes and they go fast, fast to Zaire."

On the roots of the old tree in the village, the chair sat empty. The colobus monkeys had retreated from the noonday heat back to the forest. I breathed in air, filling and expanding; light tingled to the ends of my fingers. The forest rustled behind, as if chimpanzees hovered in the canopy. It was the wind that we'd never heard in the forest, skirting its edges and bending its trees. Trumpets of orchids blared from the roof of the canopy and poured on vines to the ground. From above, the forest was a garden.

With that strange knowledge that Africans had about the movements of other people, though we'd told no one here we were coming, the forest guard came to meet me on the circle where the road ended in forest. He took my hand in both of his and held it.

"I am very sorry you are leaving. Very sorry."

We walked up to the village together.

"You know they are coming to arrest you very soon."

"I know."

57

Toilets at the Border

On the deck of the homebound boat, Emerson thought about what he would do back in New England with nowhere else to look for an answer. Perhaps there, without earth beneath his feet, he began to think of America, the land that had never had a king.

Emerson left the tilting deck and, below in his cabin, rewrote his manifesto "Nature." We were not an unpeopled nation. Our country was settled long ago, with something older than human lives. Europe had books and ruined fountains and poetry, but we had mountains as old as time, and as untouched.

Transcendence, Emerson called it, the feeling that everything human has disappeared and one has been filled with light and emptied and spread upon the horizons. He built his theory upon Kant, the Romantics, Eastern philosophies, and some unbearable grief.

We grow to the size of our surroundings. I had been as big as an ocean of grass, and as waves of mountains, and now was only half the size of a bus seat. Jammed in among humans and their business, I felt frayed and torn with noise. I'd moved the notebook from waistband to thigh pocket, safe from pickpockets, but it was early in the morning and no one grabbed me.

In a blur of red dust and black fragments of road, the last leg of the bus trip to the border passed. A chain-link fence rose from the dust beyond a line of small huts. Each hut held on splintered shelves a few dusty oranges and some used batteries. I climbed down the stairs of the bus, slinging my backpack over one shoulder. It would have gone missing in seconds if I had left it there, but I let it hang loose because my stomach hurt too badly to close the buckle. I moved slowly, feeling sick and afraid of what would happen once I stepped into the official building and put my passport in Ugandan hands. The sun burned down on dust and a haze of diesel fumes. The border to Kenya stretched out of sight past a hill of no-man's-land.

Long rows of people stood in the sun outside three buildings. I didn't know which line to stand in, and neither did any of the BaKiga. They just stood in a line and waited until it was their turn to be told they were in the wrong one. A man in a blue suit, with a small suitcase, came up to me.

"Do you know which line you should be in?" He looked hard at my backpack.

I said no.

Still staring with fixed intent, he offered to watch my bag while I checked, and I thanked him but said I had to find a bathroom first. Taking me by the arm, he pulled me around the corner and pointed to a white cement building with two bushes of pink flowers outside. Very Colonial. I waited until he had joined a line.

At the end of the nearest group, a woman with three children stood laughing because of the wait.

"Jambo, Mama. Please can you watch my bags? I have to go to the choo."

"Eeeeh, eeeeh, Mzungu. She wants me to watch her bags so she can go to the choo!" she shouted to no one. "No problem, Mzungu. Eeeeh, eeeh."

I put the day pack on my back and walked toward the toilets.

The man in the suit watched me go, then turned to look at my bag. The sun beat down so hard in the dust that the air wavered.

The bathroom was enormous and cool, tiled with white porcelain all up the walls. At first I thought it was the pink flowers that smelled rotten, and the heat that buzzed and shifted the walls on the inside. There were no doors on any of the toilet stalls, but that didn't bother me. The African hiking of the skirts by a bush is more sensible than guilt. Ten women squatted in front of the stalls with their kangas pulled up high. I didn't understand why they used the floor instead of the toilet pits.

Then the flies rose with my entrance, and I saw the sea. The women stood in four inches of urine. It washed over their feet, with lobes of feces bobbing in the tides. I hovered at the doorsill in my hiking boots. Frills of urine swept over the rubber soles and darkened the leather above in ripples. Stepping back, I looked around the compound.

The border was ringed by a fence, and each building had a line of waiting people snaked around it. No bushes, no walls away from sight. The flies, nervous because I had stood there so long, buzzed around me and crawled on my face with feet both cool and wet. I whapped them away and stepped back into the sunshine. Two women tiptoed out of the bathroom with their fabric held up around them, clicking their tongues. They took off their sandals outside and tried to wipe them on the grass, then found a tap on the wall. I thought of unlacing my boots and walking barefoot into that sea, but in the shadow where my nails had been, the skin of my toes was still raw and as wet as a sponge.

Walking back through the dust to the woman with my backpack, I asked her if there was another toilet. She laughed at me, and I admitted that I needed it badly. She poked the man in front of her.

"Hey, you, where is there another choo for the Mzungu?"

He shrugged.

The man in the blue suit poked the man in front of him and told him to save his place. He came over. "You want a choo? Come with me."

A border guard wandered by. The man in the jacket stopped him.

"You, this Mzungu needs a choo."

The guard jerked his head toward the toilet building.

"No. That one, it is not good."

With three other officials, the guard got a key and took me to a building behind the border. The walls were striped with handprints of feces, and stood so close together that to undress one had to lean on one or another, but the floor was dry. I came out and thanked my escort. The others laughed and disappeared, but the guard asked me which line I was in. I pointed to the backpack, and he said it was the wrong one. I asked him where I was supposed to be, and he dragged me and the backpack past the longest line and into another building.

There, the fifteen people allowed in the office were all shoving their passports in the face of the official seated at a pine table. He took them one at a time, scowling, from the person who got the closest to his jowls, read them closely, and stamped some. One, he refused to stamp, shouting at the man and throwing the papers back. The man held the papers to his chest and backed out of the room.

The man who held me by the arm snapped an order at the people pushing in toward the table. They pulled their papers back and stepped toward the wall.

"This Mzungu, she wants to go to Kenya."

The official looked up. Most Ugandans then had red-rimmed

eyes, especially the big, fat men. This one had large cheeks, as solid as those of a wrestler. Two deep trenches plunged up from his nose into the scowl lines on his forehead. He glared at me. It was so hot in the office that his nostrils flared to pull in oxygen. I offered my passport, weak talisman against Cerberus.

"You want to go to Kenya? Show me your passport." I held it farther out, leaning over the table.

He opened the blue cover and looked at the visas for a long time. Then, slowly, ominously, he reached into a drawer and pulled out a list marked with red ink. He read the list and looked back at the passport. Then he looked at my face.

He got me, I thought. *The rumor was true.* The flawed of eye, like the blind, do not always reflect emotions back as facial expressions. He stared at me hard in the eyes, and I knew he was about to tell me that I was under arrest. I also knew that Ugandans did not feed their prisoners, that women had to earn their beds with prostitution, that AIDS was sweeping across the country, that no one lived more than a year in a Ugandan prison anyway, and that no one would know I was there.

He leaned across the table, and the whole room hushed down into a deathbed quiet. Several seconds passed. Twenty moles spread across his cheeks. From head-on, they spread like freckles, but from the side they looked like the prickly mold one sees on oranges. He looked down at the passport again.

"You have been in this country for six months. Where have you been in this time?"

The government in Ecuador evicted peace corps workers after the assassination of an anti-American politician, claiming that most of the volunteers were CIA agents training the guerrillas. I didn't know what to say, whether I should admit that I had been camping in the forest or not.

I laughed. "Me, I am coming from Ruhizhia," I said in picture-perfect, amiable Rukiga.

Even the flies on the wall stopped buzzing and waited. The cheeks, with their crop of sharp moles, quivered and swelled. I felt like an idiot. If I had been a mercenary soldier or CIA, I might easily have gone to Ruhizhia to recruit, as it was nothing but forest between three countries.

He stared at me. I waited. Suddenly, he roared. Just that, a roar. We jumped, and the flies swarmed out into the sunshine. A guard ran into the room. The official waved his arm, and the people in line receded out with the flies. He scowled at the guard as if he were about to court-martial him.

"Get me some tea."

There is a swelling, with parasites, first of air in the stomach, then later of the spleen as it struggles to replace the blood that is taken. There are no symptoms except that the stomach hurts if touched, and as the air presses against the chest cavity, the lungs have less room to fill.

A border guard pulled a chair over for me and laid the papers and my passport aside. Another guard took my backpack and rested it in the corner, and then they flanked the door.

"So. You speak Rukiga."

"A little, only a little. I speak like a child."

"Where did you stay in Ruhizhia?"

"Me, I go to a village near Kayonza."

"*Eeeeh.* Me, I come from a village near there."

We talked for a while, with me slipping into KiSwahili after I'd used all the words from my notebook. I told him about the work I had been doing and the problems I had had with the insects and the rain, and he told me about the village he came from and how long it had been since he'd been back or had spoken Rukiga. I think he had been taken from his village during the war and had washed up like seaweed into this job, a very good one. He had never had a reason to go home. But when you are raised on matoke alone, or beans, it is hard to live somewhere else, even with the best food. He talked for a while.

I didn't understand the danger I was in, because after a while I was even a little bored, and remembered how much my side hurt, and wondered why it hurt. He drank the tea, and the line of Africans stood silent outside the shuttered door.

At last, he slapped down his cup and stood up. I stood up too, trying not to look at my passport. With a grand flourish, he picked it up, whacked it down on the table, and stamped it with a solid thwack. My exit visa lay on top of a Kenyan stamp, but it was clear enough. He handed it to me and I tried to take the passport, but he held on and shook my other hand.

Still holding both hands, he said, "You know, me, I was supposed to arrest you."

I tried hard to look perkily inquiring.

He nodded. "Yes. I have here a list of persons in this country illegally. You know, you should be arrested for that."

I looked shocked, and he nodded again.

"Yes. It was very bad that you did not leave the country when your visa was revoked. That is a severe violation. How are we to know that you are not a spy, if you refuse to leave?"

"But no one told me that they had taken away my visa. I was told I could stay in the forest for six months."

"That is no excuse. It is your business to find out."

I thought of protesting that I had had no reason to ask whether the government had decided it wanted to get rid of excess white people while I was in the forest. Instead, I looked apologetic.

He waved a hand at the list. "But I did not see you in this office."

I was never quick on the uptake and almost corrected him.

He continued, "So if I do not see you, I cannot arrest you." Then as I started to thank him, he held up a hand. "But you must be more careful in the future. Never do this again."

I promised, "I will never do this again."

In 1880 Emerson told the raw new country of America that it should no longer be ashamed of its uncultured expanses. In the trees and mountains, we had our own culture and history. Transcendentalism, he called it, the opening of the eye to nature, the discovery of spirit in the bark of a tree and not in a ruined cathedral. As if they had been waiting, others wrote about their moments of ecstasy. When they read Emerson, each had a minute of "Ah-ha, so it's not just me."

58

A Separate Skin

Mountains of red jacaranda bushes peeped over the railing of the veranda. Hummingbirds flitted between flowers, sipping here and there, though each blossom was wide enough to hold a whole day's food. The city stretched gray and dusty beneath, twice as wide as it had been six months before, but at each corner golden grasses rippled into the horizons. I ate spaghetti Bolognese with a steady hand, one bite after another. Suzan had told me that Batuko had been fired for poaching, so he was roaming free somewhere in the forest, and that Dr. Tom had followed my recommendation that Simon and Patrick be accepted into game-guard training. The Land Rover had been broken into in Nairobi and she'd lost all her notes and photos.

"You have schistosomiasis," the English doctor had said.

"No, I can't. I've never touched any type of water."

"Have you ever," he asked, looking in my eyes, "felt a prickling of the skin?"

I thought for a second of the chimpanzee rain dance, then remembered the night we were told that the soldiers were coming. "Once, I didn't wait for the water to boil before I took my bath."

"That was it, then."

"But it was a mountain stream, straight down from the top."

"Take two of these three times today."

The pain was just an ache, and the savanna flowed before me. I ate spaghetti and watched zebras moving through gray light. If Nairobi continued to spread at this pace, in a year the savanna would be invisible from this terrace.

I wondered how many BaKiga had liver flukes from that stream. It is always dangerous to take something from the sky after it has touched the earth.

The population of the hostel had swirled and changed, but the rules never altered. There were always people leaving for safari, instant family. Some Australians had hired a car. "Tanzania?" they asked.

No one knew why the weaverbirds chose one thorn tree out of all the green clouds that dotted the savanna to the horizon. Driving by the weaverbird tree was like walking through a waterfall. The sound, the color, and the splashes of light all increased as we approached; then there was a sudden burst of noise and movement as the birds exploded out of their nests and scolded us, and then we were through and gone, slightly shaken. The tree drooped under the weight of hundreds of mud-and-stick nests, and fluttered with yellow like a daffodil tree in a high gale. The birds never left the nests alone and never finished revising them, finding here the perfect floor in an egret's feather, and there the perfect parasitic vine to tuck around a door. The tree bustled and flowed with hovering, chirping, busy-making birds. They hopped among the branches without looking down, as if they had memorized the pattern of the thorns as well as the nests.

In my last few weeks in Africa, I traveled with backpackers in cars and buses and matatus from one reserve to another in Tanzania, separated from all human things. We lived out of our backpacks and slept in tents under stars as bright as flashes of water in the sun. I talked to scientists along the way, trying to find a job to come back to but wishing instead that the safari could go on forever, just lions and eagles and elephants and an eternity of lighted horizons. I was home as I had never been before, all senses as filled with pleasure as were the eyes, and surrounded by Africans and backpackers who also wanted simplicity.

A lilac roller perched nearby on a stump. It sat still, alone, while it watched us, then dipped and twirled away in a flash of blue so bright it looked like a tear of light from a sky ripped open. The roller fluttered, swooped, and soared up and along the savanna, then came back again to perch on another thornbush, wings folded, treasures unseen.

I saw two lion cubs abandoned in a tree, one on top of the other. The larger one, with wisps of mane already starting under his ears, draped his shoulder over the other cub, and they peered out with heads together, massive paws flopped over the crotch of the tree. Pale but complacent, they blinked their gold eyes in dapples of sunlight through the leaves. Perhaps the pride had gone to hunt, leaving their treasure, like pirates, in an old tree. As our van drove nearer, the heads stretched out straight over the monster paws, and the cubs tensed together. Then we were past, and I looked back to see them relaxed again, all ears.

The van slowed, then stopped, for a hyena in the road. It was a spotted hyena, the kind people think of when they hear the word "hyena"—a dirty, matted creature, dripping with blood. It must have made a good kill. The prey must have been large enough for the hyena to have thrust its whole head in, up to its blocklike shoulders. This is perhaps why the hyena has such a snake of a neck—so it can delve deep into a dying animal and eat the best parts before thieves chase it away.

Hyenas always reach first for the softest parts, such as entrails, although they have jaws stronger than a lion's and can eat bones. This hyena's belly bulged over its legs, and it sat in the road, musing, making no attempt to clean off the blood. The slurs that human beings cast at the species fall as useless as gossip about Greek gods. The hyena sat there despite all our encouragement to it to move. Long past the point when a lion would have slunk peevishly away, we had to slither over a ditch to pass by.

As we drove away, I saw other hyenas stretched flat on the gold-flecked savanna. They were all dipped in blood, but every stain was different. One could see which animal had gnawed at a leg, cheek pressed to bloody flank, or which had held a piece to its chest and embraced it there as it chewed. The prey animal, a wildebeest or a zebra, like one of the human shadows of Hiroshima, was left only in negative, fragmented about the savanna in ghostly prints of blood.

The deathbed was almost clean. A crowd of vultures squabbled and pounced over pieces of skin ripped free when the hyenas pulled off their parts, and a few insects had already stripped clots of blood from the soaked grass. Nothing else was left.

Africa takes something out of the body and leaves it in the horizon. I might have walked and talked in the years after that first trip, but part of my eyesight stayed back there on the savanna, with the light on the grasses. As the savanna and the possibility of return died away, the acacias faded out, reduced, retreated to memory. But in the back of my mind, I saw at all times that halo of fire now held in a clump of cells, strangely larger than myself, as if it were body and mind that had shrunk and were smaller than that unfading image. A separate skin.

59

Undergraduate Thesis

From February 14 through June 4 (except for the month of March) of 1987, research was performed in the Impenetrable Forest of Uganda at 53 degrees latitude and 52 degrees longitude, on the behavior and ecology of chimpanzees (Pan troglodytes), and redtail (Cercopithecus ascanius), blue (C. mitis), and L'Hoest's (C. L'Hoesti) monkeys. A three-week preliminary study was done in order to formulate a feasible research design. At the end of this time, some aspects of the data were analyzed, and it was found that there was a fascinating ecological problem existing in the forest. Four (Cercopithecus ascanius, C. mitis, C. L'Hoest, and Pan troglodytes) out of the five primates in the area were feeding on the same foods, yet only limited quantities were available. It is one of the most fundamental theories of ecology (competitive exclusion) that the competition evoked by two species feeding on the same type of limited food will force one species to become extinct in that area. Alternatively, one species could switch to a different food source. However, in this situation, four primates continued to coexist under competitive conditions. Two possibilities have been isolated to explain this phenomenon: either the overlap is minimized in some way that is difficult to observe in the dense forest, or there are benefits to the associations that outweigh the disadvantages. The ecological niches of three of the primates have been well documented at several research sites, but L'Hoest's monkeys were difficult to habituate to humans and infrequently seen. Consequently, little is known about them. It is vital for the understanding of interspecific relationships that the survival strategies of all species be understood.

60

Cage Neurosis

For millions of years, animals have bred for a purpose: leopards to leap from trees, gazelles to run, weaverbirds to build nests. Separated from the land and all its tasks, animals create new work. They pace up and down the borders of their cages as if miles must be covered by evening. Fences become mountains; the rut their feet have worn in the dirt, a centuries-old trail; and this place contained within, den and lair and protected center of the herd.

Cage neurosis is a known phenomenon in the zoo world. For hundreds of years, animals captured on fantastic journeys lived on stone floors in small rooms, like hermits settled away from the wind into silence. Some of them ate and walked and watched the world go by. Others—no one could predict which—paced back and forth along a chosen edge, sometimes beating their heads at one end or another, or stopping to chew their paws, as if head and foot had imprisoned them there. Wild animals, they were thought to be, impossible to tame. But humans too, caged and separated, have been found to beat their heads upon one section of a wall, and sometimes to walk the cage's edge from front to back with swift, eternal purpose, as if upon a horizon that must be crossed.

Spotted hyenas are the sharks of the savanna, superpredators and astounding recyclers of garbage. They hunt in large, giggling groups, running alongside their prey and eating chunks of its flesh until it slows down through loss of blood, or shock, or sheer hopelessness, and then the hyenas grab for the stomach and pull the animal to a halt with its own entrails or let it stumble into the loops and whorls of its own body. They eat the prey whole and cough back up, like owls, the indigestible parts, such as hair and hooves.

Hyenas in the wild can roam dozens of miles a day. They leave their young in small dens and trot or lope across the savanna, head down or held high and rear tucked under, until they've found a hare or a pregnant gazelle or a nicely rotted piece of flesh. But when the herds begin to migrate, the hyenas leave their dens to follow them and — passing over hills, through rifts and acacia stands, and along dry riverbeds — they reach the open plains of the Serengeti, where wildebeest beyond count mill and groan in clouds of dust.

I had never wanted to work anywhere except in Africa, but after I graduated from college, a wildlife reserve director in Israel told me that he needed someone to set up a breeding site for endangered animals, and I decided to go. When I got there, I was told that the project had been postponed and was asked if I'd mind taking a job as a volunteer at another reserve, cleaning enclosures. The reserve was dedicated to biblical animals, many of them predators from the Israeli wild — hyenas, wolves, foxes, and one unmated leopard — attackers of kibbutz livestock. It was something to do, and it involved animals, so I trudged off every day in the 114-degree heat with half a sandwich and a water canteen. I was being groomed for the job I'd first been offered, but for the moment I sifted maggots for the lizards and snakes, and cleaned the fox, cat, hyena, wolf, and leopard corrals.

As the days got hotter, my fellow workers and I carried gallon jugs of water in our wheelbarrows, poured it over our heads, and drank the rest until our stomachs were too full for food. It became a steady rhythm: sift dung, pour, drink, sift. For safety, we worked in pairs among the larger animals, but toward the end of the month I was allowed to feed a young hyena named Efa and clean his cage. He'd been taken away from his parents so that he wouldn't mate with his mother, and had been raised as a pet until he bit a worker. Then he'd been put in an enclosure, alone.

I stopped to talk to the leopard, who was in heat. This was my first chance to get near her; when she was not hormonally sedated she lunged at passersby, swatting her claws through the chicken wire.

"You're so beautiful."

She purred and rubbed against the mesh. The men said you could stroke her like a house cat when she was in these moods. I wanted to touch her, a leopard from the oases of Israel's last deserts, but I stayed away in case she changed her mind, squatting out of reach to talk to her. I didn't want to force her to defend herself.

It might have been the attention I gave the leopard, but Efa was in a frenzy of "Mmmmaaaaaaaa"s when I returned to his cage.

The hyena had turned his water bucket over and was panting in the early stages of heat exhaustion. As I leaned over to put a water tray in the sand of his cage, he attacked. The mind, I found, is strange. It shut off during the attack, while my body continued to act, without thought or even sight. I don't remember him sinking his teeth into my arm, though I heard a little grating noise as his teeth chewed into the bone.

Everything was black and slow and exploding in my stomach. Vision returned gradually, like an ancient black-and-white television pulling dots and flashes to the center for a picture. I saw at a remove the hyena inside my right arm, and my other arm banging him on the head. My body, in the absence of a mind, had decided that this was the best thing to do. And scream. Scream in a thin, angry hysteria that didn't sound like me. Where was everyone? My mind was so calm and remote that I frightened myself, but my stomach twisted. I hit harder, remembering the others he'd nipped. He'd always let go.

Efa blinked and surged back, jerking me forward. I tried to kick him between the legs, but it was awkward, and he was pulling me down by the arm, down and back into the cage. I lost hope and felt the slowness of this death to be the worst insult. Hyenas don't kill fast, and I could end up in the sand watching my entrails get pulled through a cut in my stomach and eaten like spaghetti, with tugs and jerks. I started to get mad, an unfamiliar feeling creeping in to add an acid burn to the chill of my stomach. Another removal from myself. I never let myself get mad. I want peace. I tried to pinch his nostrils so he'd let go of my arm to breathe, but he shook his head, pulling me deeper into the cage.

I think it was then that he took out the first piece from my arm and swallowed it without breathing, because a terror of movement settled in me at that moment and lasted for months. He moved up the arm, and all the time those black, blank eyes evaluated me, like a shark's, calm and almost friendly. By this time, my right arm was a mangled mess of flesh, pushed-out globs of fat, and flashes of bone two inches long, but my slow TV mind, watching, saw it as whole, just trapped in the hyena's mouth, in a tug-of-war like the one I used to play with my dogs—only it was my arm now instead of a sock. It didn't hurt. It never did.

The hyena looked up at me with those indescribable eyes and surged back again, nearly pulling me onto his face. I remembered the first lesson of self-defense class: "Poke the cockroach in the eyes." It was for my family and my friends that I stuck my fingers in his eyes. I just wanted to stop watching myself get eaten, either be dead and at peace or be gone, but other lives were connected to mine. I'm not sure if I did more than touch his eyes gently before he let go and whipped past me to cower against the door to the outside, the Negev desert.

Events like this teach you yourself. We all think we know what we would do, hero or coward, strong or weak. I expected strength, and the memory of my tin-whistle scream curdles my blood, but I am proud of the stupid thing I did next. He cowered and whimpered and essentially apologized, still with those blank unmoving eyes, and I stood still for a second. My arm felt light and shrunken, as if half of it were gone, but I didn't look. I had a choice of two doors: the one through which I'd entered, leading back to the desert, and the one opening onto the corral. I didn't think I could bend over him and unlatch the door to the desert. He'd just reach up and clamp onto my stomach. And I didn't want to open the door to the corral, or he'd drag me in and be able to attack the men if they ever came to help me. My body, still in control, made the good hand grab the bad elbow, and I beat him with my own arm, as if I had ripped it free to use as a club. "No!" I shouted. "No, no!" *Lo lo lo,* in Hebrew.

It was the beating that damaged my hand permanently. I must have hit him hard enough to crush a ligament, because there is a lump on my hand to this day, years later, but he didn't even blink. He came around behind me and grabbed my right leg, and again there was no pain—just the feeling that he and I were playing tug-of-war with my body—but I was afraid to pull too hard on the leg. He pulled the leg up, stretching me out in a line from the door, where I clung with the good hand to the mesh, like a dancer at the barre. It felt almost good, as if the whole thing were nearer to being over. In three moves I didn't feel, he took out most of the calf.

I opened the door to the desert, and he ran out, with a quick shove that staggered me. I couldn't move the right leg, just crutched myself along on it into the Negev. He waited for me. The cold in my stomach was stabbing my breath away. The hyena and I were bonded now. Even if someone did come to help, there was still something left to finish between us. I was marked—his. I saw, in color, that he was going to knock me over, and I thought, in black-and-white, No, don't, you'll hurt my leg, I should keep it still.

A workman stood by a shed uphill, leaning on a tool in the sand. He watched me walk toward the office, with the hyena ahead and looking back at me. He was the only spectator I noticed, though I was told later, in the hospital, that some tourists, there to see the animals, were screaming for help, and three—or was it five?—soldiers had had their machine guns aimed at us throughout the whole thing. Israeli soldiers carry their arms everywhere when they're in uniform; but they must have been afraid to shoot. I don't know. Stories get told afterward. I didn't see anyone except the workman, looking on impassively, and the leopard, pacing inside her fence, roaring a little, with the peace of her heat gone as suddenly as it had appeared.

I had expected the hyena bite in Africa, not in Israel. I had expected the price I paid for Africa to be high. The need that had driven me since I was eight years old had made me willing to risk anything, even death, to be in Africa, watching animals. Anyone who works with animals expects to get hurt. You are a guest in their lives—any intrusion is a threat to them. It is their separateness that makes them worthy of respect.

For three weeks, the doctors left the wounds open to wash out the bacteria from the hyena's mouth, and I watched my arm and leg floating in buckets of saline solution, open in a wall from bone to skin, with thin shreds of dying flesh fluttering in the currents of my pulse. As if, with the loss of flesh, strings tying me to earth had been cut, I felt freed. No more preparations for Africa; I was going to go to graduate school and to earn a life on the savanna.

Back in America, I stood on a boulder above a slow-moving sea. The air was cleaner here than at my parents' house, but on the horizon a thin black line spread. Pollution is not a dark haze; it is a lack of clarity. Nothing sparkles beneath it. Only on the horizon can we see the air we breathe.

From floor to ceiling, almost every item of every home I visited was made of and washed in chemicals. Instead of air tinged with the dust of dried grasses and a multitude of animals, every breath inside and out of the house was dark with smoke. Petrochemical-residue carpets, flame-retardant and pesticide-sprayed furniture, stain-guarded and mercury-soaked fabric, toxins in every food, and cleansers for it all that burn the lungs.

Pesticide warning signs waved from suburban yards like daffodils. Trucks poured black smoke into the air even on the quietest roads. I couldn't breathe. It was a nightmare of painful clothing, anonymous faces, food that tasted like paste, and a wasting of good things. Plastic bags that would have saved lives by protecting identification cards in Uganda littered the ground here, and everything bought was wrapped in plastic. Every day, most Americans threw out more than a Ugandan owned. I couldn't breathe. The lack of oxygen and scent gave me a pounding headache that blurred the ocean.

The hyena bites didn't hurt, but parasites from Africa that had coexisted peacefully in my body had multiplied and conquered after the antibiotics at the hospital. Too ill for school, I hid in my parents' house and read about animals on my own.

As physical therapy for the hyena bites, I lifted weights and slowly jogged on a treadmill. And then one day, as I was buying new glasses, the salesman told me that I didn't have depth perception, and that a contact lens would work better.

The thin slice of plastic resting on the cornea reflected light inward and downward not only into the open cells of the brain, which magnified it and sent it out in rays, but back along the darkened line of the past. So as the third dimension crept slowly into my plastic-wrapped eye and I could see time and movement, the years leading backward deeper and deeper into a flawed and immobile world lit up too, and I could see my past for the first time as it happened.

As I lifted weights, I saw the arc of the dumbbell and held it steady. I jogged, then ran, on the treadmill, and one day I decided to run outside, and soared past the trees. But I still couldn't breathe.

The worms and hyena had thrown me into a suspended animation, but when I emerged, at a time when most women find themselves slowing down, I was stronger and faster, each day bringing new muscles into play. Depth perception was sinking into the bad eye. A moth attracted to flame reversed into chrysalis, mutation of cycle.

For five years, my brain had tried to understand Africa. While it ran its circuits over and over the information in different combinations, it still froze me. My face moved and talked, I worked and made friends, but behind my expressions, every spare electron and the smallest emotion churned and turned and pulled apart, all of it running through the memory cells of childhood, Africa, and afterward so quickly that there were no chemical combinations left over for the present eye.

The human mind, as it disintegrates, throws the contents of the cells that hold our memories forward as they die, where they flash scenes in light and color on the inner eye and are turned upside down, changed back to electricity, and flown up the optic nerve to sink into and fill new cells. Again and again. The older the memory, the more often it has been reabsorbed and the greater the chance it has of holding on.

So, in old age, as the cells die, the oldest ones or the most often recalled ones are fixed the most firmly, spread widely. And they are our last memories—the first ones, or the most often replayed.

Against all odds, I got into graduate school. But, as with all my human plans, I had been wrong about it. Like the box on the floor of the gorilla center, the library I sat in was filled with formulas. My mind froze shut, no longer willing to go forward with science or to look back at a world that was disappearing. I ran through the year, looping endless circles around their track. After they kicked me out—because I wasn't capable of graduate-level thinking and because I argued that it is not illogical to assume that animals have emotions—I ran outside, long, hip-wrenching uphill struggles.

I had filled my mind with pictures of Africa, and for five years they were shut away there. Small fragments crept through now and then as I learned to see. The half-blind lion, weaverbirds turning in flight, the eagle feeding its young in silhouette, foxes leaping, spring-hare eyes at night, the lion lifting its head into the wind, and images of people too. Small pieces—I wrote them down as my brain let them slip because I knew they were gone. Only captured on paper could they be relived.

And when I finally returned to Africa, I felt as if I were running still. The school was right; I was an anecdotalist.

61

Return to Africa

With the contact lens on my bad eye, I could finally see animals instantaneously; I only wished I had had it during my semester in Africa. Then, in 1993, a primatologist wrote to me and offered me a site in Kenya beyond my qualifications. She was one of the great anecdotalists that had changed the field, and I could do whatever research I wanted to on her famous band of baboons. It should have been everything I'd been looking for: the savanna, a teacher who knew the animals as if they were her family, and all the freedom I could want. I didn't know why I was reluctant to step on the matatu.

The site was in the north, where goats had eaten the grass down to the red dust — now more desert than savanna — and the nearby town was filled with traffic and shouting. The reserve too was shrinking, eaten away by tentative farmers and poachers who had moved into the very foothills of the baboon research center. Thomas, the site manager, picked me up from the matatu and gave me a ride to the center on his motorcycle. On the way, we saw tracks that I was sure were lion's, and I argued with Thomas, who said the pads were too small. We drove on. A few minutes later, skidding to a stop, he pointed at a depression in the dust. "That is lion."

I saw, of course, with that giant's spoor, that the first tracks must have been a hyena's or a jackal's. This paw circled the dust like a tree stump. It was a peaceful print. Large and soft, more footprints ambled across the road with little extra touches to the ground. Here a tail rested, there a foot dragged one long claw in the dust like a child kicking up sand. The tracks turned a bit at the end: the lion had stopped there and looked back over his shoulder. They always do that. All animals look back over their tracks as they cross a road. Even a dust road is an intrusion on the savanna. Nowhere else does the land stop completely. Plants grow on the other side, but an animal with all four feet in the dust needs to look back and see the vegetation it used to stand on.

The road was a palette of the richness of life in the reserve. Small birds had strutted across the canvas in search of insects. Doomed ants and beetles ran from the shelter of the grasses to the road in an endless search for something better. Here a jab showed where a bird had caught one. The hyena that I'd thought was a lion still walked on the road up here; behind its tracks lay a print that I thought was a cheetah's but that was probably a serval's. Animals' feet spread in the dust, so a track is always wider than the paw that creates it. The serval, like the lion, had padded across the road and disappeared.

Little clover prints darted and dodged across the hyena tracks, zigzagging with them up the hill — those of some small insect-eating rodent. Down the next ditch, we chased an ostrich, destroying its prints as it made them. The three toes, like stiff worms, threw back puffs of dust that settled on the tracks just as we drove over them. I was glad when the ostrich veered off the road and ran in the grass instead.

The motorcycle rose toward a sharp hill. Then, with a final curve, we flew down a long slope to the research station with the sun setting in front of us. I looked back and saw the road with its puddles and waves of feet shadowed in the sunset. Smooth as a snake and riding over all, our motorcycle tracks spread, like the other prints, larger than reality.

I left the baboon research site after a few weeks; I didn't get along with the owner of the ranch, and the site was too close to roads and noise and edges of black air. For the next seven months, I traveled around East Africa, looking for somewhere clean to live. Such a place was not easy to find.

During one of my many trips through Nairobi, I visited Nairobi National Park. In 1986 it had been somewhat of a joke: a patch of savanna adjoining the savanna. Six years later, however, the entire park was surrounded by dirty, tall buildings, like a ring of ash. The animals who lived there, no longer able to migrate, were often sickly and listless. As we drove into the park, a serval strolled down the road before us, uncaring, not even turning an ear, as if life and danger were all the same to it. The serval is usually nocturnal, and thus it was strange to see it walking about in the day, as if ill. Stepping off the road into the grass, it passed an old den dug into a red termite mound that was now filled with weeds. The little cat picked through the grass and lay down behind the mound.

Driving closer, we sat on the windows of the car and leaned out: I couldn't believe it was the same animal. Unlike the miniature cheetah that it had resembled as it walked down the road — bright and slender in the sunshine — this cat had a very small and tattered head, with one eye missing and closed, both ears ripped to velvet tatters, and even the whiskers bent like old nylon. The spots and stripes so sharp on the body were smudged like dirt in the rumpled face; it looked like a handful of old hay tangled in the grass. Despite our pity, we took pictures, and it got up and bumbled away. Driving again, we left it there, moving without interest away from the old den.

There were other animals injured as well. The park had not been turned into a glossy showcase of culled animals, of nature man-made. An old buffalo stood under a bridge, ankles in the mud. We thought he had an umbilical tumor, but when he heaved up his head to look at us, the mass beneath him swayed; we could see it had spilled from a hole in his belly, and he stopped breathing until it was still. He looked at us the way buffalo do, straight and ready to charge or run, but with head low and taking only careful sniffs with upturned nose, not the deep sucks with raised head. As he stood there on the side of the pool, herons stabbed through the reeds, and a tickbird perched on his back. He had probably been cooling the mass in the water, which now ran down his sides or spiraled off dried shreds stiff with blood. We drove past to leave him in peace, but he left the pool and crossed the road anyway. He moved slowly, waiting after each step for the pendulum to swing back to center.

I changed the film in the camera to take a picture of him silhouetted against the red road with the tickbird facing front and the mass swaying below, but then he stepped into the tall grass, which camouflaged his belly. He didn't know he was dead. He picked up a mouthful of straw and stood there watching us, chewing his cud carefully for a stomach trapped outside his skin. The tickbird moved up to his head and clung underneath, picking off insects in a flurry of jabs while the buffalo waited.

By the time of this trip to the savanna — my last — East Africa had been wiped clean of condoms, because President Reagan had told the World Health Organization he'd withdraw funding if they associated with the pro-choice institutions that had customarily provided birth control. AIDS and overpopulation and erosion had spread together across the continent. Where there had been giraffes and lions and acacias, there were now deserts and sky-scrapers and slums.

With my miraculous contact lens, I could see humans clearly for the first time, but now the haze of pollution left a film over the entire country and a bitter taste on my tongue. I didn't have the courage to live on a savanna that was disappearing day by day. Grieving and heartsick, I returned home.

62

Epilogue

In the woods, we return to reason and faith. . . . Standing on the bare ground, — my head bathed by the blithe air, and uplifted into infinite space, — all mean egotism vanishes. I become a transparent eye-ball; I am nothing; I see all; the currents of the Universal Being circulate through me.

— *Ralph Waldo Emerson,* Nature

I rolled out of bed one morning in 1997, washed, and lifted up my right eyelid to put in my contact lens. A curtain of blood slid down over my eye with that swift languor that only blood, of all liquids, possesses. The clear eye saw none of the signposts of my history — the red veins of late-night reading or pupils shrunken from solitude. Thus separated from character, the other eye had achieved Dionysian splendor: it glowed red like a glass of wine or a stained-glass window. The injured eye saw the world through a red curtain, but in the mirror it stared back at me, calm and impassive.

By this time, I took my depth perception for granted. When my surroundings had stopped whirling around me, it had become much easier to move through space. When I could read people's facial expressions, it was less of an effort to enter into their worlds. But that morning I knew instantly that things would never be the same. The contact lens, bestower of humanity, had done this in some way.

I was in a graduate program in writing at Columbia that year, desperately trying to cut and shape the thousands of pages I'd written on Africa into some pattern. I was also reading books on vision and transcendence and neurology. (What was it about the light on the savanna that had caused this obsession?) I sensed that both the question and the answer I'd been searching for now lay somewhere within the forest of words before me — a forest I had created but was now lost in.

After my eye bleed, I could no longer wear the lens: without it, the human world was as hard to navigate as it had been before. My body was failing me in other ways as well. My liver had been badly damaged by both the liver flukes and the antibiotics I'd been given after the hyena bite; it could no longer filter chemicals out of my blood. By 1996 my blood pressure was dangerously low, and any random toxin — a newly painted hallway, a blast of exhaust — could make me pass out.

I had gone to one of the purest places in the world to live among the animals and had carried home enough of them in my bloodstream to kill me; Western medicine had saved my life but left me allergic to my own kind. Feeling hemmed in by my failure to get well and to bring Africa alive on the page, I packed up my belongings in boxes and traveled around America from one hostel to another, looking for a clean place to live. For six years, I was on the road.

Whenever I passed through the Northeast, I would go see my grandmother, whose mind was failing her, and play on the floor with her dog, Charlie. "Hello, darling," she said warmly each time, unable to remember precisely who I was. She asked Charlie as she stroked him, "Whose dog are you, sweetheart?" clearly hoping he was hers. "Who will take care of him if something happens to me?" she murmured. "I will, Grandma," I promised, even though I'd never had a home of my own.

In 2003 a woman told me of a yoga retreat in the mountains. It was lonely there, without the affections that spring up so swiftly among travelers. People had come to the retreat to be by themselves rather than to make friends. But I found something I needed in this place — the yoga teachers showed me how to slow down by living through the senses like an animal, to return to the present again, to recognize, even in a dangerous world, the flashes of beauty all around me. The teachers asked me the same questions the backpackers had, nearly twenty years earlier: What was I leaving behind? What was I looking for? What was I trying to become?

Maybe, my teachers gently suggested, I didn't have to travel as far as I thought I did to find out. I rented one house for eight weeks; another for a year and a half. I slept on a friend's couch; I pitched my tent in someone else's backyard. Slowly, slowly, I began to mark a territory.

In 2004 my brother and his wife had their first child; two months later, my grandmother died. I had to find a house to keep my promise to take Charlie, to finish the book, and to be near my family: I went looking for someone who would rent to a woman with a dog. Lying in the dark in our new home, listening to Charlie snore, I started remembering Africa with greater clarity. I wondered if, as I learned to live with fewer and fewer things, I might begin to hear the echo of the forest within my walls.

The human world has strayed too far from its fur and teeth. We've evolved into gears in a machine, each with our separate chores;

we keep our babies in separate rooms and eat food made by other machinery. Our teeth are refashioned with mercury, our hands wear formaldehyde and oil, and we sleep in a bed of chemicals — flame retardants and pesticides alter our dreams.

But my lake house, which I leave and circle back to like a border collie guarding nonexistent sheep, has purple thyme and strawberries pushing up through the crumbling tar of its driveway. And though it lies between a fast road and a highway two miles away, there are moments on the lake when the traffic, by some consensus, dies down and the Canada geese call like chimpanzees across blue hills. I stand in sharp thyme with Charlie sitting on my foot, his eyes closed in the sun, and through his muscles I suddenly feel a crow protesting change, a bluebird rising with a squawk of morning delight, and two mallards dipping their heads below the water's surface with slow glurks. The mountains in the distance are only slightly tinged with carbon, and sometimes, after a rain, the air fills with smells of pine and lake water.

Africa can come back now. I am leopard and redtail and L'Hoesti in the sun, Shaveleg in a column of light — separate, but now and then drawn into the human world. This is my home, and this book is my breath. The savanna is still too bright to look at, but perhaps, if I can hold the good eye closed, in the whirling haze of the other eye, I will see lions.

Author's Note

REUSE: Reuse everything you can and find new purposes for anything possible. Buy antique furniture at auctions; it is usually incredibly cheap, beautifully made, holds its resale value, and will outlast almost all modern furniture. It was almost certainly made without formaldehyde, fly ash, toxic glues, and polyurethane, and it might be thrown out if you don't buy it.

USE LESS: Think hard about any purchase. Take shorter showers, don't leave lights on in an empty room. Try to buy things with less packaging.

RENEWABLE ENERGY: Solar thermal hot water, solar heat, photovoltaic panels for electricity, tankless water heaters, geothermal heating and cooling, tide power, wind power, water power, passive solar. The federal government and many states have grants and subsidized loans that make the payoff time for installation a matter of years, and will give you decades of savings. DSIREUSA.org has up-to-date listings of grants, incentives, and subsidies.

GREEN CLEANING: Use baking soda, white vinegar, and hydrogen peroxide and the essential oils of flowers to clean everything in your house. Most cleansers are extremely toxic; the green ones are healthier, cheaper, and usually work better.

Acknowledgments

About once a week I would call my brother Matt and ask him if I could read a new paragraph. After I'd read about a thousand words to him, he'd ask how long the paragraph was, and I'd tell him three pages, but he never refused to listen. This book would never have been written without him. He convinced me to keep writing, and to turn the pieces into a book. He asked Alice Quinn, then the poetry editor of *The New Yorker*, to look at the manuscript and make a suggestion about which publishing house I should send it to. Instead, she published the hyena chapter in the magazine and, in the process of editing it, combined various parts of the manuscript to form a piece that broke my heart.

Lyll Becerra de Jenkins taught me that in the battle between scientific impartiality and emotion, emotion should win. Don Faulkner read an enormous amount of work in a short time, digested it, and suggested that I begin tying my random fragments into a book. Dr. Richard Selzer gave comments and inspiration. I read his masterpiece *Raising the Dead* whenever I had to write something that hurt. Rebecca Goldstein's astoundingly stimulating conversations gave me the courage to leave in the eye meditations, and Richard Locke convinced me to make sense of thousands of pages of writing with a chronology. Jonathan A. Levin taught one of the most inspiring classes I've ever had — on

Emersonian transcendence and sense of place — and gave comments on this book that were full of insight.

For the first trip to Africa, I am indebted to Art Mitchell, who taught me how to find a research site. Dr. Tom Butynski was enormously generous in giving a college student a chance to do her own research on chimpanzees through the Impenetrable Forest Conservation Project. He gave me transportation, food, and advice when he could, and provided half the salaries of all the men working with me. For three days, he hiked around Kampala arguing with bureaucrats to get me research clearance, risking his own. Ed Wilson from the World Wildlife Fund helped me find a research site in Kenya. Dr. Carol Lynch taught me how to sort out the Ugandan data and turn it into a thesis that won high honors and membership in Sigma Xi, the Scientific Research Society. I'm grateful to Wesleyan University for the thesis research grant that paid for the chimp research, and to the Mellon Foundation for the grant I used to go back to Africa.

I owe a tremendous debt to the men I worked with in Uganda — whom, for their safety, I have called Gabriel, Olin, Patrick, Simon, Akit, Kamumbo, and Brother Odel — for everything they did for me. I cannot thank Simon enough; he is one of the shining people on earth. I thank Ruben and others at the Nairobi Youth Hostel for being my family for so long. I am grateful to Hosteling International. Most of my writing was done in hostels across America over more than a decade of travel without a home. It is a wonderful institution that helps people of all ages from all countries create friendships in new places.

Heartfelt thanks to Jessica Green for selling this book, to Bill Phillips for buying it, and to Sloan Harris for supporting it through to the finish. I'm grateful for the warmth and tact of my editor, Asya Muchnick, who played me like a fish to get me to stop cutting and pasting in circles and work with what I had, and for the deft assurance with which she helped me incorporate transitions and a preexisting piece into *The Lion's Eye*. I'm grateful to my fact-checker, Carol Holmes, for keeping me honest. I'd like to thank the copyeditor, Karen Landry, for her unfailing professionalism and good cheer in the face of the massive amount of extra work I unintentionally sent her way, up to the very last minute!

I thank my friends for always standing by me and, last, my parents, who gave me roots and wings. My mother, who nursed me through the illnesses of the first trip, says I turned her hair gray; I thank her also for encouraging me to go back the second time.